GREAT
GOLF COURSES
OF THE WORLD

GREAT
GOLF COURSES
OF THE WORLD

GALLERY BOOKS
An imprint of W.H. Smith Publishers Inc.
112 Madison Avenue
New York, New York 10016

CONTENTS

Designed by Tom Debolski
Written and edited by Timothy Jacobs

Published by Gallery Books
A Division of W H Smith Publishers Inc.
112 Madison Avenue
New York, New York 10016

Produced by
Brompton Books Corp.
15 Sherwood Place
Greenwich, CT 06830

ISBN 0-8317-4082-5

10 9 8 7 6 5 4 3 2 1

Page 1: Looking down the ninth fairway
of legendary Spyglass Hill Golf Course, on
California's Monterey Peninsula.

Pages 2–3: This is the seventh hole at Pebble Beach Golf Links. Here, we are looking out over the Monterey Peninsula's
Carmel Bay, toward the vast Pacific Ocean.

These pages: A view over the massive
bunkers surrounding the sixteenth
green at The Australian Golf Club, near
Sydney, Australia.

Introduction:
The Designs of Greatness

One golfing ground has been preferred over another as far back as the annals of golf record. Exactly where and when it all originated is still a matter of dispute. Historian Steven JH van Hengel had evidence of the fact that the townspeople of Kronenburg played a game quite similar to golf on 26 December 1297, to celebrate the anniversary of the liberation of Castle Kronenburg from invaders: for 'holes,' they used doorways and portals of various kinds.

The French, Italians and Spaniards have similar tales to tell, and The Netherlands abounds with pre-fifteenth century inferences that a golf-like game was played there. Gloucester Cathedral has a fifteenth-century stained glass window that contains a figure swinging a golf club-like implement.

The Old Course at St Andrews is our earliest known golf course in continuous operation: historical references indicate that it was in play as early as 1552. It is, for us, the archetypal golf course, a splendid piece of well-aged linksland that is, at turns, beguiling and terrifying. Shaped from a deposit of Ice Age sand dunes, its architect was none other than nature's own hand, working a truly unique magic via the modifying effects of wind, water and the grazing habits of various livestock. The Old Course at St Andrews presents the golfer with the primal 'man against the forces of nature' contest that perhaps we all seek in the game of golf.

It is a truism at this point that, whatever the year and decade, and whatever the selecting committee, the Old Course at St Andrews will never—as long as it is in play—be absent from the top 10 of any truly comprehensive listing of the world's great golf courses.

Our criteria for inclusion in this book are a number of outstanding qualities. Greatness in a golf course is a combination of quality of play, aesthetic appeal and general ambience. Some courses have more of these considerations than of others, and some courses have all three.

Some courses—like Old St Andrews—could not possibly be excluded. Others, like Mauna Kea, combine breathtaking aesthetics with remarkable qualities of play. Still others have been recognized for their greatness by committees of experts: they have been included, and will likely continue to be included, in *Golf Magazine*'s '100 Greatest Courses in the World' and other notable rosters.

Some have been named the best in their state, shire or prefecture, and others have been crowned with legendary status solely by small coteries of golfers who have recognized a unique challenge—or a classic quality—inherent in the lie of the bunkers and fairways of a favorite course.

Herbert Warren Wind has stated that Pebble Beach may be the greatest golf course in the world. Augusta National has been called 'Golf's Sistine Chapel.' The contours of Muirfield linger in the heart like one's first memory of an ocean vista.

Some courses have outstandingly intimidating holes, like the third at Mauna Kea, or stretches of holes, like the 'Amen Corner' at Augusta National (or the seventh through tenth holes at Pebble Beach).

Difficulty in itself is insufficient to qualify a certain hole or a course overall for greatness, but its ability to generate interesting golf is much more to the point. The great Bobby Jones said, during the construction of the Augusta National course:

'There should be presented to each golfer an interesting problem which will test him without being so difficult that he will have little chance of success.'

The legendary golf architect AW Tillinghast described his conception of a *truly* complete golf course in this way:

'Every hole must have individuality and must be sound... .[If a hole] has nothing about it that might make it respectable, it has to have quality knocked into it until it can hold its head up in polite society.'

At right: **A view of the sixth hole at Spyglass Hill Golf Course. This mountain-terrain course has spectacular altitude changes.**

Therefore, a course having one great hole does not make that course a great course. Neither does greatness adhere to a course that is composed of repetitions of a single, great hole. The same can be said of a course that is simply a repetition of another great course. Uniqueness, aesthetics and rigorous, yet plausible, challenge are among the criteria by which golf courses are commonly judged.

There are also the 'traditionalist' versus 'modern' viewpoints of course architecture to consider. St Andrews, Muirfield, Pebble Beach and a clutch of others well represent the traditionalist view. Quite simply, traditionalists feel that a piece of land either lends itself to golf or not. Therefore, the architect's job is minimized to a refining touch here and there—the land's golf-testing contours having already been provided by God.

The 'modernists'—of whom the premier architect is (and has been since the term was coined) Robert Trent Jones Sr—see the architect's role quite differently. Modernists feel that nothing should prevent the building of a golf course in a given place, and nothing should prevent the designing in of rigorous or merciful characteristics as the architect pleases. The landscape is sometimes radically changed, with thousands of tons of earth rearranged.

(It should be said that—lest anyone think otherwise—many modernists do indeed have a commitment to ecology, striving to meld their designs with natural surroundings, and relocating or incorporating native flora and fauna with surprising success, and at great cost.)

Extensions of these two ways of thinking carry through to the actual playing of the courses. The traditionalists hold that the

luck of the bounce is an inherent part of the chance you take when you make your shot. If the ball unexpectedly pitches in the middle of the fairway and kicks off into the rough, why, that's part of the game, and serves to make it even more interesting. Such challenges also include blind shots, which further increase the role of the unexpected.

The modernists hold that the role of serendipity (or lack thereof) should be more restricted, and the golfer should be rewarded according to his efforts. 'A good shot should have a good result, and a bad shot, a bad result.'

St Andrews, which was molded entirely by the hand of nature, is the supreme example of the traditionalist school. Mauna Kea,

which was literally carved out of a lava mountainside in Hawaii, is a grand example of the modernist school.

Most courses lie somewhere in between. The work of architects such as Pete Dye, Robert Trent Jones Jr and Jack Nicklaus tend to be a blending of the two. Desmond Muirhead's latest creations assuredly partake more of the modernist school, while Robert Trent Jones Sr himself, the epitome of modernism, has tried his hand at one traditionalist course, at least. Some fine traditionalist courses—Turnberry, in particular—have had to be reconstructed by rearranging great amounts of earth, after various calamities.

Also, of course, there are regional characteristics that affect design. In the British

Isles, for instance, greens favor a rolling approach, while many American greens favor approach shots that take a short hop on the putting surface.

Weather is also an outstanding factor, with typical linksland courses enduring months of rainy weather, and unpredictable winds at any time of the year. In fact, the success of a course design often depends on climate and terrain in very specific ways.

Seaside linksland is the terrain on which such traditional courses as the Old Course at Saint Andrews were formed, and upon which such newer linksland courses as Harbour Town Golf Links are based.

Mountainous terrain, in which the architect combats erosion with rock riprap

underlying the course, has its own unique features. Courses built on mountainous terrain are unusually variegated and feature an extraordinary variety of slopes. The weather of mountainous regions must be taken into account when designing such a course, and the wind and other elements are considered, in addition to hillside gradients, when plotting the defenses for each hole. Representative of this kind of course are the three layouts at The Homestead, in Virginia, and the spectacular Mauna Kea, in Hawaii.

Below opposite: **One of the few remaining primordial links courses, Royal Dornoch, in play for over 400 years. The eleventh through fifteenth holes stretch away into the distance.** *Below:* **Pebble Beach Golf Links.**

Desert terrain, with its ruggedness, lack of water, stunted trees, sandstorms and general resistance to 'civilization' is a challenge indeed to the golf course architect. Robert Trent Jones Jr's Cochiti Lake Golf Course, in New Mexico, is a fine example of an ingenious solution to these problems.

Temperate conditions allow a great breadth of approaches, and the very beautiful Augusta National layout, in Georgia; Medinah Country Club, in Illinois; and SentryWorld, in Wisconsin, are fine examples of courses that have been designed for such conditions.

In the end, the choice fruit of any set of design considerations is the course itself. Greatness comes from both camps, and many a golfer has been humbled by

a course from the 'opposing' school. The courses in this text include examples of both traditional and modern philosophies, as well as nearly every kind of 'conditional' course extant. Each is possessed of a uniqueness for which it is included here.

We have endeavored to present as full an accounting of each course as is presently possible and, with the help of those two truly excellent photographers of Scottish and Irish golf courses—John James and Don Blank—have been able to depict several courses in the hallowed golfing grounds of the British Isles with some degree of completion. Most of all, we hope that you will have as much fun touring the courses in this text as we have had organizing the tour for you.

Augusta National Golf Club

Augusta, Georgia USA

Augusta National Golf Club was ranked third in *Golf Magazine*'s '100 Greatest Courses in the World' listing for 1989, up from fifth in the 1987 poll. The Augusta National is the home of the Masters Tournament, and is steeped in golfing lore that evokes the names of Bobby Jones, Arnold Palmer, Dwight D Eisenhower and Jack Nicklaus. It all began with Bobby Jones' incredible Grand Slam victories in the 1930 US Open and US Amateur Championships, and in the 1930 British Open and British Amateur Championships, all in one season.

Jones retired from competitive golf at age 28, that same year. He turned his thoughts to building a golf course to his own liking. He was soon to receive an assist in his dream. An investment banker from New York, Clifford Roberts, spent his winters in Augusta at the resort there. An avid golfer, he idolized the great Bobby Jones, and when the two met, they became fast friends. When Bobby talked of his 'dream course,' Roberts offered to help.

The two soon formed a partnership: Jones would oversee the design of the course, and Roberts was to organize and run the financial apparatus. They agreed that the course would be the centerpiece of a national golf club, and would be located in Augusta. Membership was by invitation to known golf enthusiasts. Social activity was to be held to a minimum, to keep the club's golfing focus clear.

Once the finances were well on their way to being established, Jones and Roberts bought a 365-acre patch of land formerly occupied by a commercial nursery. For expert assistance in the design of the course, Jones turned to the man who had created Cypress Point, on California's Monterey Peninsula. This architect was the Scotsman Dr Alister Mackenzie.

Mackenzie and Jones agreed upon Jones' basic approach, which emphasized the preservation of the natural attributes of the site. The two worked closely together, and created a true masterpiece—Mackenzie, whose contributions currently account for 10 of *Golf Magazine*'s '100 Greatest

At right: A floral map of the US invites players and spectators to Augusta National Golf Club, the renowned home of the Masters Tournament.

Courses in the World,' considered Augusta National to be his finest creation ever.

Unfortunately, he died before the course was ready for play. It was strikingly beautiful from the beginning—the tees, greens and fairways seemed to have been gently coordinated with the dogwood, azalea and other flowering trees that emblazoned the site with a rare natural grace.

The course was formally dedicated in January, 1933. The course immediately had such prestige that the US Golf Association considered holding the US Open there. Augusta National declined, feeling that if a great golfing event were to be held on the course, perhaps it should be an event sprung from the golf club itself.

Bobby Jones and company decided that it would be an invitational event of 72 holes at stroke play, and that the invitees would be the best players in the game. Roberts suggested calling it the 'Masters Tournament,' but the modest Bobby Jones declined that title as too presumptuous.

Therefore, the tournament was known as the Augusta National Invitational Tournament until Jones relented, changing the name to the Masters Tournament four years after its inception. The first such tournament was played in March, 1934.

While that first Invitational (Masters) cost far more than Roberts and Jones had estimated it would, it was a great success—attendance was estimated at 10,000, second only to that year's US Open. After a four-year layoff, Jones returned to play in this tournament, and shot a 294 for the thirteenth place. Horton Smith won with a 284, and won again in 1936 with a 285, becoming the first two-time winner in the Masters.

Smith's stiffest competition in 1934 was runner-up Craig Wood. Wood lost another close one to Gene Sarazen in 1935, in a sudden-death playoff. Byron Nelson won in 1937 and again in 1942—this latter win being one of the most exciting in Masters history. He tied with Ben Hogan at 280, and in the ensuing playoff, gained five shots on Hogan in 11 holes, even though Hogan played those 11 holes one under par. Nelson won by one stroke.

Jimmy Demaret became the Masters' first three-time winner with his wins over Lloyd Mangrum, Byron Nelson and Jim Ferrier, in 1940, 1947 and 1950, respectively, with scores of 280, 281 and 283.

Except for the year 1950, 'Slammin'' Sammy Snead and Ben Hogan alternated championships from 1949 to 1954. Snead won three times, in 1949, 1952 and 1954, scoring 282, 286 and 289, respectively. (The 1954 tournament resulted in a playoff between Snead and Hogan, who were considered to be the two best players in the world at that time.)

Ben Hogan, on the other hand, won the Masters in 1951 and 1953, with scores of 280 and 274, respectively. 'The Hawk,' as he is affectionately known, had been a contender since 1939, placing in the top ten nine times, and coming in second a career total of four times. His 1951 Masters win is especially gratifying in light of the fact that a near-fatal auto accident in 1949 had caused him injuries so severe that doctors said he would never play golf again. He obviously proved them wrong.

Hogan believes that the 1953 Masters saw him playing the best golf of his career, while Masters Tournament officials believe that he achieved the *best* 72-hole stretch of golf ever achieved by anyone, anywhere. It was, in fact, the year that Ben Hogan won

the Masters, the US Open and the British Open, and was named US Athlete of the Year.

Arnold Palmer became the Masters' first four-time champion with his wins in 1958, 1960, 1962 and 1964. His scores were, respectively: 284, 282, 280 and 276. In the 1960 Masters, he led the field at the end of each scoring day, joining Craig Wood (1941 Masters winner) in an elite club of the only two men to do so. Palmer also became part of the Masters' first triple tie, with Gary Player and Dow Finsterwald, in 1962. He won in the playoff by shooting 31 on the last nine, after being three down to Gary Player on the first nine.

Gary Player won the Masters in 1961, 1974 and 1978, scoring 280, 278 and 277, respectively. Player, from South Africa, became the first foreign entry to win the Masters with his 1961 win. In a tight contest with Arnold Palmer and Charles Coe, Player made a four from the bunker on the right of the eighteenth green, while Palmer pulled a six, leaving their scores 280 and 281, respectively. Coe, meanwhile, had a two-day finish of 69-69, to gain four strokes on Player and five on Palmer, to tie Palmer for second place.

In the 1974 Masters, he made a spectacular nine-iron approach shot to within inches of the pin, which proved the decisive stroke in a close contest with Tom

Weiskopf and Dave Stockton. The 1978 Masters was another close contest, despite Player's seven birdies on the last ten holes.

The year 1963 saw the first win by the phenomenal Jack Nicklaus, who at 23 became the youngest winner of the Masters, up until 1980, when Seve Ballesteros edged him out of this record by a few months difference in birthdates. Nicklaus was to go on to win a total of six Masters—1963, 1965, 1966, 1972, 1975 and 1986, with scores of 286, 271, 288, 286, 276 and 279.

The 1965 Masters saw Nicklaus breaking Ben Hogan's tournament record 274 with a 271, and tying Lloyd Mangrum's 18-hole score of 65. Nicklaus won by nine strokes—the largest margin in Masters history—over Arnold Palmer and Gary Player. In 1966, Nicklaus became the first Masters champion to successfully defend his title, in a three-way playoff with Tommy Jacobs

tively. In the final round of the 1977 tournament, Watson's 20-foot birdie putt on the seventeenth forced the great Jack Nicklaus to gamble for a birdie—only to come up with a losing bogie. Watson won by two strokes.

Nicklaus and Johnny Miller were the competition for Watson in the 1981 Masters, but Watson's 280 defeated the second-place tie at 282 shared by Nicklaus and Miller.

At left: Arnold Palmer at the 1982 Masters, where Craig Stadler defeated Dan Pohl in the second-ever Masters sudden-death playoff. *Above:* A Masters fan wears her loyalty on her hat.

and Gay Brewer Jr. Nicklaus shot a 70, to defeat Jacobs' 72 and Brewer's 78.

Nicklaus joined Arnold Palmer in the four-time Masters winners' club, and while his winning score was 286, conditions were such that he was the only player to finish the tournament under par. Nicklaus became the first five-time winner of the Masters in 1975. It was a tight contest, down to the finale, as runners-up Tom Weiskopf and Johnny Miller had tying scores of 277 to Nicklaus' winning 276.

Perhaps the sweetest of Nicklaus' Masters victories was his sixth, when, at age 46, he became the oldest Masters winner with a dramatic charge in the second nine of the final round, shooting an eagle, two birdies and a par to overcome a four-stroke lead by Severiano Ballesteros, and fending off serious challenges by Greg Norman and Tom Kite. His closing round was a masterful 65.

Tom Watson's two wins came in 1977 and 1981, with scores of 276 and 280, respec-

Severiano 'Seve' Ballesteros won the first of his two Masters in 1980, at the tender age of 23, becoming the youngest Masters champion ever. He finished the tournament at 275, four strokes ahead of runners-up Gibby Gilbert and Jack Newton.

Over the years, Masters play has resulted in various changes to the course. First tournament winner Horton Smith suggested changes to the seventh hole, as he felt the hole was too short, and too easy. The seventh was thereupon lengthened, and bunkers were added; now the seventh is one of the premier tests on the course.

Again, in the mid-1960s, Jack Nicklaus had the canny habit of dropping his tee shot onto the extreme left side of the eighteenth fairway, which was unguarded, save for the roped gallery. The green was an easy goal from that lie, and other strong shooters followed suit. The Augusta National club committee resolved the situation by constructing a two-part bunker there, reducing the fairway width by more than 30 yards, and adding challenge to the green approach.

In the 1970s, club officials felt that the greens no longer had the speed and firmness that they should. Over the years, drainage problems with the clay subsoil that underlies the greens had caused the putting surfaces to soften. Very cautiously, the club explored the idea of using bentgrass greens with a sand base, following the example of Robert Trent Jones' Greenville Country Club course in South Carolina.

Augusta National experimented with bentgrass on its 'par three' course for three years before making their decision. They went with Penngrass and a sand base. While the project cost was enormous, the original contours of the course were carefully preserved, and the greens now have a lightning-like speed.

The sixteenth hole, a par three, was subject to a radical revision which gave extra length and a more substantial water hazard than it had before. Originally, its tee lay just behind the fifteenth green, and there was a

stream carry off the tee, but the hole was only 110 yards long.

The management committee brought in Robert Trent Jones to redesign the hole. The stream was modified to provide an elongated pond that runs from tee to green, and the green features several difficult pin placements. Altogether, the sixteenth has become one of the most challenging par threes in America.

Each of the holes at Augusta National is named for one of the plants or trees on the course—and, speaking of such flora, the privet hedge that borders the practice range is said to be the mother of all privet hedges in the US, and the wisteria in front of the clubhouse terrace is said to be the oldest in America. Together with the more-than-200-year-old oak in front of the clubhouse and the beautiful abundance of plants, flowers and trees in general at

Augusta National, these add to the extraordinary richness of the aesthetic experience of Augusta National.

Augusta National was designed to provide a pleasurable round of golf for the average player, and to provide a tough challenge for players of tournament caliber. Augusta has very little punishing rough and few bunkers; mounds are often used in place of bunkers to emphasize strategic aspects of play; and while greens and fairways are large, the implementation of slopes and fast surface creates a difficult situation for the player who plays his approach shot indifferently. The course does not punish severely so much as it rewards the finely played shot.

The following is a hole-by-hole description of the championship course at Augusta National, as set up for the Masters Tournament. The first hole, Tea Olive, is a 400-yard

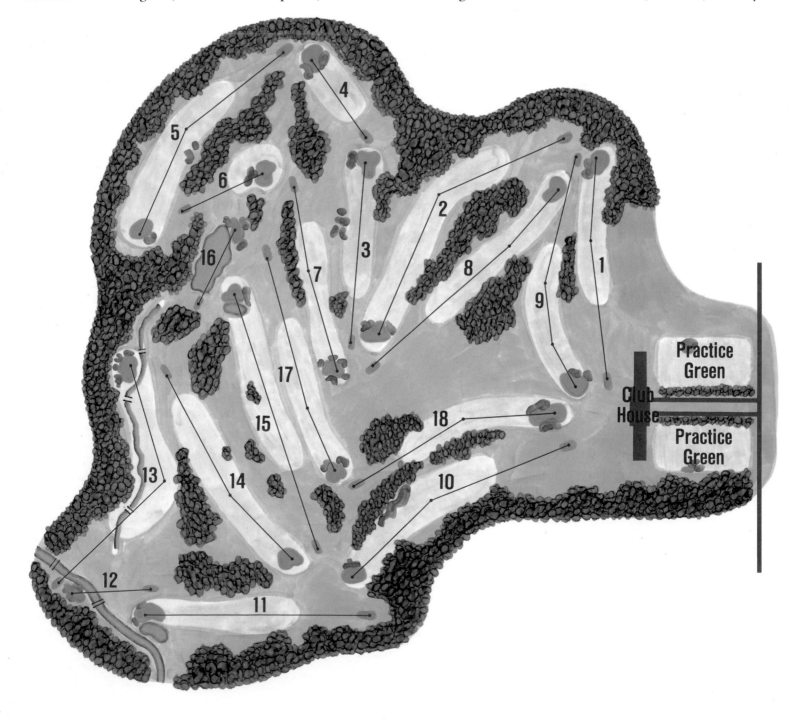

Above: **Arnold Palmer, a favorite Masters winner, draws the attention of a Masters gallery.**

par four that tees off just behind the Augusta National clubhouse. It is tree-lined, with a large bunker on the right near the landing spot. The green narrows from back to front and is guarded on the left by a deep bunker.

Hole number two, Pink Dogwood, gives you a chance to limber up, as it's technically the longest hole on the course, at 555 yards. It's a dogleg left, lined with flowering trees and trees of the plainer—but still quite beautiful—green, leafy variety. Those who cut the corner on the dogleg will probably save a stroke in reaching the green, but should be careful of the trees. A bunker on the outer bend of the dogleg may also collect errant tee shots. The irregular, tri-lobed green is guarded right and left with two large bunkers.

The third hole, Flowering Peach, favors shots to the right side of the fairway, but a tendency to hook can land your shot in the bunkers at left. Another tri-lobed green, smaller than the second, and with a single bunker on its left-most lobe, awaits your putting expertise.

Hole number four, Flowering Crabapple, is the first par three on the course. Guarded at left and right with bunkers, the green is shallow on the right, and the deep bunker on that side cuts into the putting surface.

The fifth hole, Magnolia, is a dogleg left. This tree-lined hole has a pair of bunkers on the left of the landing spot, in position to frustrate some golfers who try to shave a stroke from their score by going left from the tee. Any way you play it, this is a hole for the adventurous, with a series of mounds that come out from either side of the green and culminate at a bunker directly blocking the approach.

Hole number six, Juniper, tees off with a mound to the left, down a short hallway of beautiful trees. The tee shot on this par three must carry a large, deep bunker directly in front of the green. The green is, as is the general rule at Augusta National, fast—it takes some artistry to stop the ball dead.

The seventh hole, Pampas, so named for the swatch of pampas grass that lies to the left of the tees, is a straightaway, 360-yard par four. Its wide fairway is lined with trees, and accuracy and judgement of wind is a crucial factor here. The green is the smallest on the course—a true 'postage

stamp.' The three bunkers across its front, and the two at its rear, have caught many a misjudged shot.

Hole number eight, Yellow Jasmine, requires an approximately 250-yard shot from the tees. Included in this is a carry over a large bunker. The second shot passes down a broad corridor of trees. This hole doglegs to the left at the green approach. It's an uphill drive, but bear in mind that Claude Harmon made this one in two strokes en route to winning the 1948 Masters. It is, however, a hole for long hitters.

The ninth hole, Carolina Cherry, is a dramatic dogleg left. The green is long and narrow, and approach shots must carry over the foremost of two bunkers on the left of the putting surface. It is a difficult—and rewarding—test of one's expertise.

Hole number ten, Camellia, is named for the flowering bushes that grow to the left of the green approach. To the left of the tees lies the Jones Cabin, one of the National's many landmarks. This is a 485-yard par four that features a carry over a long, massive bunker on the second shot. Tee shots down the left side have the advantage, as the right side is the domain of the greater extent of the aforesaid bunker. A slope in front of the green, and a bunker at right front, add to the challenge here. This is, however, where Arnold Palmer made a 40-foot putt for a birdie, leading off a total of five birdies that enabled him to win the 1962 Masters.

The eleventh, White Dogwood, is the first of three holes in the rigorous 'Amen Corner,' of which the following is said: 'No Masters is won until you're safely past Amen Corner.' The best route to take on the eleventh is in the center or right center of the fairway—anything to the left will bring a greater portion of the lake that hugs the left side of the green into play. Overflights may find the bunkers at right and left rear of the putting surface.

Hole number twelve, Golden Bell, is the mid-point of Amen Corner. It's a par three and features a carry across Rae's Creek. Just to the left is Ben Hogan Bridge. The scores established on this hole and on the thirteenth have often decided the outcome of Masters Tournaments. When the pin is placed on the left, the cut that the creek takes toward the green on that side has much significance. When the pin is on the right, the tee shot is longer, and the creek and bunkers front and rear can make a real difference in your score. The premium is on accuracy—at this hole, you can lose two strokes, or gain substantially on the competition.

The thirteenth, Azalea, is a dogleg left that plays back and forth across Rae's

Augusta National Golf Club

Hole	1	2	3	4	5	6	7	8	9	Out	
Masters	400	555	360	205	435	180	360	535	435	3465	
Par	4	5	4	3	4	3	4	5	4	36	

Hole	10	11	12	13	14	15	16	17	18	In	Total
Masters	485	455	155	465	405	500	170	400	405	36	6975
Par	4	4	3	5	4	5	3	4	4	36	72

Creek. This is the last hole of the Amen Corner, and continues the extraordinary challenge that began with the eleventh hole. You'll tee off with the Byron Nelson Bridge to your left. To get good position for the second shot, you'll actually carry across two segments of the creek, and shave your shot past the stand of trees on the left. Then you go for a green that is protected by the creek on its right side from front to rear, and has a series of large bunkers on the left all the way from front to back.

Hole number fourteen, Chinese Fir, is a driver's hole, and plays along a wide corridor of trees to a large green that is surrounded with mounds.

The fifteenth hole, Fire Thorn, is another test of strength. A 500-yard par five, trees close in on the left of the fairway can cause trouble with hooked tee shots. A large pond guards the front of the green, and a longitudinal bunker guards the right-hand side. To the left is the Gene Sarazen Bridge. In the 1935 Masters, Sarazen scored a double eagle on this hole, and went on to win a playoff against Craig Wood. The water carry to the green may tempt one to put too much behind the approach shot: it's entirely possible to overshoot this green. A bunker and a spectator mound lie to the right.

Hole number sixteen, Red Bud, a par three, features a long lake carry to an obliquely-set green that is well guarded by three strategically-placed bunkers. This is another make-or-break hole, and adds yet one more reason to those provided by the previous holes as to why the back nine of Augusta National is such a tough test of golf. The pin is often placed, on the last day of the Masters, in the narrow neck of fairway to the far left, making for an exceptionally difficult birdie. Arnold Palmer and Jack Nicklaus both scored birdies on the sixteenth, en route to their respective Masters victories in 1962 and 1963.

The seventeenth, Nandina, tees off down a hallway of trees, a few of which lie close in on the left, challenging those who want to place their tee shots on the left side of the fairway, for a more direct access to the green. The putting surface is guarded with bunkers at left and right front.

The eighteenth, Holly, is a gentle dogleg right with bunkers placed strategically near the landing spot. The green is set end-on to the fairway, and two bunkers—one at right, and the other at left front—guard the putting surface. It is an elegant and rewarding challenge to complete a truly great test of golf.

Jack Nicklaus is the only six-time Masters winner, and Arnold Palmer, shown at the Masters _at left_, is the only four-time Masters winner.

The Australian Golf Club

Kensington Australia

Jack Nicklaus was invited to submit ideas for the enhancement of this course in 1976: the course had been put in its previous championship form by Dr Alister Mackenzie, and his predecessors Hutchinson, Martin and Clark (see below).

The Australian was ranked 87th among *Golf* magazine's '100 Greatest Courses in the World' in 1987, and was ranked 97th in 1989—not as great a fall as it would seem, as, in the latter 20 placements of this particular poll, the difference in standings is often the separation of a few decimal points—hence, a rounded-off fraction in this sector can cause a significant decline (or rise) in ranking.

The new construction work began in 1977, and resulted in a recontouring and reconfiguring of the course. The introduction of numerous water carries and the replanting of the fairways with the new hybrid Couch 329 changed the course from what had been a wind-swept, virtually treeless linksland course to a lushly tree-lined layout similar to many American courses.

Nicklaus worked in cooperation with Mr Kerry Packer, the sponsor of the Australian Open—which is now permanently based at the Australian Golf Club Course. A bit of historical review on this layout may give an inkling as to the kind of excitement that the

remodeling project generated. The Australian Golf Club—one of the most prestigious clubs in Australia—was founded in 1882, at which time golfers played on a course situated near the present-day Sydney Cricket Ground. This location was not quite what was needed, so a further venue for play was sought.

After a search for a suitable site, 99 acres of land were leased on the shore of Botany Bay, an inlet of the Tasman Sea, just southwest of Sydney. Here, two distinguished firsts were inaugurated—the Country Golf Week Tournament, and the Australian Open Championship. In 1903, the club bought the present site—175 acres in Ken-

sington, which is due south of Sydney. The original eighteen hole design at Kensington was the result of a competition between three professional golfers who are known to us as 'Hutchinson, Martin and Clark.' Alterations to this design were made in 1926 at the suggestion of renowned course designer Dr Alister Mackenzie.

Tragedy struck in 1932, when the club-house—then located at the present sixth tee area—was completely destroyed by fire. The new clubhouse was built on newly purchased land to the west of the then-existing layout, and this necessitated further changes to accommodate the first and tenth tees in the vicinity of the new building. In 1967 the club was informed that a freeway, known as Southern Cross Drive, was to be built on the course's western and southern boundaries. This freeway would connect Kingsford-Smith Airport with Sydney. The necessary course changes were designed by Sloan Morpeth. Then came the hand of Jack Nicklaus, and the transformation wrought thereby has added challenge to this, which was already one of Australia's finest courses.

After a second total fire loss of their club-house—before the Nicklaus course changes were completed—a more modern clubhouse was built on the original club-house site.

This beautiful course is adorned with flowers at aesthetically advantageous points, and has hosted a plethora of national and state championships, both amateur and professional, in addition to many commercial tournaments. This great course was included among the '100 Greatest Golf Courses in the World' by *Golf* magazine, and will no doubt only grow in stature as the years continue to roll by. The following is a hole-by-hole description of this fine golf course, which measures 6443 meters from the back tees.

Hole number one is a tree-lined dogleg right having four bunkers situated on its inside bend. The fairway then veers back to the left for a pinched green approach, and a well-bunkered green. The second hole is a well-wooded par three featuring longitudinal bunkers to the right and left of the two-tiered green. Hole three is the first of the water holes. This par four doglegs left at a

cluster of bunkers—two right, one left—and bends around the edge of a lake to the right. A dogleg right brings you to the split-level green, which has bunkers at left and behind, and the lake to the right.

The par three fourth hole plays around the same lake that we met on the previous hole. You tee off to a fairway which bends right around the limb of the lake, which provides most golfers with an obvious water carry for a savings on strokes to the green, which itself is bunkered left and right. Hole number five, at 526 meters, is the longest hole on the course. A tree-lined par five, its opposing bunkers at the first dogleg introduce a long fairway that will give you a good chance to test your driving abilities. A trickily bunkered, two-level green provides a satisfying target to conclude this hole.

Hole six gives you a 'gunsight' of trees to aim at the fairway with—straight and narrow here. The fairway features a ridge early on, and has a massive bunker to the right front of the split-level green. You tee off

Below: **The fairway of The Australian's daunting and beautiful seventeenth green approach.**

down a hallway of trees on the seventh hole, and unless your shot tends to the right or lays up, you'll find the two fairway bunkers lying left. The split-level green is situated snugly beside a lake. The tees of hole eight are sandwiched between two lakes, and staggered, opposing bunkers guard the fairway early on. This hole's asymmetrical, two-level green is bunkered left and right of its narrow 'jaw.'

The ninth hole fairway bends to the left, with a bunker set to the left of its bend. Bunkers right and left of the green keep shots straight and narrow; a long lake to the left beyond the bunkering should keep your calculations toward not letting shots go too far afield. Trees and an access road are to your right. Well treed, par four hole ten leads you past two right-lying fairway bunkers to a green having a slope at right and behind, and a cannily-placed bunker at left. Hole eleven, a par three, has trees all along its left, and a 32 meters-long green. This green is very well bunkered.

The twelfth hole has you teeing off into a dogleg surrounded with bunkers. Down the tree-lined fairway from this is a two-level green with bunkering right and left. The golfer tees off down a long hallway of trees on hole thirteen. These trees compose a daunting psychological barrier, as they tend to force tee shots to the rough and trees at left, not to mention the large fairway bunker that lies just beyond the fairway's dogleg. The green is elevated, with bunkers set right and left in the approach.

Hole fourteen, a reasonable par five at 512 meters, forms a long serpentine. You tee off somewhat obliquely to a fairway which has two bunkers on its right to catch overlong tee shots. A long bunker guards the right of the green approach, and the green itself is bunkered at front—left and right. The green is also backed directly into several trees, and *that* could mean trouble! The fifteenth hole, a par three, features a split-level green that is virtually surrounded by three hefty bunkers. The sixteenth is tree-lined all the way, and has a gang of bunkers on the right front of the green, and two more on the left rear. This three-tiered green is obliquely set and oblong—be careful here.

Hole number seventeen winds you up for the conclusion. Shots from the back tee are forced to the left of a fairway which fades to the right—not much to land on from that perspective! Trees on both sides line this hole, and the fairway bends left to tuck the green partially behind a left-lying

At left: **The Australian's challenging par three fourth hole. The green is as viewed from across a lake that comes into play on the fourth.**

lake. Bunkers on either side of the green complete the scenario for a spine-tingling challenge. The tree-lined eighteenth bends to the right, for a balancing act with the previous hole. A fairway bunker squeezes in from the right early on, and hummocks on the left give a hint of Scottish linksland. Nearing the green, two left-lying bunkers guard the outside of the fairway bend, and a longitudinal lake guards the inside of same. The green has a bunker on its left, and widens away from the lake (which guards the green from the right), toward the trees behind it. It's a cleverly arranged set of defenses, and is sure to provide an exhilarating and challenging finish for your round of golf at The Australian Golf Club.

Opposite: A view from behind the bunkers on the sixteenth green approach. Your view of the green could be from inside one of these bunkers if your attention lapses on the approach shot. Even so, the beauty of the course is strikingly evident here. *Above:* The skyline of Sydney, seen from The Australian.

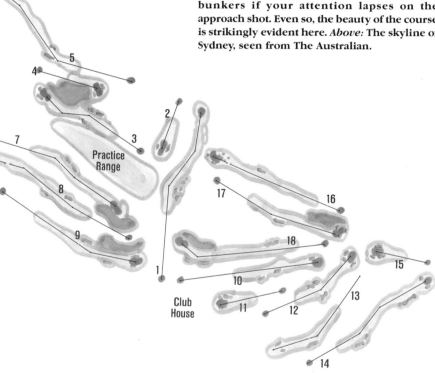

The Australian Golf Club

Hole	1	2	3	4	5	6	7	8	9	Out
Member Blue	457	168	343	159	526	384	382	397	405	3221
Member White	440	156	327	136	497	378	320	387	388	3029
Associate	403	146	291	105	453	366	312	379	305	2760
Par	5	3	4	3	5	4/5	4	4/5	4	36/38

Hole	10	11	12	13	14	15	16	17	18	In	Total
Member Blue	379	173	367	351	512	187	388	390	475	3222	6443
Member White	361	140	354	346	490	173	368	359	459	3050	6079
Associate	313	120	278	325	465	152	353	309	430	2745	5505
Par	4	3	4	4	5	3	4/5	4	5	36/37	72/75

Note: all distances are given in meters.

These pages: The seventeenth green at The Australian, with a view down the fairway. The challenge, playability and aesthetic qualities of this course are of the highest level. The Australian is one of several outstanding reasons—including the National Golf and Country Club, and the Royal Melbourne Golf Club—that Australia is the place to golf in the southern hemisphere.

Ballybunion Golf Club

Ballybunion Ireland

The Old Course at Ballybunion is rated ninth in the world by *Golf Magazine*'s 1989 listing of the '100 Greatest Courses in the World.' The same listing for 1987 pegged Ballybunion as the eighth greatest golf course in the world. This drop in the rankings is probably more a reflection of changes in the ranks of *Golf Magazine*'s panelists than any actual decline on the part of this great course, which is one of the most highly revered venues in the world of golf facilities.

Ballybunion, a true seaside course, is located on the Shannon Estuary, where Ireland's most beloved river meets the Atlantic Ocean. It has a wild look, with long grass covering dunes that undulate throughout the course. Ballybunion is full of sharp contours, and is virtually treeless. In the words of golfing great Tom Watson, 'It looks like a course laid out on land as it was in the tenth century.'

The first Ballybunion Golf Club was inaugurated on 4 March 1896, but suffered financial failure in August of 1898. The good golfers of the Ballybunion area were not ones to give up that easily, however, as the present Ballybunion Golf Club was formed in 1906. The founders were Colonel Bartholomew, BJ Johnstone of the Bank of Ireland, Patrick McCarthy (Honorary Secretary of the Original Club) and John Macauley of Listowel.

Lionel Hewson, who served for many years as the editor of that renowned publication, *Irish Golf*, laid out nine holes for the new club, and by 1926, the links had attracted so much attention that a plan was under way to expand the course to a full 18 holes. The work was finished in 1927, and the ensuing five years saw a maturing process on the links, until, in 1932, Ballybunion was chosen as the venue for the Irish Ladies' Championship.

In 1937, Tom Simpson, one of the leading golf architects of the time, was called in to make the course ready for the playing of the Irish Men's Close Amateur Championship. Simpson was generally pleased with what he found at Ballybunion, and chose to make just a few changes, which included the repositioning of the second, fourth and twelfth greens, and the creation of a bunker in the midst of what is now the first fairway. This bunker was playfully dubbed 'Mrs Simpson,' in honor of the braking effect domesticity has on most lives.

Ballybunion saw its next major championship when the Irish Professional Cham-

At right: **Putting on the Old Course second green, with the sea in the background.** *Below:* **A tee shot at the Old thirteenth.**

pionship was played there in 1959. It was to be the last of 10 national titles for the great Harry Bradshaw. Again, in 1970, the public's attention was riveted on Ballybunion when the 'World of Golf' television series commissioned a match between Ireland's Christy O'Connor and the USA's Bob Goalby.

The year 1971 saw the purchase of an adjoining patch of land for the construction of what is now known as the New Course at Ballybunion. That same year saw the construction of a new and larger clubhouse to accommodate the increasing numbers of overseas visitors, who were eager to play this extraordinary golf course.

The age of international travel has indeed struck Ballybunion full force, and its management is looking forward to the challenges of the future. The renowned Tom Watson—to mention just one golfer from 'beyond the sea'—has been playing Ballybunion's Old Course every year since 1981, as an essential part of his preparations for the British Open.

It is a course that rewards good play and good shots, and requires the full range of shots. There are all sorts of slopes and gradients—uphill, downhill and sidehill, and

the small greens require sureness and accuracy. The greens confront you with contours that will challenge your putting, and require a rolling approach.

Combined with the seaside winds at Ballybunion, the contours and naturalness of the Old Course make for an unforgettable challenge.

As indicated above, Ballybunion Golf Club is also the venue for a second 18 holes of golf—the New Course, which, in itself, is a magnificent golf layout. Robert Trent Jones Sr, the architect of the New Course, has this to say about the New Course: 'When I first saw the piece of land chosen for the New Course at Ballybunion… I was

thrilled beyond words… it was the finest piece of linksland that I had ever seen, and perhaps the finest… in the world.'

Mr Jones collaborated with nature on this course, saying 'There is no more natural golf hole in the world than the tenth, an outrageously beautiful stretch of God-given terrain.' The New Course at Ballybunion is a unique and majestic golf course.

The following is a hole-by-hole description of the world-famous Old Course at Ballybunion. To begin with, the Old Course has five par threes, one of which is the downhill eighth hole, which, in a wind, requires one of the most demanding shots

in golfing. Tom Watson feels that the eleventh, a par four, is 'one of the toughest holes in the world.'

As you stand on the first tee of the Old Course, the graveyard just off to the left may well erase any cavalier attitude on your part concerning the round of golf you're about to play. This hole demands excellence off the tee, as a sand hill surmounted by a grassy hollow stands off to the left, and just right of the landing spot lie two bunkers, and just ahead of these and in the midst of the fairway is a mound. The fairway bulges off to the right beyond the two bunkers, but rough lies perilously close on that side. Beyond this set of haz-

ards is an ample green with two bunkers on its left and two on its right.

The second hole features a stream carry off the tees, and a mound and a hollow that are cannily placed to catch shortfalls to the fairway. Further, there is a rise in elevation just beyond the landing spot (unless your valor is such that you can unhesitatingly carry from the tees over the top of this rise). To the left and right of the landing spot are bunkers, and a row of bunkers on the left continues on up past the rise, where a hollow, and then a sand hill, further complicate the green approach, which features yet another change in elevation. To the right of the green approach, a sand hill,

complicated by a mound and a hollow, stands guard. The green itself is protected by a wondrous array of defenses, including bunkers on both frontal faces, mounds on either side at rear, and a slope and a sand hill at left rear.

The wind will be coming from the left as you play the third hole. A large sand hill stands to the right of the line of shooting from the tees. The green is large and undulating. Hollows at left and right, plus a mound at left, guard the frontal surfaces of the green. Also, a single bunker guards the right rear, and two bunkers and a slope guard the left front, left and left rear surfaces, respectively.

guarded on either side by ridges, and the irregularly-shaped green, which narrows front to rear, has bunkering at left and right front.

The sixth is a perilous dogleg left that heads toward the sea. With the wind usually pouring in from the left, your tee shot must avoid a mound and a hollow on the left of the fairway's leading edge, and a mound on the right—just in the line of flight from the tees. The green, long and comparatively narrow, is notoriously hard to hit. Rough and out of bounds lies to the right, where mis-hit balls often find their way. A ravishing, and quite distracting, face-on view of the Atlantic Ocean is yours

The Old Course. *At left:* **Playing out of the bunker at left front of the fourteenth hole.** *Above:* **On the seventeenth tee.**

Now two par five birdie chances (depending on wind conditions) present themselves—the fourth and fifth holes. The fourth hole requires a tee shot straight down the fairway, avoiding the sand hills that lie to either side of the fairway's leading edge. The second shot will probably take place from between the ninth green, on the left, and the house on the right. This requires a carry over and past a large, central hollow, a left-lying mound, and a mound and a hollow at right. The green is quite long, and reasonably wide, with bunkers at left and right front, and hollows at left and right rear.

The fifth hole, at 508 yards the longest hole on the course, is a great chance to limber up your driving muscles—considering, of course, that your attention to accuracy is on par with your strength. To the left at the 200-yard mark lies a bunker, and at the 300-yard mark two bunkers in a row occupy the center of the fairway. Prefacing the green approach is a bunker, backed by a mound, on the right. The green approach is

as you combat the rigors of this hole.

On hole number seven, the wind will be coming in from the right. As on much of this course, stunning vistas are availed to golfers on this hole. With the surf just to your right, you tee off to a fairway that has a mound to the left and a set of ridges a bit farther down on that same side. If you manage to get your ball going right, just beyond the ridges lies a slope. The green approach is guarded by a central mound, and off to the left of the green is a huge sand hill, while closer in lies a bunker, and on the right is another slope. At rear and left rear are substantial hollows, and at right rear is a mound.

The eighth hole, a par three, is a strict test in a wind. This hole plays downhill to a deep, highly contoured, serpentine green that is protected on the left, front to back, by a bunker, a compound mound, another bunker and a large hollow. On the right of this green, in the same sequence, lie a bunker, another compound mound and a hollow.

The ninth hole usually has wind coming in from the right. Par on this hole requires two perfect setup shots. Huge sand hills

Above: A view of the Ballybunion Old Course fourteenth green. *Below:* The Old tenth green, with its magnificent vista in evidence. As can be seen by the photos in this chapter, Ballybunion, a seaside course, is subject to the wiles of seaside weather, which only adds to the challenge here.

guard both sides of the leading edge of the fairway. Behind the hill on the left is a cunningly-situated little pond, tucked into the inner surface of the hill at right is a hollow. Just beyond these is a swale, a hill, and then another swale. Then you have a transverse central hollow called 'The Crow's Nest,' which is accompanied on the right of the fairway by a gigantic sand hill that stretches from the second slope all the way to the green. The green approach is guarded on the left center with another mound, and the split-level green has two bunkers on its right side, with an additional bunker lying farther out on that side, and has slopes practically everywhere else.

Hole number ten is a another test of perfection. The tees face a fairway that is a conglomeration of mounds, slopes and hollows, and features a canny 'ell'-shaped slope just when you might think the worst is over. Off to the left of this is a large sand hill that overshadows most of the left side of this fairway. The green approach is guarded by a mound and a large hollow,

which slopes to the green, which is backed up to the sea, and is sandwiched between two of the eleventh tees. On the right front of this green lies a bunker, and a slope is located at left rear.

The eleventh hole plays along the sea, requires a long carry to a complex fairway that is broken into three parts, features two central slopes and is guarded on the left by a sand hill and a mound, in that order. On the right lies a mound that is backed by a slope down to the ocean, and another mound, respectively. The green approach is guarded on either side with large sand hills. The long, slender green has a hollow on its left front surface and a slope on its right.

A little more simple is the par three twelfth, which features tee shots between large sand hills to an ample green that is guarded by three hollows, a bunker and a sand hill on the left, slopes in front, and is guarded on the right by a mound, a ridge, a slope and a large hollow. The green has a slope in back, as well.

The thirteenth, a par five, has a long carry from the tees. The fairway is guarded at left by a procession of hazards that begins with a sand hill, then a hollow, two bunkers, a mound and another bunker. The wind generally comes from the right here. At approximately 250 yards from the tees lies a fairway slope, and beyond this, a central mound and a mound to the right keep up the defenses. The green approach, which is traversed by a stream, is somewhat obscured by a ridge. Beyond this lies a central mound, to the left of which is a massive sand hill. The green has bunkers at right front and right, with a hollow at right rear and the fourteenth tee off to the right. On the left front, the sand hill, compounded by a bunker, a mound and a hollow, provides the defense. All along the rear of the green is a slope.

The fourteenth hole is another great par three on the Old Course. The wind generally comes from the right here, and the tee shot is presented with a 'gunsight' of two sand hills. The tendency is to want to go right, to counteract the wind, but beyond that right-hand sand hill lies a huge hollow. The green is further preceded by a bunker, and off the left side of the green lie two sand hills, while closer in, on the left rear, is a longitudinal hollow. At the rear of the green is a slope, and on the right rear is a sand hill, while at right front is a hollow backed by a mound. This green is 34 yards long, but is comparatively narrow.

The fifteenth hole, a par three, features a long carry past a left-lying sand hill to a two-tiered green that has a slope on its frontal surface as well. At right front and right lie bunkers, and at right rear is a mound. On the left lies a complex of a hollow, a bunker and a mound. At rear is another mound. The ocean breezes are coming at you from the left front, and the glorious expanse of water is in view. Sean

Ballybunion Old Course

Hole	1	2	3	4	5	6	7	8	9	Out	
Championship	392	445	220	498	508	364	423	153	454	3457	
Medal	366	394	211	490	489	344	400	134	430	3258	
Forward	328	379	186	483	476	319	386	116	411	3084	
Par	4	4	3	5	5	4	4	3	4	36	
Hole	10	11	12	13	14	15	16	17	18	In	Total
Championship	359	449	192	484	131	216	490	385	379	3085	6542
Medal	336	400	179	480	125	207	482	368	366	2943	6201
Forward	312	385	166	477	118	197	476	350	358	2839	5923
Par	4	4	3	5	3	3	5	4	4	35	71

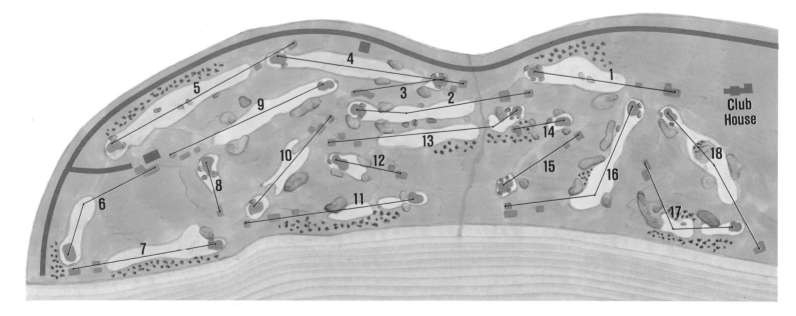

Walsh, Manager of Ballybunion Golf Club, considers this to be the best short hole on the links. Your tee shot on the sixteenth hole receives wind from the right side, but then as this dogleg bends left, the wind is at your back. This tee shot must negotiate a series of sand hills and two hollows, one of which is called 'Saucer,' but both of which could be deadly to your game. It is a perilous setup for the second shot, which must pass down a short, narrow valley called 'Gap,' and skirt a left-lying sand hill and a right-lying slope. The green approach is guarded by the slope and the sand hill, and a bunker set into the sand hill. The green is roughly oblong, and has two bunkers guarding its right-hand surface, and a hollow guarding its left.

The seventeenth hole tees off into the wind, with the ocean sparkling just beyond this dogleg left's fairway. The tee shot must negotiate a left-lying slope and a right-lying sand hill, and must pass over a large bunker en route to the fairway. Just to the left of the landing spot is another bunker. A slope occupies a break in the fairway, just as the dogleg bends left. At the outside of this curve is a mound. The second shot passes down a fairway that is open on the right. You will have to try to keep your ball from being blown against the large sand hill on the left. The green approach has a mound on the right, and the green is protected by two mounds on the right, and a mound and a bunker on the left. To the back of this green is a pathway and a slope.

The eighteenth hole is also a dogleg left, with the wind coming in obliquely from behind. Close by the tees, on the left, is the seventeenth green. to the left and right of the landing spot are large sand hills, and at the 250-yard mark, just after the bend in the fairway, and hidden from view by the sand hill, is a patch of rough that contains a hollow and the central, lateral bunker known as 'Sahara.' The green approach is severely pinched by a mound on the right, and an arm of a large, 'ell'-shaped sand hill on the left. The green is protected on the right by another mound, at rear by a hollow, at left rear with a bunker and at left front with another bunker. Off to the left, at the foot of the nearby sand hill, is a slope, and all along the right is the Atlantic Ocean.

Now, let's consider the New Course at Ballybunion Golf Club, from a hole-by-hole perspective. The first hole is a slight dogleg right, whose tees lie in the back of a funnel-shaped hallway that is formed by a slope at left and a ridge at right. Just left of the landing spot is a bunker tucked into the side of a large sand hill, and some 40 yards from this lies a mound and a ridge on the right and a sand hill on the left. The green

has a longitudinal bunker almost directly in front of its broad forward surface. At right rear are a bunker and a mound, and at left rear are a slope and a sand hill. The slope continues on around to the rear of the green.

You'll be playing into the wind at hole number two, which is also a dogleg right, with a large, concealing mound directly across the fairway, which steps treacherously down after the mound. At the midpoint of the fairway, two mounds form a line with a bunker, emphasizing a carry or a flight over to the right side of the fairway, which is guarded on the outside by a longitudinal bunker and a large mound that extends all the way to the mouth of the green. Just off the front and right front of the green are two bunkers, and to the right and left rear of same are two more.

At left: **The practice green, near the graveyard.** *Below left:* **Finding an overflight past the Old tenth hole.** *Below:* **In an Old second green bunker.**

The third hole, a par three, plays with the wind coming in from the left. Tee shots pass down a hallway composed of two sand hills on the left, and a long sand hill and a massive hollow on the right. The green is fronted by two bunkers, and has a sand hill topped by a hollow at right rear. Beware the wind.

From the back tees, hole number four is a dogleg left, with a cluster of three bunkers, a mound and a hollow surrounding the landing spot. The green approach is pinched by one bunker at right and two left, while the green has bunkers at right front and at rear, and a large mound off to its left front. You're playing near the ocean now.

Hole number five plays along the ocean, with the wind at its back and left. An extremely long carry (260 yards from the back tee) hopefully gets you to the fairway. A battery of hazards on the right includes a sand hill, an incursive valley and another

sand hill, leading up to the green approach, which is narrowed considerably by bunkering on either side. The green is long but narrow, and has a mound off of its left front surface.

The sixth hole is a highly threatening par three that features a 145-yard tee shot across a large, circular valley—usually in a headwind. The green has a slope at front, and bunkers at right front, left front and left rear. A sand hill is located to the right rear, just off the green. At 154 yards from the back tees, this is the longest par three on the course.

The seventh hole plays away from the wind, with some breezes coming in from the left. It's a dogleg right that has a mound directly in the line of flight from the tees. The fairway is guarded on the left with a large sand hill, and wraps around a valley on the right. The green is broad but shallow, and has a bunker directly in front, and at left and right rear. It's a thrilling shot

Ballybunion New Course

Hole	1	2	3	4	5	6	7	8	9	Out
Championship	437	397	153	404	445	154	346	615	501	3452
Medal	413	377	142	341	425	140	316	600	486	3240
Forward	364	365	131	322	405	124	300	588	469	3068
Par	4	4	3	4	4	3	4	5	5	36

Hole	10	11	12	13	14	15	16	17	18	In	Total
Championship	328	142	262	387	398	489	145	484	390	3025	6477
Medal	317	133	251	370	351	476	133	476	369	2876	6116
Forward	306	121	240	358	337	453	126	470	361	2772	5840
Par	4	3	4	4	4	5	3	5	4	36	72

across the valley, and in a strong wind, it's downright spine-tingling.

The eighth hole is, at 615 yards from the back tees, the longest hole on the course. A dogleg left, this hole plays away from the ocean, but does receive some wind from the left and rear. To the left of the landing spot is a large sand hill, and directly in line with tee shots is a bunker on the perimeter of the fairway. The second shot must negotiate a slope, a hollow and a ridge—on the greenward side of which are two left-lying bunkers. The green approach is guarded by a mound and a sand hill at left, and a 130-yard-long sand hill on the right. The green has bunkers at left and right front, a slope and a hollow at left rear, and the two sand hills off to the left and right.

The ninth hole is lined with sand hills left and right. A large depression lies off to the left of the leading edge of the fairway, and a break in the fairway features a broad valley, beyond which lies the green approach. The green has two sand hills on its right, a single large sand hill on its left, and a bunker at left front. Beware the crosswind at the valley.

Hole number ten is a dogleg right that heads toward the ocean, and into the wind. Tee shots pass along a right-lying sand hill. A mound lies on the left of the fairway, on the outside of the curve, as does a large sand hill that shelters a bunker on its inner flank. The green is long but narrow, and has grass bunkers at right and right rear, as well as a bunker at left front.

The eleventh hole, a par three, has an ample green that is protected by a slope approximately 20 yards out, a hollow to the left front and a sand hill to the left of this, and (immediately surrounding the green) a hollow and a mound at right, and bunkers at right front, left front and left. The wind is coming from the right here. On the same side, the sea is a magnificent spectacle that also serves to distract.

Hole number twelve on the New Course is a dogleg right that plays away from the sea. A sand hill to the left of the line of flight can become a real threat, depending on conditions, and three bunkers on the left of the fairway have been known to catch miscalculated shots often enough. To the right of the fairway is a hollow. Some players will want to go for the green from the tees. In this situation, the green will present a smallish target, with two bunkers on its right side. Remember, the wind can absolutely foil such valorous attempts—but then again, it may be worth a try. A slope lines the right side of the fairway.

The thirteenth hole is a real beauty. Three mounds surround the landing spot. At this point, you'll face a downward slope, beyond which lies the green, a magnificently situated putting surface. Directly in front of the green is a bunker. On its left, a slope leads down from a sand hill. On its right, a slope leads down to a hollow. The ocean lies beyond, and the sound of it mingles with the whistling wind to conjure dreams of the perfect golf hole.

Hole number fourteen plays back inland, and is a straightaway hole, with a ridge on the right and a mound on the left forming a 'gunsight' for tee shots to pass through. At perhaps the 230-yard point lies a sand hill at left. This hole is a chance to drive for a birdie. The green is deep but narrow, and has one treacherous bunker on its right front.

The wind comes from ahead and to the right on the fifteenth hole, which plays back out toward the ocean. It's a dogleg right, and becomes quite complex at about 167 yards out from the green, perhaps 90 yards past the bend in the fairway. At this point of complication, a break occurs in the fairway, and to the left lies a ridge, while to the right is a sand hill. Right of center when the fairway resumes is a mound, and to the left and right of the green and green approach are large sand hills. On the right and right front of the green proper are bunkers. This is a small green, some 15 yards deep, and will be a difficult target.

The sixteenth hole requires a tee shot over a rise in front of the green. Frontal bunkers right and left further protect this putting surface, and a sand hill and a hollow protect the left rear, while a sand hill protects the right rear. The wind comes in from the left, where lies the Atlantic Ocean.

Hole number seventeen also plays along the ocean, again with the wind from the

left. It's a dogleg left, with a sand hill to left, near the landing spot. The tee shot from the back tees requires at minimum a 210-yard carry to reach the fairway. On the outside of the dogleg curve, a mound awaits errant shots, and beyond this, on either side of the fairway, sand hills stand sentinel. Between these sand hills, there is a change of elevation in the fairway, and then a long stretch to the green, which is protected in front and at right front with bunkers.

The eighteenth is a great finishing hole for the superb New Course at Ballybunion Golf Club. A dogleg left, its plays inland

The great Old Course. *Above opposite:* **Locating a windblown ball near the eighteenth fairway.** *At top, above:* **A practice swing on the eleventh tee.** *Above:* **Walking by the graveyard, near the first.**

from the ocean, heading toward the new clubhouse. Sand hills—three on the left and one on the right—line the fairway. The green is prefaced by a slope, and has bunkers at right front and left front. It's a pleasure to accomplish par or better on this hole, and then head for the Ballybunion clubhouse, which serves the two extraordinary golf courses at Ballybunion Golf Club.

Carnoustie Golf Links

Carnoustie Scotland

Located between Dundee and Arbroath on Scotland's North Sea coast, Carnoustie Golf Links has long been held in the hearts of golfers everywhere as one of the world's finest golf Links. *Golf Magazine* has rated this course as 22nd and 23rd in their '100 Greatest Courses in the World' listings for 1987 and 1989, respectively.

Golf has been played at Carnoustie for hundreds of years, yet it was not until 1850 that Allan Robertson laid out a 10-hole course. Within the span of the following 20 years, Old Tom Morris encouraged several changes, and the expansion of the course to 18 holes. In 1926, James Braid designed in more bunkers, new tees and new greens, to lay the groundwork for the course as it is known today.

The eighteenth was shortened from a relatively simple par five to a tougher par four in the early 1970s. Just recently, the eleventh green was moved; a few green approaches and driving areas are being reworked and better defined; and bunkers in various parts of the course are being reshaped and brought more into play, to compensate for improvements made in clubs and balls over the years.

The expanse over which the original, championship course at Carnoustie was built could easily accommodate a good number of courses, and in fact now encompasses three courses—the Championship, the Burnside and the relatively new Buddon courses.

The Burnside rides the northern perimeter of the site, and borders on a railway, before looping around and into the center of the Championship Course. The course is well-treed, has plenty of bunkers, and has been used as a qualifying course for British Opens held on the Championship Course.

The Buddon Course is on open ground, and lies between the Championship Course and the sea. It is longer than the Burnside Course, and has been undergoing some adjustment and upgrading.

The Championship Course is the layout we're most interested in here, though. It is 7263 yards long from the championship tees, and requires strategy and awareness of conditions on every hole. No more than two holes face the same direction—therefore, the wind is quite changeable.

The Championship Course is unusually varied for a links course, and the three par threes are especially tough. For example, in the 1968 Open, Jack Nicklaus, using a driver, was the only player to go beyond the pin on the sixteenth in the final round.

Carnoustie was chosen to host its first British Open in 1931. An expatriate Scotsman, Tommy Armour, born in Edinburgh, won with a 71. In doing so, Armour beat the favored Argentinian, Jose Jurado, and local hero Macdonald Smith.

Then came the 1937 Open, in which the Englishman Henry Cotton won with a 71—in high wind and driving rain. Ben Hogan, still recovering from a near-fatal auto accident, won the 1953 Open by four strokes, posting scores for consecutive days of 73, 71, 70 and 68. He had just won the Masters Tournament and the US Open. See the reference to this feat in the chapter on Augusta National.

In 1968, the South African Gary Player beat Jack Nicklaus by two strokes to take the British Open title. It was a contest that saw Jack Nicklaus make a 340-yard drive on the watery seventeenth.

The 1975 Open saw American Tom Watson's one-stroke playoff victory over Australian Jack Newton, which was accomplished in driving rain. It was Watson's first British Open title. (He would go on to win an astonishing five in all.)

We have no doubt that the Championship Course at Carnoustie Golf Links will be the venue for many more memorable rounds of golf. There are no less than 12 par fours on this course. The holes are, naturally, given pertinent names in accordance with the grand old Scottish tradition. It should also be noted that streams are called 'burns' in Scotland. Now, let's take a hole-by-hole tour of this world-famous golf course.

The first hole, Cup, is a par four that requires a carry over a stream—Barry Burn. Just to the right of the landing spot are a number of trees, a small slope and a series of pot bunkers. At the 260-yard

At right: **Teeing off on the first hole, named Cup, which plays over Barry Burn.**

mark, the fairway has a cup-like depression, and making an incursion from the right on the green approach are three bunkers and a mound. The green is a 35-yard-long ovoid, with a slope to its right and two mounds on its right. The wind is from the left rear.

Hole number two, Gulley, requires a carry from the tees over Jockie's Burn, and Braid's Bunker is set in the center of the landing area. The wind comes from the left on this hole. Slopes to the right and left of this fairway, a depression off to the right, and pot bunkers cannily situated on the right and left, contribute to the hazards here. The green approach has two pot bunkers and two mounds on the right and a pot bunker on the left. The green is long and narrow, with a pot bunker, a slope and a mound on the right, and a row of mounds behind these. To the rear of the green is a slope and the out-of-bounds line; and a pot bunker and a slope lie on the left of the green.

The wind is from the right on the third hole, Jockie's Burn (named for the stream that comes into play here). This hole has a slope all along the right, trees (and out-of-bounds) to the midpoint on the left and two bunkers at the left of the landing spot. Jockie's Burn flows from the left to the

right, across the green approach. The green is 34 yards long, with 12 of those yards taken up by a streamward slope at front. On the right front of this green are two mounds, and at right and left are pot bunkers. At right rear is a hollow.

Hole number four has Jockie's Burn flowing down its left side. The wind comes in from the rear. Just to the right of the landing spot are two bunkers. Perhaps 100 yards further, a pot bunker is at mid-center of the fairway, and the green approach has one bunker on the right. The split-level fairway is long and narrow, with a bunker and three small mounds on its right, and two bunkers and a slope at left.

Below: Blasting out of the left greenside bunker on the sixteenth, named for Barry Burn. *Below right:* Playing out of a ditch beside the fairway of the ninth, Railway. *At left:* At the tee.

A burn, or stream, runs diagonally in front of the tees on the fifth hole, Brae. This hole plays into the wind, and is a dogleg right, with a pot bunker to the right of the landing spot. Trees line the left of this fairway, and Jockie's Burn flows across the middle of this fairway. The green approach has out-of-bounds to the left, and three pot bunkers to the right. The split-level green has slopes at right, left rear and rear, and a pair of bunkers at left.

The longest hole, at 575 yards from the back tees, is the sixth, appropriately called Long. Two central bunkers and an additional bunker on the right guard the landing spot. Just to the left of these central bunkers is a narrow strip of fairway, with out-of-bounds on its left, that has been dubbed 'Hogan's Alley,' in honor of Ben Hogan's final-day feat during the 1953 Brit-

ish Open. This was the flight route for his ball for both of the birdies he scored on this hole that day. To the right of the fairway, running on toward the green approach, is a stream. This entire hole is has out-of-bounds very close on the left. Two bunkers and clumps of gorse guard the right of the broad green approach, and the narrow, obliquely-set green has three pot bunkers on its right front, and one large bunker on its left rear, with trees beyond the rear, and gorse off to the right.

The seventh hole, Plantation, features a row of trees that stretches down the right side of the tees to a point one-fourth of the way down the fairway. Bunkers at left and right guard this fairway against both short and long hitters. The wind comes in obliquely here, so be alert. Close by on the left is out-of-bounds. The green approach is

guarded on the right with a mound and on the left with a bunker. The green is broad, with a pot bunker near its right front surface, and with a slope all along the rear.

From Long we come to Short, the par three eighth hole. The green is long but narrow, with slopes at front and rear. Two bunkers protect its left surface, and one large bunker protects the right. Out-of-bounds is close by on the left, and the wind comes in from the right rear.

The ninth, a straightaway hole, is named Railway. All along the right is out-of-bounds, beyond which is a row of trees. All along the right is a stream, or burn. The wind comes from the right here. A cluster of bunkers, one of which is named Jack Nicklaus (in honor of that great golfer), protects the landing spot. The green approach has a bunker at left, and the green has a bunker at right front, another at left, slopes to the right and left, and streams farther out on both sides. Off to the rear is a copse of trees.

Hole number ten, South America, features a precarious shot from the back tee — trees close in on the left and a stream to carry over to a fairway that is lined with gorse on the left, with a headwind. The landing spot has three bunkers at right, and a slope stretches from these to a bunker on the left. Three more bunkers lie off the fairway to the right. Barry Burn flows across the green approach, and wends up past the right front of the green. The green also has two bunkers at left front, another bunker on its right side, and a slope at rear.

The twelfth hole, Southward Ho, plays in a southerly direction, as its name indicates. The wind here is from the left front, a challenging situation considering the stream that flows down the right side of the tees and the fairway. Two bunkers lie right at the 260-yard mark. A mound lies by the stream on the right, and trees, a section of stream and gorse lie to the left. On either side of the green approach, gorse threatens errant shots, and the right-hand side is intruded upon by two bunkers, while two more guard the left. The split-level green is broad but comparatively shallow, and has slopes to the front and rear.

Whins, the thirteenth hole, has a massive clump of gorse on the right rear of the green. This par three plays into the wind. The long, narrow green is protected at front, left and right with a large bunkers, and additionally has slopes at right and all along the rear.

The fourteenth, Spectacles, is so named for a pair of pot bunkers on the green approach. Its split tee approaches must both negotiate patches of gorse on the left and center. This hole has wind at the right

front, and a complex of trees on the right, plus bunkers at left and right protect the landing area. Mounds and gorse extend these defenses, with gorse on either side of the fairway up to the green approach. As indicated above, you'll find the two 'Spectacles' bunkers at the head of the green approach. The green is protected by bunkers just off its left and right frontal surfaces. This putting surface is long but narrow, and is split-level, with three mounds at left, next to the change in gradient. At left rear and right rear, more bunkers add to the defenses. Out-of-bounds lies along the left side of this hole.

Lucky Slap, the fifteenth hole, is a dogleg left, with a cluster of bunkers on the curve to the right of the landing area, and a gorse ridge running a bit farther on to the left.

Trees and a hollow lie left, and gorse, mounds and trees lie right. The green approach is guarded at left with two bunkers, and the green has a slope that wraps around from left front to right rear, and has another slope on its left side. A bunker off to the left and another off to the right front this slope. A copse of trees lies to the rear. It will take a 'lucky slap' indeed to achieve par on this hole.

The sixteenth hole, Barry Burn, is the longest par three on the course, at 250 yards from the back tees. The wind comes in from the right front, and a cluster of bunkers off to the right, and a loop of Barry Burn off to the left provide more than adequate hazards here. The long, narrow, split-level green has a diagonal slope a small distance from its front, as well as slopes on

all other sides. Two bunkers on the slope at right and two off to the left front add further defenses.

Hole number seventeen, Island, has wind coming in from the right front. The landing area is on an island of fairway that is formed by a loop of Barry Burn. On the left of the fairway are clumps of gorse, a bunker and a hollow. The green approach has gorse, two bunkers at center and right, and one bunker and a slope at left. The green has a bunker and a slope at right front; a slope at left front; and gorse off to the right and at left rear.

The eighteenth is a par five from the championship tee and a par four from the inner tees. Appropriately called Home, this is an extraordinary challenge with which to complete a round of golf on this great golf course. Close by the left of the tees is out-of-bounds. Barry Burn wends its way in front of the back tee, comes back around to enfold the right rear, rear and left side of the fairway, and returns right again to cover the green approach. To the right, on the fairway, are three bunkers, the one closest to the green being named Johnny Miller for that great golfer. To the left is a compound mound, and between the fairway and Barry Burn, out-of-bounds. The green, fronted by Barry Burn, has a slope to the rear and bunkering at left front and right front, with out-of-bounds close by the left side. A memorable conclusion to your round of golf on the world-famous Championship Course at Carnoustie Golf Club.

Carnoustie Golf Links

Hole	1	2	3	4	5	6	7	8	9	Out
Championship	416	460	347	434	393	575	397	174	474	3670
Medal	407	425	342	375	387	524	390	168	420	3438
Ladies	370	374	306	358	350	490	350	133	405	3136
Par	4	4	4	4	4	5	4	3	4	36

Hole	10	11	12	13	14	15	16	17	18	In	Total
Championship	452	358	475	168	488	461	250	455	486	3593	7263
Medal	446	353	477	161	483	456	245	433	444	3498	6936
Ladies	332	327	395	118	437	414	212	382	383	3000	6136
Par	4	4	4/5	3	5	4/5	3/4	4	4/5	36/37	72/73

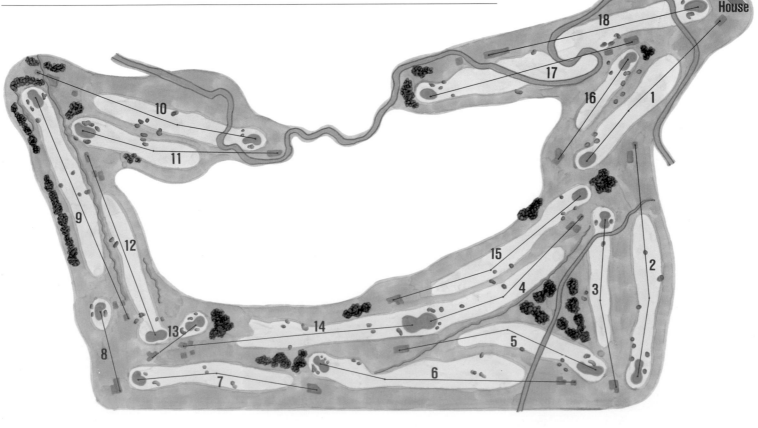

Below: Teeing off on Island, the seventeenth hole, with a barely visible Barry Burn in the foreground. *Above:* A vista at Carnoustie. The famed Carnoustie Championship Course, featured in these photos, is intermingled with the Burnside Course. Please refer to the course map.

The Colonial Country Club

Fort Worth, Texas USA

The Colonial Country Club was ranked 46th in *Golf Magazine*'s '100 Greatest Courses in the World' listing for 1989, not far from its 43rd ranking in that same poll for the year 1987.

The Colonial Country Club was the brainchild of Marvin Leonard, the pioneering co-founder of the Leonard Brothers discount store that opened in downtown Fort Worth in 1918.

With his brother Obie, Marvin worked long hours to make the enterprise a success. The brothers succeeded phenomenally, and their enterprise became the pride of Fort Worth, and would eventually extend into the oil, gas, ranching, banking and real estate businesses.

In 1923, Marvin was invited to join the Glen Garden Golf Club, and he accepted the invitation, but found little time for golf, and quit playing. His hard work had started to wear him down, however, and in 1927,

Above: **A view of the seventh green at the Colonial Country Club. As can be seen *below*, play at the ninth hole involves plenty of water.**

his doctor ordered him to find time for recreation in his life.

Marvin took up the golf clubs again, and this time, his interest became intense. Playing at Glen Garden, and also at Rivercrest Country Club, he developed his own game to the point that he regularly shot in the low 80s, and often shot in the 70s when he was really on his putting game.

He studied all aspects of the sport, including the makeup of golf courses. On family vacations in California, he had the chance to play on bentgrass greens. Unlike the uneven texture of the Bermuda grass greens that predominated in Texas, bentgrass greens are smooth. Additionally, with Bermuda grass, you are more or less at the mercy of the idiosyncracies of the putting surface, while with bentgrass, if you strike a putt true, you're likely to overcome the wiles of the green.

Leonard dedicated himself to bringing bentgrass greens to Texas. He was told by one and all that bentgrass would wilt in the hot Texas sun, while Bermuda grass thrives in intense heat. Marvin was not dissuaded, and went so far as to tell the Rivercrest governing board that, if they'd let him convert two or three greens to bentgrass, he'd foot the bill—and, if it didn't work out, he'd pay for the change back to Bermuda grass.

The president of Rivercrest, grown weary of Marvin Leonard's badgering, suggested that perhaps Leonard should build his own course, and Leonard declared that he would.

He began to put his plans in action in late 1934, acquiring 157 acres of land in southwest Fort Worth, near the Texas Christian University campus. Then he called in noted golf architects John Bredemus and Perry Maxwell to submit five alternate designs each for the course. When he had reviewed these, he asked them for five more, and took elements from both architects' submissions to shape the course.

By early 1935, Marvin Leonard's course was taking shape under the supervision of Claude Whalen—who would later be the club's first manager, golf pro and greens superintendent. To develop the bentgrass greens, Whalen's crew planted seaside bentgrass in a bed of sand and cow manure.

To combat the fierce Texas heat, the groundskeepers kept the greens watered frequently.

Late 1935 saw the golf course and the clubhouse—with its stately pillared portico in the Colonial style—nearing completion. The grand opening was held on 29 January 1936, and by that time, approximately 100 Fort Worth residents had joined the Colonial Golf Club. No membership fee was exacted from the first members. They merely had to pay a $50 security deposit against charges to the club.

Mr Leonard had a keen appreciation of golf, and his avid study had given him the expertise to develop the Colonial Country Club into one of the best in the nation. He naturally wanted recognition for his creation, and in the late 1930s, started lobbying the USGA to bring the US Open to Colonial. With the aid of two more Fort Worth golf visionaries—Amon Carter, Sr and Dr Alden Coffey—he besieged the USGA.

Finally, he and several other golf aficionados guaranteed the USGA $25,000 (at the time, a small fortune) if the Open were to be held at the Colonial Country Club. An agreement was then struck whereby the Open would be held there, in 1941.

A USGA committee came to Fort Worth and inspected the course. They recommended toughening the fourth and fifth holes for the tournament. Marvin Leonard, never one to stint on what he felt to be a worthy project, purchased several acres of undeveloped ground adjacent to the course, and brought in golf course architects Perry Maxwell and Dean Woods.

The product of this venture was the notorious 'Horrible Horseshoe'—a very demanding cul-de-sac containing the third, fourth and fifth holes. They created a new fifth hole, the extraordinary 'Death Valley' hole that follows the banks of the Trinity River.

The committee also lengthened the third and fourth holes. The changes added, altogether, 300 yards to the course, making it a 7100-yard par 70 that demands accuracy from the golfer. Mr Leonard and company implemented the redesign in six short months, and the revised Colonial Country Club layout was ready just in time for the Open.

On 7 June 1941, Craig Wood won the US Open at the Colonial Country Club, over leaders Denny Shute, Ben Hogan and Johnny Bulla. Other greats that played in that championship were Byron Nelson, Gene Sarazen and Harold McSpaden. Wood won with a 20-foot hillside putt that brought a thunderous ovation from the

spectators. Wood was to become known as 'champion for the duration,' as six months later, golf championships were suspended when the US entered World War II.

In 1942, Mr Leonard stated that he didn't expect to live much longer, due to persistent health problems (he actually lived a vigorous life for 30 more years), and he wanted to sell the Colonial Country Club to the members. His asking price was the

Above: **Pristine and dangerous—the thirteenth green, looking toward the tree-shrouded tees.**

amount of his personal investment, roughly $300,000.

A dinner meeting to discuss the proposal was arranged for late 1942, and heavy debate ensued. At the end of the meeting, a vote was taken, and the measure passed by 12 votes out of a total of perhaps 300. (Membership at the golf facility was to rise above 700 by the end of 1946.)

On 6 August 1943, the ballroom, lounge, kitchen and dining room of the clubhouse were damaged in a fire that resulted from a short circuit in the club's electrical system. Since the war was in full stride, construc-

tion materials to rebuild were impossible to come by. Marvin Leonard therefore bought an abandoned schoolhouse, had it taken apart, and used the wood to rebuild the Colonial clubhouse.

The success of the 1941 Open convinced the membership that a yearly championship was in order. It was seen that The Masters had put Augusta, Georgia on the map of the world of golf, and the Texas

Open did the same for San Antonio. What was wanted for the Colonial was a similar prestigious annual tournament.

The plans laid, under the leadership of Marvin Leonard, were as follows. The tournament would be over 72 holes of medal play with a field limited to a set number of professionals and amateurs. It was to be an invitational, and to add even more interest, the purse was set at $15,000—then the third largest on the pro circuit—with $3000 going to the winner, and the rest going to players who at least 'placed' in the standings.

In a move that was rare for the 1940s (when touring professionals were not nec-

COLONIAL COUNTRY CLU

U.S. OPEN CRAIG WOOD 1941 284	BEN HOGAN 1946 279	BEN HOGAN 1947 279	CLAYTON HEAFNER 1948 272	SAM SNEAD 1950 277
MIKE SOUCHAK 1956 280	ROBERTO DE VICENZO 1957 284	TOMMY BOLT 1958 282	BEN HOGAN 1959 285	JULIUS BOROS 1960 280
BRUCE DEVLIN 1966 280	DAVE STOCKTON 1967 278	BILLY CASPER 1968 275	GARDNER DICKINSON 1969 278	HOMERO BLANCAS 1970 273
LEE TREVINO 1976 273	BEN CRENSHAW 1977 272	LEE TREVINO 1978 268	AL GEIBERGER 1979 274	BRUCE LIETZKE 1980 271
DAN POHL 1986 205	KEITH CLEARWATER 1987 266			

WALL OF CHAMPIONS

RY MIDDLECOFF 1951 282	BEN HOGAN 1952 279	BEN HOGAN 1953 282	JOHNNY PALMER 1954 280	CHANDLER HARPER 1955 276
DOUG SANDERS 1961 281	ARNOLD PALMER 1962 281	JULIUS BOROS 1963 279	BILLY CASPER 1964 279	BRUCE CRAMPTON 1965 276
GENE LITTLER 1971 283	JERRY HEARD 1972 275	TOM WEISKOPF 1973 276	ROD CURL 1974 276	T.P. CHAMPIONSHIP AL GEIBERGER 1975 270
FUZZY ZOELLER 1981 274	JACK NICKLAUS 1982 273	JIM COLBERT 1983 278	PETER JACOBSEN 1984 270	COREY PAVIN 1985 266

essarily granted such prerequisites as meals and lodging), amenities for the visiting players were to be of the first rank. This was calculated to build respect for the organization among golfers everywhere.

The tournament was to be named the Colonial National Invitational Tournament, or 'NIT.' The first NIT was held on 16 May 1946, and among the field of 32 players (including four amateurs) were Ben Hogan, Byron Nelson, Raymond Gafford, Harry Todd, Cary Middlecoff and Ben Hogan's older brother, Royal Hogan.

Ben Hogan won that inaugural NIT, and defended his championship in 1947, winning the NIT five times altogether. Hogan is closely connected with the Colonial Country Club—in the early years of his career, Marvin Leonard, believing in Hogan's ability, helped him to stay monetarily solvent.

Also, Hogan remains as the NIT's only five-time winner—hence the Colonial's nickname, 'Hogan's Alley.' In 1953, when he won The Masters, the US Open and the British Open, he was greeted on his return to the US with ticker-tape parades in New York City and Fort Worth—and the Colonial awarded him with a lifetime honorary membership to the club.

The Colonial Country Club then instituted the Ben Hogan Trophy Room on the first floor of the clubhouse, containing many of Hogan's trophies, including the 1953 Hickock Belt, which recognized him as the US Athlete of the Year. This was just four years after a disastrous head-on collision with a Greyhound bus that caused his physicians to say he would be lucky to walk with crutches—if at all.

On 15 April 1953, the Colonial clubhouse burnt severely for the second time. It was decided to temporarily repair the clubhouse in order to host the 1953 NIT, and afterward to consider building an entire new clubhouse. After lengthy discussions and numerous revisions of architectural plans, it was decided to build anew, and to finance the building through a series of bond sales.

The entire process, including construction, came to completion on 7 October 1955, with the formal opening of the new clubhouse. The next major item on the construction agenda was to come to the attention of the Colonial Board of Directors just a little over a decade later, and it was to be the course itself.

A disastrous flood stemming from torrential rains had inundated Fort Worth—and much of the Colonial's golf course—in 1949. It was precisely the recurrence of

At left: The Wall of Champions, honoring winners of the US Open, the Tournament Players Championship and the National Invitational.

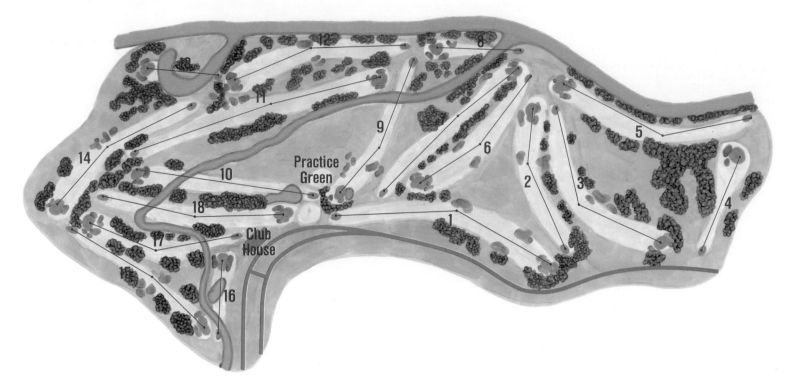

flooding in the Fort Worth area that caused the Tarrant County Water Control and Improvement District to mandate, in 1967, the rerouting of the Trinity River, including segments that bordered the golf course.

This necessitated changes in the course. The Board elected to bring Ben Hogan in to supervise said changes. Hogan demanded complete control over the work if he were going to rework the course. Hogan and other representatives from Colonial met with members of the Water Control and Improvement District to discern the extent of what was required, and what was possible, without ruining the course.

It became clear at this meeting that the Corps of Engineers were going to straighten the river channel that ran by the eighth and thirteenth holes; add a levee that would run along the ninth, eleventh,

twelfth and fourteenth holes; and install a drainage system that would cut across the tenth, eleventh, fifteenth and seventeenth holes. The course would therefore have to be partially redesigned.

Shortly thereafter, Ben Hogan set forth before Colonial's Board all the changes that he would make, and they gave their assent. He began by reshaping the seventh hole, and had to remove several pecan trees, causing the membership to complain, as the pecan trees add verdant splendor to the course, and have always been a source of pride for the membership.

Next came proposed changes to the eighth and fourteenth, which would have required the removal of a grove of pecans that surrounded the thirteenth green. At this point, the reality of Hogan's proposed changes hit home, and the membership

requested that Hogan not redesign the fourteenth, and thus spare the grove of pecan trees. Mr Hogan replied that he had agreed to work on the course, provided there would be no interference—if the membership wished to interject their changes, then he would respectfully resign from the project, which, after further discussion, he did.

Garrell Adams, Chairman of the Greens Committee, was assigned the task of revamping the course. He worked in close collaboration with Course Superintendent Joe Cano: Adams relocated the thirteenth green, and Cano personally laid out and built the eighth green. As a result of the changes, the Colonial had a tamer course, and meant an average difference of two strokes to tournament players. Changed, for instance, was the terrifying par three eighth, which Byron Nelson described thusly: 'It was so dangerous. You hit it down the river to this little-bitty green. If you pushed it a hair or didn't hit it exactly solid, you'd go in the river. And you had to hit it again from the green. There wasn't any drop area... .'

Even so, the course remains a great course, with its share of rigors, as is witnessed by Arnold Palmer's remarks regarding the fifth hole: 'Nearly every great player has experienced the rigors of the hole, and many wish they hadn't. I consider it a great hole because, sooner or later, you must play a difficult shot.'

Through the 1970s, tree and flower plantings added visual interest, and the thirteenth hole was restored to the way it was before the Trinity River Project began. The greens were all rebuilt for better drainage

Colonial Country Club

Hole	1	2	3	4	5	6	7	8	9	Out
Championship	572	401	470	226	466	415	453	192	405	3600
Mens	550	356	441	199	416	385	420	178	390	3335
Executive	539	328	426	186	397	370	403	162	362	3173
Par	5	4	4	3	4	4	4	3	4	35

Hole	10	11	12	13	14	15	16	17	18	In	Total
Championship	416	609	435	172	431	436	176	387	434	3496	7096
Mens	390	582	391	154	400	384	167	364	390	3222	6557
Executive	369	564	370	107	385	369	132	355	371	3022	6195
Par	4	5	4	3	4	4	3	4	4	35	70

in the late 1970s, and in the early 1980s, a flood control plan instituted by the Fort Worth Water District widened the channel that runs by the sixteenth to eighteenth holes. After landscaping and excavation, the channel was beautified with a terraced rock wall. Other changes throughout the years were made, including refurbishment of the clubhouse, and other of the Colonial's extraordinary facilities (which include championship tennis courts).

In 1974, Joe Dey, commissioner of the PGA, approached NIT Committee Chairman Joe Cauker with the proposal that the Colonial NIT become the PGA's first 'designated' tournament, at which touring pros would be required to play. Dey had made his offer based on the intense enthusiasm for golf that is evident in the Fort Worth area, and he knew that the course was highly regarded among touring pros.

Colonial would have to make some changes in the NIT if they were to comply. The purse would have to go from $100,000 to $250,000, and the tournament would have to become an 'open,' not an 'invitational,' tournament. While that was a sore subject with some of the older club members, the Board, seeing that such a move could increase club revenues and help cover some of the expenses of the renovation projects the club had undergone, agreed.

During the 1974 NIT (which saw Jack Nicklaus coming in second to Rod Curl), Joe Dey and associates again lobbied the Board—this time, they wanted the club for the 1975 Tournament Players Championship, or 'TPC.' Again, an agreement was struck, and the 1975 TPC was an immense success, with Al Geiberger carrying the field.

This is an honor roll of past NIT and TPC champions at the Colonial Country Club, with the dates of the their triumphs: Ben Hogan, 1946—47, 1952—53, 1959; Clayton Heafner, 1948; Sam Snead, 1950; Cary Middlecoff, 1951; Johnny Palmer, 1954; Chandler Harper, 1955; Mike Souchak, 1956; Roberto De Vicenzo, 1957; Tommy Bolt, 1958; Julius Boros, 1960, 1963; Doug Sanders, 1961; Arnold Palmer, 1962; Billy Casper, 1964, 1968; Bruce Crampton, 1965; Bruce Devlin, 1966; Dave Stockton, 1967; Gardner Dickinson, 1969; Homero Blancas, 1970; Gene Littler, 1971; Jerry Heard, 1972; Tom Weiskopf, 1973; Rod Curl, 1974; Al Geiberger, 1975, 1979; Lee Trevino, 1976, 1978; Ben Crenshaw, 1977; Bruce Lietzke, 1980; Fuzzy Zoeller, 1981; Jack Nicklaus, 1982; Jim Colbert, 1983; Peter Jacobsen, 1984; Corey Pavin, 1985; Dan Pohl, 1986 (with a 205 for rain-shortened tournament of 54 holes); Keith Clear-

At top, above: **A view down the fairway of the second green.** *Above:* **The verdant fifth hole.**

water, 1987; Lanny Wadkins, 1988; and Ian Baker Finch, 1989.

The following is a hole-by-hole description of this great golf course. The course begins with a sweeping gesture in the form of a 572-yard dogleg right. Trees left and right, and a bunker to the left, guard the landing spot, and bunkers left and right guard the green approach of this first hole. The green has a bunker on either side, up front. This green is larger and slopes a bit more than any other on the course, but it's a chance for a birdie.

The second hole demands accuracy off the tee and on the drive. Pecan trees encroach on the fairway from both sides, the one on the right being especially hazardous from the tees. Bunkers also cut into the fairway from both sides, lying in wait

for hooks and slices. The green is protected at left front, and right and right rear with bunkers. This putting surface is deceptively shallow, and overpowered balls will find bad fortune here. The bunker at left front of the green is voracious, so take care with your approach shot.

The third hole begins the much-feared 'Horrible Horseshoe' that golfers must survive in order to reach the sixth hole with a reasonable score. It's a long way from tee to green on this 470-yard par four. This dogleg left has a tree just on the left off the tees, and a group of bunkers on its inside bend that are dangerous for inattentive golfers who try to cut the distance by carrying the inside curve. The green is well protected.

Hole number four is the longest par three on the course, at 226 yards. It's a rugged test, with a 'gunsight' composed of trees bracketing the tee shot, and a green that is heavily bunkered on the left, and a boundary line abbreviates the margin on the right. The green slopes away from the tee, creating a 'slippery' situation for long shots.

A dogleg right, the fifth hole plays along the Trinity River. This hole is the Colonial Country Club's calling card, and has been included in innumerable 'best hole' lists. It is unarguably one of the greatest—and is perhaps the best—par four in the world of golf. The landing area is narrow, with trees and the river to the right, and trees encroaching all along the left, where also lies a ditch. The green is extremely well bunkered. It's best to play this hole conservatively—the river beckons for hooks and overcuts, and the ditch awaits the big draw shot. See Arnold Palmer's comments, above.

With the sixth hole, you are out of the Horseshoe, and have either established a strong score or are considering the coolness of the clubhouse. The sixth is a dogleg right, playing away from the river. Trees close in on the right may distract you from the presence of the bunkers guarding the landing spot. From there, you face the short approach shot to a long, narrow green that is bunkered in front and right and left front. Balls missing the left of the green will have difficulty coming back into play.

Hole number seven is a straightaway, tree-lined hole. The trees are close by the right, and the approach shot depends on the wind. The bunker that lies off to the left, by the trees on the riverbank, has some significance. The green is elevated and well-bunkered, and a pecan tree overhangs it on the right.

The eighth hole is a par three that demands a carry over Hill Creek, a channel of the Trinity River, from the tees. While it's

let you exercise your driving prowess. A ravine on the right presents additional hazard, and the green is large, guarded by five bunkers. Be attentive, and this hole will reward you.

The twelfth is a dogleg left that plays along the Trinity River. The wind is very much a factor here, and over-lengthy drives have often been blown into the river. The green is narrow and somewhat shallow, and three strategically situated bunkers increase the premium placed on good shot-making at the approach.

Hole number thirteen is a par three. The tees are set back in a cul-de-sac of trees, and face a long carry over a lagoon to a split-level green that slopes left to right. This green is set into a grove of trees, and has bunkers along its rear.

The fourteenth hole is a dogleg left with trees to the right just off the tees and a trio of bunkers on the outside of its bend. Opposite the bunkers is a grove of trees. On the right of the approach is another grove of trees that can affect the second shot, depending on the wind. The green is long and narrow, with bunkers on either side, and trees to the right.

Trees and bunkers lie along the right of the fifteenth hole, which is notoriously unfriendly from the tees. Opposing bunkers pinch the landing area, demanding either caution or valor in the length of your tee shot. The green is set obliquely to the fairway, with a bunker at left front, and a large bunker along its right face. Hill Creek winds across the rear of the green.

The final par three at the Colonial Country Club, the sixteenth hole is yet another challenge that has proven decisive in tournament play. The tee shot should land below the pin, for this long, narrow putting surface is severely sloped. The tee shot must carry over a lake and a segment of Hill Creek, and longitudinal bunkers guard either side of the green.

A dogleg right, the seventeenth is yet another hole that features a water carry from the tees. Trees on either side of the fairway narrow the playing area, especially on the right green approach. The green is small, and is very heavily bunkered.

The eighteenth hole is a gently-curved dogleg left, with incursions of trees that tighten the landing area, on a sloping fairway, for a tee shot that must carry over Hill Creek. A 434-yard par four, this hole will exercise your driving ability. The green is long and narrow, with longitudinal bunkers on either side, and a lake on the left. It's a rewarding challenge with which to complete your round of play at the Colonial Country Club, one of the great courses in the world of golf.

not the same monster that Byron Nelson described, it's not exactly easy, either. The green has three levels, and pin position can make this a trial, indeed. The quadrilateral bunker setup here provides enough sand for any hole.

The ninth hole crosses back over the channel, and the tee shot must carry over water. On either side of the late-breaking bend of this dogleg right, bunkers await hooks or slices. The green is surrounded by a grove of trees, and limbs can be a problem. Additionally, bunkers to the rear, and a lake to the front, challenge your mastery of this hole. The green slopes toward the lake. It is, in the words of Roland Harper, a 'sneaky tough' test of golf, and is, like

Above: **The eighth hole at the Colonial Country Club. This view is a close-up of the green, and hints at the extensive crescent bunkering here.**

the 'Horrible Horseshoe,' a make-or-break challenge, especially in tournament play.

A carry down the length of a lake awaits golfers at the tenth tees. The approach shot on this straightaway hole must carry across a water channel, and the green is protected by bunkers and trees. Accuracy is all-important here.

The eleventh, a 609-yard par five, is the longest hole on the course, but is also somewhat of a relief. Comparatively open, with bunkers at left and trees at right guarding the landing spot, and trees intermittently lining the fairway, this hole will

Glen Abbey Golf Club

Oakville, Ontario Canada

Glen Abbey was Canada's first public golf club to be specifically designed for major tournaments, with the spectator very much in mind. Jack Nicklaus, the renowned golfer and course designer, is quoted in Glen Abbey's *Pocket Pro* magazine and course guide as saying 'The idea was to build a championship golf course, a tough but fair golf course, but most of all an easily viewable golf course.'

This has been admirably accomplished, with Glen Abbey having celebrated its 10th year of hosting the Canadian Open Golf Championship. At Glen Abbey, the spectator mounds that have been built on the course come into play on several of the holes, as do the four lakes and Sixteen Mile

Creek, not to mention such other spectacular defenses as steep canyon walls and magnificent trees.

Glen Abbey was originally a large country estate. When its owner died, he bequeathed it to a group of Jesuit priests for use as a retreat. After several years, the Jesuits left the estate, as it was too large to be properly taken care of. A group of Oakville businessmen purchased the property and turned it into the Upper Canada Golf & Country Club. It then became the Clearstream Golf & Country Club, and finally, it was renamed Glen Abbey.

Glen Abbey, host to the Canadian Open Golf Championship since 1978. *Below:* Teeing off on a typically tree-lined hole during tournament play.

The Jesuits left their mark on the property, in the form of the old stone building that is now the Royal Canadian Golf Association Headquarters. Hence, the figure of the Jesuit monk who is shown swinging a golf club is the club logo.

The success of its hosting of the Canadian Open has earned Glen Abbey a reputation as a good tournament course, and many corporate tournaments are held here. The Glen Abbey clubhouse is an unusually striking tri-level structure with a central spiral staircase adjoining various accommodations for receptions, dinners and business meetings.

The Jack Nicklaus Suite is ideal for small dinners, cocktail receptions and business

meetings; its outside balconies offer a magnificent view of the course. The main restaurant, with its full-length windows, offers an unobstructed view of the eighteenth hole and the lake.

In addition to this, 'The Champions' Club' allows you to unwind after a challenging round of golf. A full locker room and whirlpool bath, plus a luxuriant private lounge and secluded patio, are available for use in conjunction with small or large tournaments. A fully equipped pro shop, plus a full selection of golf clinics, lessons and workshops, complete the facilities at Glen Abbey.

The following is a hole-by-hole description of this fine course. Golfers at the first hole face a carry over bunkers through a hallway of trees to a landing spot on a narrow fairway that is guarded at right by a bunker. The tree-lined fairway leads to a green that is multi-level and heavily bunkered. Pin placement is also an important factor on this hole.

Hole number two has a tree and a bunker at left that make tee shots here a matter of extreme accuracy. The landing area has trees to the left and bunkers, a mound, and trees to the right. The green approach is lowland, and the green is elevated, with one bunker at front left and one bunker at right rear. This is a good test of golf.

The third hole is a par three, with a long water carry to a wide, shallow green, with large bunkers on both sides at rear and a smaller bunker at front center on the edge of the lake. Balls hit too hard will find an absolutely terrible lie behind the green, so just the right touch is required here. Players at the fourth hole have a water carry from the back tees. The landing area has trees to the right and bunkers to the left, and the approach has trees, a bunker and a mound to the right. The green has heavy bunkering on its left front, and trees to the right and behind.

Hole number five is a dogleg right that plays through a hallway of trees. A large oak on the right of the landing area presents an obstruction to be avoided—as does a tree farther down on the left, near the green approach. The green approach has trees on both sides, and a bunker and a mound on the right. The green is tucked into a grove of trees, with bunkers on all sides leaving just the very center front open. Contouring makes the putting surface here very interesting.

The sixth hole has bunkers to the left of the landing area, and trees on both sides of the fairway all the way to the green approach. The green has a large spectator mound on its left and rear, and a large bunker on its right front. The seventh hole

is a par three that plays into the wind. Trees to the right and left make this tee shot over a lake a rigorous test, and the bunkers on the left and right of the green add to the challenge here. Water is on the front and right of the green, and a spectator mound occupies the right rear. Trees lie over to the left. The lake here has swallowed a lot of balls.

Hole number eight has water and trees to the right of its tees, and the landing area has bunkers to its right and trees to the left. Two bunkers are on the left front of the green, and a large single bunker is on the right front. A grass bunker guards the green approach on the right. Trees surround the

green on three sides, and mounds are present to the right and rear. The green is narrow on the right side, so a shot to the middle or left is recommended.

The ninth hole has elevated tees, and the landing area is quite narrow, with trees on the left and mounds and bunkering on the right. The green approach is a carry over a lake to a small green with water on its front and right sides. A bunker at right front may serve as a saving grace for balls that would otherwise find the water. Trees at rear and left lie downhill. At this point, you might want to make a quick visit to the halfway house for refreshment, as the clubhouse is off-limits until you've completed your round.

The tenth hole is a water carry from the back tees. The landing spot has mounds and bunkers to the left, and trees to the right. The green approach has trees on both sides, and a bunker on the right. The green is long and narrow, and heads into a pocket of trees. On the right is a bunker, behind which is a stand of trees.

The eleventh hole takes you into the valley portion of this course. This hole is an extremely tough challenge, with a 220-yard carry from the back tee. Trees to the left and bunkers to the right make this long carry also a real test of accuracy—for those who can reach the fairway. The green approach is a carry over Sixteen Mile

Creek to a small, narrow green having bunkers on both sides, trees behind and the creek along its front.

Hole number twelve is a par three that features a long carry over Sixteen Mile Creek to a green having bunkers all along its front, and a bunker and trees behind. The creek will swallow balls hit short, and still other underpowered hits will find a lie on the shore in front of the green; it's best to go long and to the right here.

The thirteenth hole has a creek carry from the tees, and the creek runs along the left of the fairway. Bunkers to the left of the landing area, and mounds farther down on the right, mingle with trees to form the

defenses on that side of the fairway. Sixteen Mile Creek cuts across the green approach, in front of the extremely narrow green. A bunker in front adds sand to the dangers encountered by short hits here; long shots will find a very tough lie behind the green. Accuracy is a premium here.

Water in front of the tees and on both sides of the fairway is to be found at hole number fourteen. Fairway bunkers to the left of the landing area form a good target—and also a serious hazard—for shots from the tees. The green is elevated and has

Below: **The second green approach, a gully that threatens under-powered shots. This hole is a challenging 414 yards from the gold tees.**

These pages: Sixteen Mile Creek figures prominently in this aerial view of the fourteenth hole.
The tees are on the right of the stream, and the
fairway is on the left. The lake on the fairway's
left is somewhat hidden by the trees on the left.

Above: The eighteenth green during tournament play. Note the spectator mounds, and the observation deck in the roof of the clubhouse.

Below: A typical Glen Abbey green—well-defended and with ample spectator mounding. Note the angle of the playing surface, the large

bunkers and the water to the left. *Above right:* Teeing off from the third hole's blue tees. *Opposite:* The eleventh.

Glen Abbey Golf Club

Hole	1	2	3	4	5	6	7	8	9	Out	
Gold	443	414	156	417	527	437	197	443	458	3482	
Blue	416	393	123	379	504	406	142	391	408	3162	
White	369	380	123	345	452	395	135	391	383	2973	
Par	4	4	3	4	5	4	3	4	4	35	

Hole	10	11	12	13	14	15	16	17	18	In	Total
Gold	435	452	487	529	426	141	516	434	500	3620	7102
Blue	489	439	182	515	367	122	466	421	455	3456	6618
White	435	426	152	481	330	115	452	390	448	3229	6202
Par	5	4	3	5	4	3	5	4	5	38	73

a gully in its middle. This is a wonderful—and also dangerous—hole. Golfers at the par three fifteenth hole tee off across a valley to an elevated green. Large bunkers at left front and left rear add to the challenge here, as does the green's tendency to roll toward the front.

The sixteenth hole is a tree-lined dogleg left. The green has bunkers on its left front and both sides in back. Overflights will find either the bunkers, the trees behind these or the hill that leads down to the thirteenth green. This is a hole for the brave, but prudent, golfer. Hole number seventeen presents a challenge to tee shots with a series of small bunkers on both sides of the fairway near the landing area. Those on the right will figure in a carry to the landing area on the middle-to-right side, near the trees there. This hole features a horseshoe-shaped green with trees to the left and rear, bunkers on its three exterior sides, and a bunker in the interior curve. Pin placement is crucial, given the shape and defenses of the green.

The eighteenth hole is a dogleg left, with heavy bunkering on either side of the landing area. Trees line the fairway from there on, and the green approach has a lake to the right that extends along the green. On the left and rear of the green are bunkers, and, additionally, a spectator mound lies to the left beyond the bunkers. Overflights produce extremely difficult lies, and shots to the left, sand—while those to the right mean lots of water. A stunning conclusion to eighteen holes of great golfing.

Harbour Town Golf Links

Hilton Head Island, South Carolina USA

Harbour Town Golf Links was ranked 29th in *Golf* magazine's '100 Greatest Courses in the World' listing for 1989, up from 30th in 1987. It also is among the top six courses of *USA Today*'s '130 Best-Designed Courses in the USA.'

Harbour Town Golf Links, home of the MCI Heritage Classic and the PGA Seniors

which also offer a fine test of golf, and were designed by George Cobb.

Now, let's take a tour. The back tees at hole one face a water carry, and the ball must be kept low to avoid the branches of the trees that line this hole. The green is protected by one large sand bunker out front, and two grass bunkers behind.

right. It's a small green, and rather hard to stay on. Hole four is a par three with a lot of water off the tees and a large, hidden bunker—and more water—behind the green. Beware of hooks and overflights here.

The fifth is a dogleg right with bunkers lining it at strategic points, and some dangerous water to the left. The green is hard to hit, and has two all-too-easy-to-find bunkers to its left. On its right are overhanging trees, and behind it is greenery that could snag your ball. The green falls off to the right and to the rear.

Hole six is a dogleg right, with a pond and an earth bunker on the right. These work in counterpoise to the trees, rooted in the fairway on the left. It's either lay up, or play long and accurately off the tees here. The green has two bunkers left, one bunker right and pampas grass at left, right, and rear.

The seventh hole is a tough little par three that features a carry over water and a massive bunker to the green. The green is narrow but deep, and sand surrounds it on all sides but right rear, where trees stand guard. Trees also guard the green at left front and left rear, with a hiatus between that is filled by yet more sand. You'll earn this one.

Hole eight is a dogleg left with trees and ponds guarding the fairway. Two trees about two-thirds of the way down form a 'gunsight' that must be negotiated, and the wayward green shot may find the water to the right and left there, or the long strip bunker on the green's left. Overflights will find the bunker behind the green, which is ominously decorated with ball-snagging pampas grass.

The ninth hole has a tight border of trees on its last 100 yards, and the vee shaped green is superimposed upon a wedge-shaped bunker that points at a companion bunker behind the green. This shallow green will be hard to hold, so accuracy and good judgement are paramount here.

Hole number ten is a dogleg left with a pond on its left, and an approach that is tree-choked. The green is nestled in the trees with a pair of bunkers to its right. The rearmost of these sports a nasty bit of

International, is the only golf club in the world to host both a PGA Tour event and a PGA Senior Tour event. Renowned golf course architect Pete Dye collaborated with Jack Nicklaus in the design of this famous course in 1969.

The rich Scottish heritage of this course is exemplified by the use of Centipede and Bahia grass in the roughs and cross-ties around the bunkers. This combination of grasses, kept long in height and cut, is rarely found on a US course of any kind. The earth bunkers at holes two, six and sixteen, and the pot bunkers at nine, ten and fourteen, lend further Scottish flavor to the Links. The greens tend to be small, encouraging accurate shots.

Harbour Town Golf Links is one of three golf layouts at the fabulous Sea Pines Resort on Hilton Head Island, with the other two being the Ocean and Sea Marsh courses,

Above: **Harbour Town Golf Links' seventeenth green.** *Opposite:* **A view over marshland of the eighteenth green, with Harbour Town Lighthouse and Calibogue Sound in the background.**

Hole number two has an earth bunker off to the left of the landing area, ready for overflights. Glimpses of ponds hidden among the trees on either side could serve as a distraction here, and the earth bunker to the right of the green approach could catch the errant greenward shot. The green is set obliquely to the fairway. The green approach is pinched by trees on either side, and other greenery complicates matters here. A grass bunker and two sand bunkers guard the sides of the green, and more trees stand sentinel behind. A challenging par five.

The third hole is a hallway of trees, with a large bunker on the left front of the green, and four smaller bunkers and water on the

greenery in its middle, making double trouble for errant balls in that quarter.

The eleventh hole is another hallway of trees, with water on either side as well. The green is protected by a tree at right front, and bunkering at left and right along its sides. This is a verdant challenge, indeed.

The twelfth hole is a dogleg right with trees guarding either side of the fairway. This calls for a long tee shot to reach the

At left: **Action in a bunker on the thirteenth. Note the wood shoring on the bank in the background—a variation on a Scottish tradition.**

dogleg, and then it's a shot to a radically-shaped green that is heavily bunkered on its forward half. The shape of the green could make a big difference in the way it is played, depending upon pin placement.

A bunker on the left side of the thirteenth hole's fairway awaits tee shots there; and a bunker farther down—on the right side of the fairway—complicates the green approach, which features trees on either side, and a massive bunker fronting the green. Behind the green, a grass bunker awaits overflights. This is a par four that

Harbour Town Golf Links

Hole	1	2	3	4	5	6	7	8	9	Out	
Heritage	397	492	399	188	528	404	165	439	327	3339	
Men's	326	474	314	146	510	363	124	385	310	2952	
Ladies'	300	413	297	125	407	302	93	341	249	2527	
Par	4	5	4	3	5	4	3	4	4	36	

Hole	10	11	12	13	14	15	16	17	18	In	Total
Heritage	418	412	404	363	153	561	373	169	458	3311	6650
Men's	350	371	379	320	121	472	294	137	428	2872	5824
Ladies'	323	312	290	300	88	407	250	85	330	2385	4912
Par	4	4	4	4	3	5	4	3	4	35	71

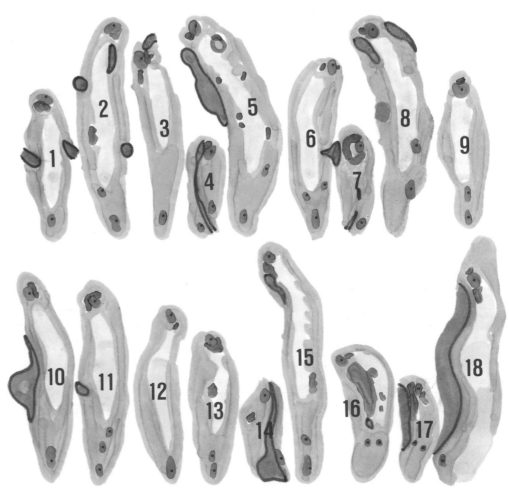

will be earned by anyone escaping without extra strokes.

Trees and grass bunkers guard the left side, while a lake guards the front and right, of the green at hole number fourteen, a par three with a small, round green that is a difficult target indeed. The pot bunker at left rear will catch overpowered tee shots, and pampas grass awaits the unlucky overflights to right rear. There's lots of water on this one.

The fifteenth hole has trees all along the right, and trees on the left, with the accompaniment of a lake along the left of the green approach. Thoughtful shot making is demanded here, as a bunker lies right, opposite the water. The very small green

Previous pages: An aerial view of the spectacular seventh green. *Below and below right:* Views of the seventeenth hole: a greenside bunker on an inlet of Calibogue Sound; and a view, over a cove, of the green. *Above:* A golfing party confronts a small sea of sand at Harbour Town's first green approach. *Above opposite:* A foursome amidst the splendors of Harbour Town Golf Links.

has bunkers left and right that form pincers at its front. A natural bunker lies at left rear, and trees guard the right rear.

Hole number sixteen is a dogleg left with trees squeezing in from the right and a massive earth bunker all along the left. In addition, a pond just to the left of the inner tees causes some distraction, and a bad hook could find its way there. The green is surrounded by bunkers and will prove to be a slippery target.

The seventeenth hole is a par three that demands a bold and extremely accurate shot to a narrow, irregular green that has a 90-yard bunker at its exposed face, and lots of water between it and the tees. A bunker behind the green will catch any overflights

to the inland side. A crosswind can easily blow shots into the lagoon at left.

The eighteenth hole is thought of as the 'gem' of Harbour Town Golf Links. A long carry off the tee will reach the bulge of fairway that juts to the left, into Calibogue Sound. The right is guarded by greenery, and less valorous players may try to avoid the water carry by playing to the right — it's a slender margin, and you'll have a terrible time with the flora. A long, golf-tee shaped bunker holds the green in its 'cup,' and a pot bunker is at the rear of the green. Calibogue Sound is on the immediate left, and there's mounding to the right. This par four is an outstanding finish to a great 18 holes of golf.

The Homestead, Virginia Hot Springs Golf and Tennis Club

Hot Springs, Virginia USA

The Virginia Hot Springs Golf and Tennis Club is home to some of the best golf facilities in the world—including the Cascades Course, which was ranked 52nd in *Golf Magazine*'s '100 Greatest Courses in the World' listing for 1989, and is widely recognized as one of the very finest mountain courses in the world.

Even so, the Cascades Course was one of two courses at The Homestead (the other being the excellent Lower Cascades Course) that were the fields of contest for the 1988 US Amateur Championships, in which defending champion Billy Mayfair lost his title to Eric Meeks, of California.

The third, and oldest, course at The Homestead is the Homestead Course, whose first tee is the oldest tee in continuous use in America.

The Homestead also has other glories of which it can be proud. For more than 27 years, it has had a continuous ranking as one of America's Mobil Five-Star Resorts. The Homestead offers 19 tennis courts; 100 miles of horseback and carriage riding trails; skeet and trap shooting; a four-mile stocked fishing stream; the South's first winter sports complex, offering skiing and skating; and a fully-equipped spa on the European model. Situated on 15,000 acres of the rolling, verdant Allegheny Mountains, it includes the site of a hot spring that dates back to the 1600s, when Indians first discovered the salutary effects of its waters.

Then, in the 1700s, white men came to also use the hot spring. Thomas Bullitt, one of George Washington's officers at Fort Dinwiddie, a frontier outpost, built the first spa around the hot springs in 1766.

The guests that have, over the years, visited the springs reads like a who's who of American history: George Washington, Thomas Jefferson, John Adams, Alexander

Above: 'The Homestead,' this hotel's name also applies to Virginia Hot Springs Golf and Tennis Club—including the famous Cascades, historic Homestead, and Lower Cascades courses. *Opposite, both:* The Homestead Course.

Hamilton, Woodrow Wilson, Henry Ford, John Rockefeller and William Howard Taft are but a few of the distinguished guests that have come to the springs—and in later years, availed themselves of the amenities of the growing resort. Royal European visitors through the years have included Lord and Lady Astor and the Duke of Windsor.

Going back to the nineteenth century, the resort embarked upon its first big growth surge in 1832, when a man now known only as 'Dr Goode' came into possession of the site, and promptly advertised the springs as it had never been touted before. He loudly proclaimed that the spa he had built around the hot springs easily

rivalled any of the finest spas in Europe, and that the health-giving properties of its waters were second to none. The hot springs soon became more popular than it had ever been before.

Several other owners followed Dr Goode's demise, until, in 1891, Melville Ezra Ingalls bought the property, and launched an ambitious plan that included constructing the main part of the stately hotel that is now known as 'The Homestead' in 1902, following a fire that destroyed a pre-existing hotel.

Additions to thi s came as follows: the west wing was completed in 1903, the east wing was completed in 1914, the celebrated clock tower was finished in 1929 and the south wing was completed in 1973.

Interest in the game of golf had manifested even earlier than that, however, with the Homestead Course opening in 1892, after Melville Ingalls brought in the legendary golf course designer Donald Ross, who was in the US inspecting a golf course site at Pinehurst, New Jersey (which was to become a great course in its own right).

Ross laid out the design, and The Homestead was commenced. It was on this course that former US President William Howard Taft created a national scandal by playing golf on the Fourth of July—at the time, a hallowed holiday. Changes and adjustments were made to The Homestead in later years by a succession of great architects—Peter Lees, AW Tillinghast and William S Flynn.

The Homestead Course was regularly played by some of the finest golfers in Virginia, including Glenna Collett (later, Mrs Edwin Vare), and Helen Hicks. One of the first member clubs in the US Golf Association, formed in 1894, was The Homestead's Virginia Hot Springs Golf Club. In addition to The Homestead, there was a nine-hole

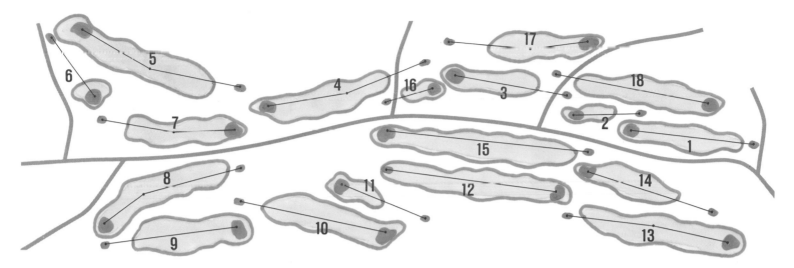

pastureland golf course called 'the Goat Course,' which was strictly for the use of employees of The Homestead. It is said that 'Slammin'' Sammy Snead perfected his 'sweet swing' on the Goat Course (now part of the ski area), when he was a handyman in The Homestead's pro shop.

The Cascades Course had its inception in April of 1923. The Homestead Course was unwontedly crowded that day, and it took one foursome that included three directors of The Hot Springs Company an hour and 20 minutes to reach the sixth hole. As they whiled away 30 minutes waiting to tee off on the sixth, these three directors decided that a second 18-hole course was needed.

Arrangements were made to purchase land for the course, and after some haggling, the land was bought. Golf course designer William S Flynn was contacted—he had assisted in the design of the fine course at Pine Valley, and it was felt that he would no doubt do good work on a solo effort.

Flynn came to inspect the site and declared that, with the addition of an adjoining parcel of land upon which stood a landmark shack, a course was possible that would be outstanding strategically, and would be visually stunning as well. The next day, negotiations were made for the indicated parcel, and the Cascades Course was soon under construction, opening for play in 1924.

Of the seven USGA events that have been held in Virginia as of this writing, five have been played on the Cascades Course, including the 1928 US Women's Amateur (won by Glenna Collett), the 1966 Curtis Cup (in which the US defeated England and Ireland), the 1967 US Women's Open (Catherine LaCoste became the first amateur and second foreign player to win this competition), the 1980 Senior Amateur (won by Bill Campbell) and the 1988 US Amateur, which we have discussed previously.

The Homestead Course

Hole	1	2	3	4	5	6	7	8	9	Out	
Blue	342	158	298	449	446	157	397	330	311	2888	
Red	334	154	294	422	404	155	346	295	264	2668	
Par	4	3	4	5	5	3	4	4	4	36	
Hole	10	11	12	13	14	15	16	17	18	In	Total
Blue	386	191	402	432	341	497	149	307	364	3069	5957
Red	319	188	354	392	262	365	145	245	275	2545	5213
Par	4	3	4/5	4/5	4	4/5	3	4	4	35/36	71/72

Thomas Lennon became The Homestead's general manager in 1952, and he and then-president Fay Ingalls added a lake on the Cascades' sixteenth hole, and engineered other subtle adjustments to the course.

In fact, Tom Lennon was instrumental in inviting the renowned golf course architect Robert Trent Jones to design a third course for The Homestead. Jones designed the Lower Cascades Course, which opened for play in 1963. It has proven to be an excellent test of golf.

In both the cases of the Cascades and Lower Cascades courses, the architects worked with the natural mountain terrain and essentially worked the course into

places that were a natural 'lie,' in the time-tested and approved manner of building natural golf courses. The results in both cases are stunning.

On Robert Trent Jones' part, the Lower Cascades presented one of the unique challenges that he has faced (and the likes of which he seems to enjoy—see also the Westin Mauna Kea portion of this text). The Lower Cascades had a railroad track, a road and two streams dividing the property, and Jones happily incorporated such into the course. Though the railroad track was removed in 1976, the course has not been altered from its original design.

The extraordinarily verdant Allegheny highlands make The Homestead courses

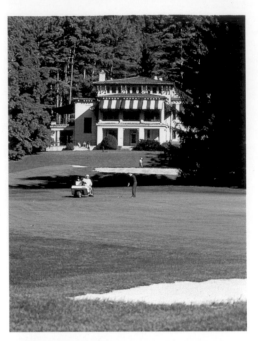

some of the most beautiful to be found anywhere. Flora and mountain vistas in profusion make for a visual feast that is newly stunning each time you encounter it.

The following is a hole-by-hole description of the three courses offered by The Homestead's Virginia Hot Springs Golf and Tennis Club. First, we'll briefly consider the venerable Homestead Course.

The first hole has a plaque by its tee, proclaiming, 'The oldest first tee in continuous use in America. No other tee has been used for a longer period of time.' This should put the course design in perspective. As we discussed previously, the directors of this facility chose to build additional courses (and we're glad they built the courses that they did!), rather than engage in continual updating of The Homestead Course. Therefore, the severity of doglegs and lengths of holes are still those that were built for golfers using earlier, less sophisticated golfing equipment than we enjoy today.

The Homestead Course has six dogleg holes, all of them fairly mild, with the most difficult pin placement being on the fifth hole, a 446-yard par five.

Four par threes—holes two, six, eleven and sixteen—test your accuracy off the tee. The shortest of these is the 149-yard sixteenth hole, and the longest is the eleventh—a comparatively lengthy 191 yards.

The longest hole on The Homestead Course is the 497-yard fifteenth, a par five. The eighteenth is a straightaway par four driving hole of 364 yards. It's a unique opportunity to be able to play The Homestead Course—you'll get a taste of golfing history when you play this one.

Now, we'll visit the world-renowned Cascades Course. Putting on the greens of this course can be confusing to those who are unfamiliar with lining up their putts by means of the irregular horizons of the mountain vistas that are everywhere to be seen here. Wind and water, mountain slopes and stunning scenery play key roles on this extraordinary course. It has five of the most challenging par threes to be found anywhere—and that is certainly not the sum of its challenges.

The first Cascades hole is straight and narrow. An out-of-bounds on the left encourages play to the right, but be careful—the fairway slopes left to right, and trees and bunkers form the defenses on that side. The long, narrow, two-tiered green is all too cannily bunkered, and is quite fast, back to front.

Hole number two on the Cascades Course is one to watch out for. The tee shot has to pass down a narrow hallway of trees,

and the slippery fairway slopes left to right, toward the woods. A large, longitudinal bunker lies along the right of the green, which itself is large and 'putter-friendly.'

The third hole is a gentle dogleg right that plays shorter than it seems it would. The tee shot ideally will shave past the trees on the left. The elevated green has a gulley in front, thick woods to the rear and a bunker at right front. Take care on this putting surface. You could, however, birdie this hole.

The Cascade Course's fourth hole is an extremely demanding par three, with a dramatically elevated tee and a large green that is surrounded with perils. On the left is a large bunker and a slope, behind is a slope and trees and on the right is a slope and woods.

The fifth hole, a 576-yard par five, is the longest on the Cascades Course. Though its two fairways are large, they require canny shotmaking for good position. The green is large and rolling, and flat ground is at a premium here. The tee shot must carry over a stream, and the green is bunkered at left front, left rear and rear.

Hole number six is a dogleg right that is reachable in two strokes, the second being a carry over a stream to a flat, easily-puttable green with two bunkers on its left. The putting surface is set like a jewel in a pocket of trees. This, like others of the first 12 holes on the Cascades Course, could conceivably be a little claustrophobic to flatlanders—due to the verdant presence of trees and slopes on every side—but such visions as this green totally supplant such impressions.

The elevated tee of the seventh hole hints at the vistas that await golfers on holes thirteen through eighteen. The fairway slopes decisively from left to right, and bunkers, rough and trees lie off to the right—the place to land is on the left side of the fairway. Wind is a strong influence of the approach, which is uphill and blind. The green has a large bunker on its left and a smaller bunker on its right: It's big and flat with—watch out—subtle breaks.

Hole number eight is the shortest on the Cascades Course. This 141-yard par three is a vision of alpine sweetness from its elevated tee—and then you tee off. The green is severely sloped, and has a huge bunker on its left, and another bunker on its right front, so keep your tee shot true. The green is a tough putting challenge.

The ninth hole is a dogleg left. The tees are elevated here, and tee shots cross over a ravine and into a valley. The approach is an upward slope. With the wind, tee shots can reach the top of the slope; against the wind, all but the strongest hitters will land in the

The Homestead Cascades Course

Hole	1	2	3	4	5	6	7	8	9	Out
Championship	394	412	283	198	576	369	425	141	450	3248
White	381	403	278	190	550	362	416	136	425	3141
Red	368	332	272	166	469	355	360	128	275	2725
Par	4	4	4	3	5	4	4/5	3	4	35/36

Hole	10	11	12	13	14	15	16	17	18	In	Total
Championship	375	191	476	438	408	222	525	491	192	3318	6566
White	366	172	434	408	396	213	488	480	184	3141	6282
Red	355	147	367	358	332	202	459	358	145	2723	5448
Par	4	3	4	4	4/5	3	5	4/5	3	35	70/71

Opposite, top to bottom: The Cascades clubhouse, viewed across the seventeenth green; the Cascades Course eighth hole (a bogey for many golfers); and the Cascades fifteenth green. *Above:* A stream is hidden in the trees to the left, in this view of the treacherous Cascades thirteenth hole. *Above left:* The Cascades sixteenth hole.

valley, leaving a blind uphill shot to the green. Situated in a cul-de-sac of trees, and with bunkers left, right and behind (and a stream beyond the bunker to the left), the green will be a challenge to 'find' for blind shots. It is long and undulating and is a stern putting test.

Hole number ten is a sharp dogleg right. To the right of the tee is out-of-bounds. There are bunkers left and right of the fairway, and bunkers at right and left front, and at right rear of the green. The best tee shot will go down the left of the fairway, where a flat spot precedes a downhill slope that is deceptive enough to cause a great many overflights of the green. It's a hard recovery, so be mindful of the slope.

The eleventh hole is the third of the five Cascade Course par threes. The elevated

green is relatively flat, and while it is heavily bunkered at front and on its sides, it should be easy to hit, and is a birdie opportunity.

The twelfth hole is a gradual dogleg left with trees guarding the inside of the dogleg. It's the toughest par four on the Cascades Course, and is the first of three par fours in a row. You tee off across a stream to a long, narrow, curving fairway. The green approach is with twin bunkers, and the green is long and narrow, with a ridge running through its center. A large, longitudinal bunker lies to the right, and two smaller bunkers guard the left of the green.

With the thirteenth hole, one begins to leave the hills and valleys, and longer vistas present themselves. The mountains, woolly with trees, and the gentle undulations of their crests, are a delightful counterpoint to the intensely verdant surrounding trees and undergrowth. A gentle dogleg left, the thirteenth has a stream and trees all along its left side. To the right, about halfway down, is a crescent bunker. The fairway is wide, but at the green approach a progressive train of three bunkers marches out from the green, crossing the line of play from left to right. The green is sandwiched between two massive bunkers. It's a deceptively tough test of golfing skill.

Hole number fourteen plays straightaway, and plays slightly uphill. Trees pinch in from the right and left at driving range—those at the left are to be avoided at all costs. Bunkers squeeze the green approach, so the second shot will be a carry over them to the green, which has a mound in its middle. It's a difficult green, and par here will be a gratifying achievement.

The fifteenth hole is the fourth par three on the Cascades Course. The tee shot must pass through a hallway of evergreens and diagonally down a footpath to a green that can be difficult to putt: additionally, its right side is tiered, and further is guarded by an overhanging tree and bunkers fore and aft. The left side of same is guarded by a single, large bunker.

Natural beauty and great golf. *Above left:* The eighth green of the Lower Cascades Course. *Above:* An attempt to chip out of a bunker on the right side of the Lower Cascades seventh green.

The sixteenth hole is the first of two back-to-back par fives. It's a sharp, 525-yard dogleg right with three bunkers on the inside of its bend. Bunkers right and left, and trees left and a stream right present hazards to be avoided, and the green is fronted by a lake that has to be dredged often to clear it of the golf balls that have sunk in its depths. To the left of the lake is a large crescent bunker. The green is large and firm, and is set into a pocket of trees, with two bunkers on its rear perimeter.

Hole number seventeen is another sharp par five dogleg, but this time it goes to the left. A mountain on its left—and heavy rough and a creek on its right—encourage accuracy on this hole. The tee shot passes close to the trees on the right, and will set up a second shot which can be played safe, or can be carried to the green, risking a pond which lies to the right of the green. With water on the right, a bunker on the left, and bunkers at rear, this is a challenging green, and makes for a very fine conclusion to an outstanding hole.

The eighteenth is the fifth par three on the Cascades Course. Shots from this hole's

elevated tee must pass over a lake to a very challenging green that has a large bunker on either side. These bunkers are a definite threat, and that's only the beginning of the test here: the green both slopes steeply, and narrows, from back to front. There is no 'breezing through' this world-class putting challenge. It is a wonderful finish for an extraordinary eighteen holes of golf.

Now, let's turn our attention to the excellent Lower Cascades Course. The first Lower Cascades hole is a slight dogleg right with a fast green. Bunkers lie on the left front and on the right side of the putting surface. Bear left off the tee for a good approach to the green. Watch out for the rough—and the stream—on the left, however.

Hole number two on the Lower Cascades Course is a slightly sharper dogleg right, and carries over the stream from the tees, and has the stream all along its right-hand side. A bunker lying left in front of the green will catch shortfalls, and hooks or slices on the approach may find the bunkers flanking the green.

The third hole is another dogleg right, with bunkers on the outside of the dogleg, trees to the right, and a bunker at left front of the green. It's perhaps the toughest green on the course, and will test your putting abilities.

Hole number four is a par three with bunkers in front of, at left and right of, and behind, the green. A putt uphill to the pin is best; downhill is 'murder.'

The fifth hole has a serpentine fairway, and trees at left, and a hill a bit farther on, are hazards to be avoided. The green presents a narrow face to approach shots, widening to the back. A single large bunker guards the left face.

The sixth hole plays in a mild arc to the left. Play down the middle and you'll be all right: the green is supremely puttable. Hole number seven is a sharp dogleg right, with bunkers protecting the bend. Get past these, and make the approach shot to a triangular green which presents a broad side to you. Bunkers at either side of this open face provide hazards.

The eighth hole, a 161-yard par three, is the shortest hole on the course, but plays longer than it seems. Bunkers at left and right front guard the triangular green, and the tee shot is a carry over a stream.

Hole number nine has a number of elevation changes, and overhanging trees to contend with. It's a dogleg left with an oval green that is protected by bunkers on its left and right sides.

The tenth hole is a dogleg left, with an elevated green. The rough here can be high and thick, so try to avoid overshooting the

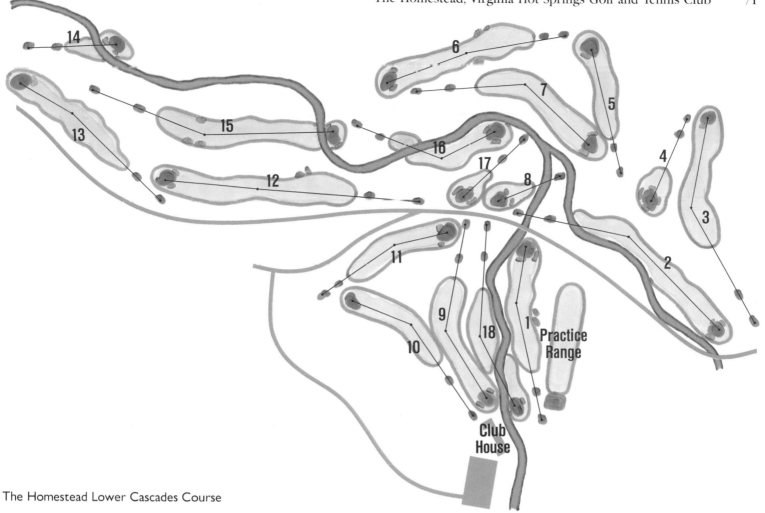

The Homestead Lower Cascades Course

Hole	1	2	3	4	5	6	7	8	9	Out
Blue	348	527	450	202	351	415	493	161	413	3360
White	332	479	388	172	344	405	480	153	400	3153
Red	223	404	261	116	235	304	367	146	322	2378
Par	4	5	4	3	4	4	4/5	3	4	35/36

Hole	10	11	12	13	14	15	16	17	18	In	Total
Blue	357	358	533	386	172	588	357	173	379	3303	6663
White	339	352	484	375	157	524	345	161	363	3100	6253
Red	231	311	364	253	92	413	284	102	269	2319	4697
Par	4	4	4/5	4	3	5	4	3	4	35/36	70/72

green, which itself is eminently puttable. It's a hole that has produced bogeys for some of the best golfers around.

At hole number eleven, trees on the right and left of the fairway make this dogleg right a challenge to your ability to drive the ball down the middle. The green presents a narrow face having a bunker on its left side, and another bunker off to the right.

The twelfth hole is very long from the back tee, and less powerful hitters will have difficulty reaching the fairway from the rearmost tee position. The left side is to be avoided. Bunkers to the right and left guard the face of the green. This straightaway

hole will test your putting with a difficult green.

Hole number thirteen is straightaway to an amenable green. If you're on your game, this hole will be a relief. The fourteenth hole is a deceptive par three—assess it carefully before you choose your club. You'll tee off over a stream to what is felt to be the easiest putting green on the course. Bunkers left and right guard the front of the green, and the water is very close by.

The fifteenth hole, a par five, is the longest on the course. Normally, the back tees measure 588 yards; for the 1988 Amateur Championships, the distance was cut to

544 yards. Bunkers guard the left and right of the landing spot, and the approach must carry over a stream to a broad, shallow, green.

The sixteenth is a tree-lined dogleg left with a stream down the left side of the fairway. You may try to cut across the dogleg, but don't take the trees—or the stream—too lightly. The green has bunkers at right front and left front, and the stream at left rear. Those in the know say it can be a dangerous hole.

The seventeenth is the last par three on the Lower Cascades Course, and plays uphill. The green is dangerous—steep from rear to front, and with bunkers at left, right and directly in front, it's a situation in which you must really be on your game.

The eighteenth hole is a dogleg left that plays longer than its 379 yards indicate. A creek winding across the fairway may tempt some players to 'go for it' from the tees, attempting a long carry. This creek has swallowed many such attempts. Walnut trees guard the right, and present a peril to the incautious. The creek guards the right side of the green. 'Slammin" Sammy Snead is quoted in the Homestead literature as saying you can make a birdie here if you play it safe.

It's a rewarding and challenging conclusion to a round of golf at The Homestead's very fine Lower Cascades Course.

Westin Mauna Kea Beach Hotel Golf Course

Kamuela, Hawaii USA

Some call this course a miracle, some call it a monster—but any way you consider such comments, they add up to the fact that this is a demanding and unforgettable golf course.

Mauna Kea was once again ranked among 'America's 100 Greatest' and 'Hawaii's Finest' and by *Golf Digest* in 1989. A popular course with the likes of Tom Watson, Jack Nicklaus, Chi Chi Rodriguez and Bob Rosburg, this beautiful course, which serves as a practice haven for Isao Aoki, was included in the 'Twelve Magnificent Golf Courses of the World' calendar by Paul Gleason.

This course was named for the nearby snowcapped volcano, Mauna Kea—which

Above: **Snowcapped Mauna Kea is a backdrop for the 'water hole' thirteenth green, also seen** *opposite. Below:* **An aerial view of the eleventh.**

literally means 'white mountain' in Hawaiian. This legendary test of golf was built in 1964 by Robert Trent Jones Sr. In 1974, his son, Robert Trent Jones Jr, was called in to re-tune parts of the course.

The elder Jones applied the full range of his considerable knowledge to overcome the extreme difficulties which the site imposed. The course was conceived as a rugged beauty rolling over 230 acres of lava hills, with the beautiful snowcapped mountains on one side and the Pacific Ocean on the other.

Greens and fairways had to be hacked out of the solid lava rock, and, to enable the moon-like surface to support life, an elaborate automatic underground watering sys-

tem was installed to pump more than a million gallons of water per day to fairways and greens—compensating for the coast's meager rainfall, this particular water supply system was an innovation among golf course irrigation systems.

Jones Sr brought in heavy construction machinery, equipped with special devices that he had invented himself, which crushed the brittle lava to a powdery consistency through repeated gradings and rollings. The crushed lava was then spread over the course foundations, which had now been carved out of the same lava flow.

The same pulverization process was, in turn, used to make lime powder out of coral dredged from the nearby Kawaihae Harbor. A three-inch layer of this material was then spread over the lava soil, followed by a blanket of fertilizer. This was then carpeted with a new variety of hybrid Ber-

muda grass, which had all the fine qualities of Mainland golf course bent grass, but was suited to Hawaii's tropical climate. The bunkers themselves were filled with crushed coral.

Hundreds of coconut palms and other trees—including rainbow shower, wili-wili, monkey pod and Chinese banyan—were brought in to accent the landscaping, and to help anchor the topsoil to the lava base.

It is a course with an incredible panoramic sweep of sea and land, including snowcapped Mauna Kea, rugged lava beds and the blue Pacific, where whales 'winter' just off the island of Hawaii's Kohala Coast.

Mauna Kea's undulating fairways, uphill holes, steep greens, doglegs, strategically placed bunkers and 120 sand traps make the course one of the most challenging in the world of golf. The *pièce d'résistance*, however, is the course's incredible hole

number three, where an inlet of the mighty Pacific Ocean forms the water hazard. This hole is rated as 'one of the Top 100 Holes in America' by *Golf Magazine*. The challenge comes both physically and mentally—the prospect of shooting 215 yards over the roiling surf ensures that.

The eleventh green, with a sheer drop of 100 feet to the ocean behind it, is part of another breathtaking hole; it measures 247 yards from the back tees—an almost unreachable distance when ocean breezes blow. Isao Aoki rates the eleventh hole as the hardest par three not over water. Hole number thirteen offers a breathtaking view of beautiful, awe-inspiring Mount Mauna Kea, which is snowcapped from December to June.

This masterwork was christened on 8 December 1964, when a 'Big Three' golf tournament featuring Arnold Palmer, Jack Nicklaus and Gary Player took place there.

Nicklaus, who won the match, gave the course the highest praise—he declared that it was 'more fun to play than any course I know.' After the course and hotel were opened to the public in July of 1965, Mauna Kea quickly became a world golf mecca.

With the ocean breaking against the cliffs below as you tee off, and a 215-yard carry across an inlet with updrafts, Mauna Kea's third hole is loaded with challenge. *Below*: **Teeing off on same.**

In 1968, Shell Oil Company's *Wonderful World of Golf*, which focused on the world's outstanding golf courses, filmed a segment at Mauna Kea. This television show featured a match between Peter Allis, Al Geiberger and the late Dan Sikes; Sikes won with a par 72.

The Westin Mauna Kea course has taken on a rich, mature patina in its quarter century of existence, and has been kept in top form under the careful supervision of

Mauna Kea's golf course superintendent, Robert Itamoto. He has been at the course since the first rocks were scraped away for the greens.

The first notable changes made to the course were made by Robert Trent Jones Jr. Due to complaints early on that the course was too difficult for players at the lower echelons of golf, Jones Jr was contracted to make refinements in his father's design. These refinements were made on holes two, three, six, eight, ten and fourteen, and involved softening the greens, thus increasing their playability.

During this four-month project, the greens were entirely stripped and their rock bases were reshaped to provide an

Westin Mauna Kea Beach Hotel Golf Course

Hole	1	2	3	4	5	6	7	8	9	Out
Black	400	390	215	420	580	350	210	534	433	3532
Blue	387	360	210	410	560	350	188	515	408	3388
Orange	372	330	180	396	514	333	178	510	380	3193
Par	4	4	3	4	5	4	3	5	4	36

Hole	10	11	12	13	14	15	16	17	18	In	Total
Black	353	247	385	414	393	204	415	550	428	3571	7103
Blue	480	208	385	335	393	204	410	550	428	3393	6781
Orange	475	198	375	332	383	191	394	534	380	3262	6455
Par	5	3	4	4	4	3	4	5	4	36	72

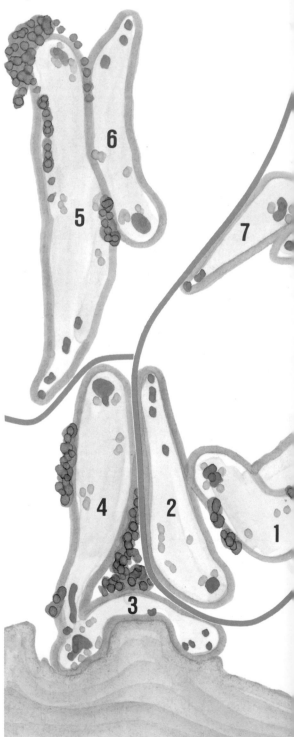

entirely different surface, and some of the rock and brush adjacent to the course was cleared away

When the revised course was opened in late 1975, the changes were greeted with enthusiasm. The following is a quote from Ben Neeley, then the head professional at Mid-Pacific Country Club on Oahu, whose team captured the annual Pro-Am tournament that year: 'It was a great golf course and it's still a great golf course....It's improved, but still it's the toughest in the state. Anyone who thinks the changes have made this an easy course doesn't know golf.'

More subtle course refinements were made in 1983 with the re-establishment of 22 championship and alternate tees. JD Ebersberger and Bob Itamoto supervised these changes, which included the reinstallation of the original back tees, creation of some new tees and the realignment of other tees for better vision of the fairways. While the black, championship tees measure 7114 yards, there are now a total of six tee positions on some holes, including the famous third hole. According to JD Ebersberger, as quoted in the *Sunday Star-Bulletin & Advertiser* of 8 July 1984:

'The alternate tees offer a challenge to all types of players. We couldn't build the black tee on the third in its original position because the promontory there was washed away in a storm two years ago. But it is 215 yards across the ocean from the new black tee, and just as challenging as when Nicklaus, Palmer and Player played here.

'Sculpturing of the fairways has been carried out, allowing the grass to grow a little higher… This helps keep the balls in play. The fairways are Tif 328 — around 60 yards wide in some areas, and narrow to 35 to 45 yards further out for long hitters. This gives a better challenge to both the high handicap country club players and the stronger players.'

Mauna Kea observed its 20th birthday with its two major yearly tournaments, a Pro Am in July, and an Invitational in early December.

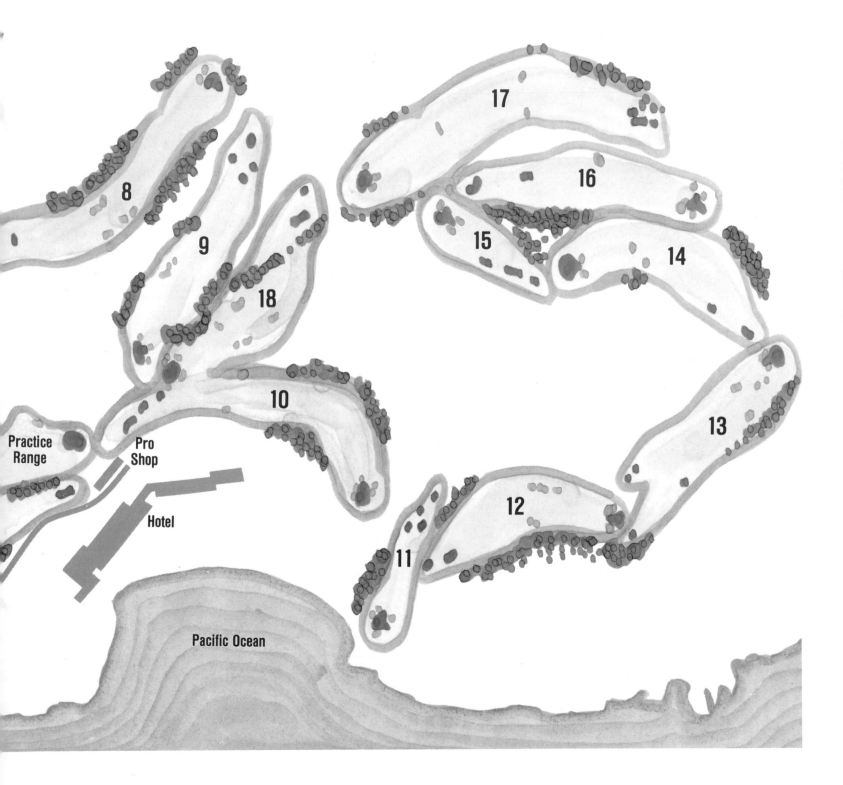

Medinah Country Club

(Course Number Three)

Medinah, Illinois USA

Medinah Country Club Course Number Three was rated 40th among *Golf Magazine*'s '100 Greatest Courses in the World' in 1989, and was ranked 12th in the US by *Golf Digest*.

In 1923, a group of Shriners from Medinah Temple in Chicago set out to build 'the best golf club in North America.' It was to have three 18-hole golf courses, a polo field, ski slides, toboggan runs, an amphitheater, riding stables and a gun club.

They purchased 400 gorgeously wooded acres from the brothers Henry and James Lawrence. Experts were hired to supervise the cutting of only the necessary trees, as an effort was strongly backed to preserve as much of the lush forestation as possible: giant oaks, elms, hickories and other indigenous trees graced—and still grace—the grounds.

Tom Bendelow—a once-maligned golf course designer whose courses are to be

Above: **The astonishing Medinah Clubhouse.** *Below:* **The first hole, looking toward the tee, with Lake Kadijah beyond. This is a well-treed course, with ample challenge and beauty.**

found throughout the US—was retained for the design of the club's golf courses.

Richard Schmid, an architect of several noted Shriner buildings, was hired for the design of the incredible clubhouse, with its central dome reminiscent of the ancient Christian church of 'Higher Wisdom' (Hagia Sophia) in what is now Istanbul (and was Constantinople).

On 5 July 1926, the nearly completed clubhouse hosted an informal opening: the scaffolding was still up in places, but it was evident that the Medinah Clubhouse was something special. Gustave Brand had been brought in to do extensive interior fresco work; and leaded glass, terrazzo floors, Scagliola marble columns and more in the way of interior detailing make the place a palace indeed.

Its styling is basically Byzantine, with touches of Italian Villa, Louis XIV and Oriental influences blended in. Of the two frontal minarets, the western was built as an observatory and search light tower, and the eastern was built as a chime tower.

Including a massive dance promenade, the clubhouse is a city block long, with lounges, dining rooms, kitchens, overnight facilities, locker rooms, card rooms, a billiard room and a gymnasium.

On 5 September 1925, Course Number One was completed, and a bottle of Medinah well water was used to christen the first tee. During the three days of festivities that followed, the championship golf events at Medinah were held, with gold, silver and bronze belt buckles for the winners. A special match was held in which Chick Evans, Jock Hutchison, Bill Melhorn and Al Espinosa—then four of the best golfers in the country—competed over 36 holes. Hutchison won with a one-under-par 71.

Course Number Two was well on its way to completion. At first, the thought was that Courses One and Two would be for the men, and Course Number Three would be for the ladies. When everything was said and done, Course Number Two became the ladies' course, while Course Number Three

became one of the greatest courses in the world.

The land for Number Three was not part of the original parcel, but was an adjoining plot that was bought on 30 December 1925. Tom Bendelow's orders for Number Three had been to construct 'a sporty little course that will become famous the country over to and for women.' Its beginnings were fertile in a humble sort of way, as the course builders had to wait for the previous owner to harvest his last crop on the land before they could begin.

By 1927, Course Number Two was open for play, and it and Course Number One saw fairly heavy use for that period in American history. Medinah's first golf professional was Amber Andrews, born in Edinburgh, and descended from a lineage of golf professionals: his father had been a golf professional at an English course, and his *grandfather* was reputed to have been the first golf professional at an English club.

Club President Morris Jepson hit the first drive off the number one tee of Course Number Three on 23 September 1928. It was immediately obvious that this course was more of a challenge than was intended. It was a 6215-yard, par 71 course. Early commentary on the new course included a statement that 'Only excellent or par golfers would enjoy it.' Complaints arose that the tee on the seventeenth was, at 160 yards back, so distant that one couldn't see the water in front of the green.

In 1929, it was decided to rework the course into a full-blown championship layout. Later that same year, the course was re-opened at 6261 yards and par 70. The $3000 Medinah Open was held on 22 September 1930, to showcase the new layout. Sixty-two professionals—including the legendary Gene Sarazen—and five amateurs came to play. The first day saw Sarazen shooting a 78, but the second day, he shot a 65. Harry Cooper shot an opening 73 and followed that with a 63.

While the course was plenty tough for the average player, if Number Three were ever again to host a pro tournament, it would need toughening. One hundred thousand dollars' worth of reworking stretched the course to 6820 yards and par 72. This involved the creation of seven new holes—three, four, seven, eight, thirteen, fourteen and fifteen—and the remodeling of holes six and nine.

After this, the course was quite formidable, with four par fours of over 440 yards, and three par fives, the longest of which was 580 yards. The revamped course was opened on 19 June 1932. In 1933, Tommy Armour became Medinah's golf professional and scored a 67 on the new Number

Above: An aerial view of the par three second hole, from just above and behind the tees, and looking toward the green, across an inlet of Lake Kadijah. *Below:* Looking up the fairway toward the green of the fifth hole. Note the intermingling of bunkers and trees.

Above: **A view of the eighth green, which is often tragically underestimated. The ninth hole** *(at left)*, **on the other hand, presents a birdie opportunity.** *Opposite:* **The dogleg of the eleventh.**

Three that same year. Even so, the course was now recognized as a 'contender,' and was ranked among the top 10 courses in America.

In 1934, a sprinkler system was installed on the course; also, Great Britain's Joyce Wethered scored 77 on Number Three — possibly still a women's record.

Then, the 1935 Medinah Open, a benefit for the Shriners' Hospital for Crippled Children, was held on Number Three. Harry Cooper won again, but this time with a not-

so-spectacular one-over-par 289 for four rounds.

The Chicago Open of 1937 was hosted at Medinah: the first round was played over Course Number One, and the remaining tournament was played over the already-famous Course Number Three. Gene Sarazen won the (very big for the time) $10,000 prize with a four-round score of 290.

The Western Open was first played on Medinah Number Three in 1939, with the great Byron Nelson posting a score of 282, six under par, to win. The Chicago Victory Open of 1946, also held at Number Three, was another Byron Nelson victory — he shot a nine-under-par 279 to triumph over a field that included Johnny Revolta, Lloyd Mangrum, Ben Hogan and Chandler Harper.

The club's silver anniversary year, 1949, saw Number Three hosting the 49th US Open: Cary Middlecoff became the man of the hour, and was awarded the $2000 prize for his two-under-par 286. The Western Open returned to Number Three in 1962, when Jackie Cupit won with a 281. Again, in 1966, Number Three hosted the Western — this time, Billy Casper prevailed with a 283.

The US Open was played again at Number Three in 1975: heavy rain had made the

course quite soggy, but an exciting tournament occurred despite turf conditions. Lou Graham and John Mahaffey tied at 287, and a playoff saw Graham getting the edge, 71—73.

By this time, tournament golf had become more popular than anyone could have anticipated: the US Golf Association rejected Medinah's request for the 1980 US Open because Number Three's eighteenth hole offered too little space for spectators.

Though there was resistance to making the extensive changes that would have to be made if Number Three were to continue to host Opens, the decision to make the changes was finally agreed upon by the membership of the club.

The general feeling was that if they could have changed only the eighteenth, which was not particularly challenging anyhow, they would have restricted the changes to that hole. However, it was seen that a change in the eighteenth would affect the entire traffic pattern of the back nine.

Chicago architect Robert Packard was called upon to make the changes. Under the guidance of the of the USGA, he rerouted the back nine, creating two new holes and lengthening another to do so. Packard's changes raised the par of Number Three to 72, with accommodation for 30,000 spectators.

Number Three's most famous back nine holes — old number seventeen and old number thirteen (named by the PGA as one of the toughest holes in the US) — remained as they were, but have received new places in the order of the back nine: old seventeen became number thirteen, and old thirteen became number sixteen.

The first 11 holes also remained unchanged, but of the last seven holes, in addition to the changes noted above, the sixteenth became number twelve; the fifteenth became number fourteen (and was also lengthened); and the twelfth became number fifteen.

Medinah Number Three hosted the 1988 Seniors Open, with a field including Defending Seniors Open Champion Gary Player, Arnold Palmer, Don January, Chi Chi Rodriguez, Billy Casper, Bob Charles and other Seniors greats. Player successfully defended his title, triumphing over this stellar field, edging out Bob Charles in a playoff.

The 1990 US Open is scheduled for Medinah Number Three, and the course, acclaimed as one of the world's greats, has a bright future to match its illustrious past. The following is a hole-by-hole description of this extraordinary golf course.

The first hole plays straight at Lake Kadijah. This tree-lined gem has a Persian lux-

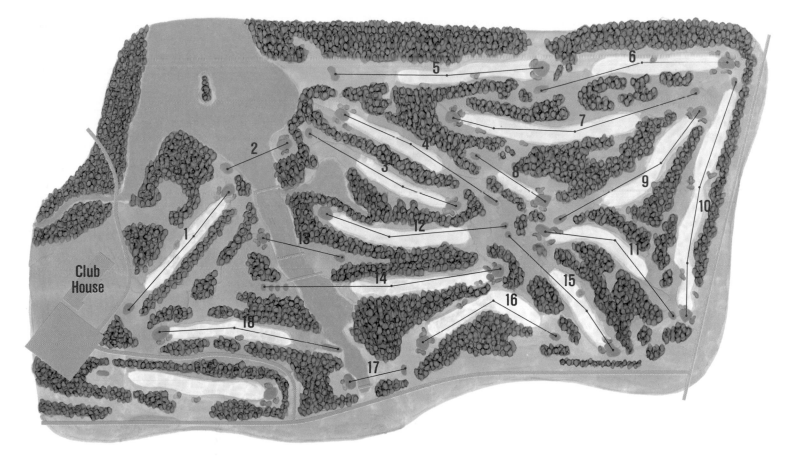

Medinah Country Club

Hole	1	2	3	4	5	6	7	8	9	Out	
Championship	373	169	404	407	505	418	571	180	417	3444	
Par	4	3	4	4	5	4	5	3	4	36	

Hole	10	11	12	13	14	15	16	17	18	In	Total
Championship	558	388	450	163	525	366	421	151	415	3437	6881
Par	5	4	4	3	5	4	4	3	4	36	72

uriance in its green setting near the beautiful lake. The elevated tees face a goodly carry across a rise to a gently undulating fairway. One bunker lies to the left about halfway down. The green widens to the rear and has a bunker on either side. It is backed by trees, with open access to the lake on the right rear. This green slopes from back to front.

Hole number two, an aesthetically stunning par three, plays across the lake. The water can be quite intimidating, but those in the know say it's not bad at all—the trouble starts when you reach the green, which slopes steeply from back to front. It's best to be short on this green.

The third hole tees off with an inlet of Lake Kadijah to the left of the ball's-flight path. Beware the trees and rough on the left. The green rolls subtly, and is elevated, with a large bunker on either side. If your ball falls short of the putting surface, you'll wish it hadn't.

The fourth hole has trees in close to the fairway on either side: straight and narrow is the way to go. The green is elevated, with a steep bank down its back: don't go too long. Additionally, there are two huge bunkers on either side of the green, for a total of four gaping hazards. This hole plays uphill.

Hole number five has a large bunker to the right of the landing area, and an incursion of young trees to the left, and another bunker directly on the fairway some yards

Above: The twelfth, a hole without bunkers. The sloping fairway more than makes up for that. *At right:* Bunkers, water and a tough green: the thirteenth. *Below right:* The fourteenth green,

farther along, also on the right: accuracy and strength are premiums here. This hole plays uphill from the second shot. The broad, oval green has two huge bunkers across its front and the green approach. Bushes behind the green will swallow overflights.

The sixth is a dogleg right, and tee shots pass down a hallway of trees to a landing spot having a large bunker, rough and ball-hungry bushes directly across the fairway: overflights are not treated mercifully. Trees line the fairway on the right, and huge bunkers guard this hole on both sides, from the green approach to the back of the green. Wind will affect your club choice for an approach to this, the largest green on the course.

Hole number seven is a dogleg right, with a concentration of trees on its inner bend. Bunkers lie to the left just beyond, so the tee shot will demand accuracy and good judgement of distance. The left side of the fairway is heavily bunkered up to and including the left front of the green. The green, widening like a pear, is 'neck-on' to the fairway, and is heavily bunkered on its right side: it slopes from back to front, and, depending on pin position, can be extremely difficult.

The eighth hole is a par three, and its tees are sheltered on both sides by trees, which makes it hard to judge the wind on this hole. The green is very hard to 'read,' and has many subtle undulations. An optical illusion often causes this green to appear perfectly flat at first glance. The massive bunker on the left approach, and the two large bunkers on the right of the green, are very dangerous.

As opposed to the preceding hole, the ninth is one of the few birdie holes on this course. Tree-lined, but not too tightly, the ninth is an easy dogleg left with a relatively flat green. Beware the large bunkers on either side of the green, and the trees and rough to its rear.

Two large bunkers on the right and one transverse bunker on the left emphasize clear-headed golfing on the tenth hole. It's a long, extended dogleg left. The green approach has heavy bunkering right and left, and the green itself is protected right and left. The green is treacherous, and slopes intensely from back to front.

Hole number eleven is a sharp dogleg left. The trees close in on either side will likely catch hurried tee shots, and the heavy bunkering right and left of the green approach and the green itself is not to be ignored.

An elevated tee on the twelfth hole faces a bunkerless fairway. However, the fairway both slopes and curves to the right, where trees crowd the inside curve. The green approach is quite restricted, and the wind tends to be a deciding factor here. An inlet of Lake Kadijah lies to the right of the green, and has been known to catch more than a few underpowered shots. Trees abound on this hole, and can be considered a hazard.

Hole number thirteen (the re-numbered old hole number seventeen) is a renowned and perilous par three that plays across an arm of Lake Kadijah. The green is hard to hold, and has heavy bunkering at front and rear, and on both sides. It's a test of accuracy—many balls have been lost in the lake, and still more strokes have been added to scores in the bunker behind the green.

The fourteenth hole is a severe test. Tee shots must carry 200 yards over Lake Kadijah to a plateau landing area. The fairway is crowded by trees from the halfway point on. With one bunker on the right of the green approach, and no less than five forming a 'beard' for the green—with an obscuring 'hump' that is integral to the central bunker—this green, a broad oval, falls off to the rear, where overflights may come to rest amidst a grove of trees.

Hole number fifteen looks free and easy, but you are forced to shave past the trees on the right of the fairway to access all possible pin placements on the green. Lose control of your shot, and a round bunker on the left will probably grab it before the trees on that side do. The green is elevated, and hides behind two built-up bunkers on its left and right front. This putting surface asks for your best, and the bushes and out-of-bounds behind that lie close behind the green are a repository of overflights.

The sixteenth hole is one of the greatest holes in US golfing. Originally the thirteenth, it was known as the toughest thirteenth hole in golf. Number sixteen is a very sharp dogleg left, heavily treed on both sides—and these trees are a certain danger. Only the most accurate shot will suffice. The green is tiny and is set atop a plateau: too-short approach shots may roll 30 or more yards back down the hill. Heavy bunkering on the right and left approach also endanger wayward shots, as does the bunker at left rear, and the slope behind the green.

Hole number seventeen, newly created by Roger Packard, is a par three that plays across an arm of Lake Kadijah. With a single, large, peanut-shaped bunker just beyond the broad, shallow green, the chances of finding sand or water here are high. The green slopes severely back to front.

The eighteenth is the second brand-new hole at Medinah Number Three. It plays away from Lake Kadijah and toward the palatial Medinah clubhouse. Roger Packard has done a good job of echoing the lushness of the original Medinah Number Three holes in his own creations for the course, adding his own preference for broad, shallow greens. A dogleg left, with a sizable bunker at its inner bend, the eighteenth's approach is to a wide, shallow green. Heavy bunkering on the left front of the green, and a subtly undulating green surface, add to the challenge of this closing hole. It's a fine culmination for the unique excellence of Medinah Number Three— one of the world's great golf courses.

Below left: The sixteenth hole. *At left:* The par three seventeenth hole, one of two new holes on Medinah Number Three. *Below:* The eighteenth—the second of Medinah's new holes.

Muirfield (The Honourable Company of Edinburgh Golfers)

East Lothian Scotland

Muirfield ranked first in *Golf Magazine*'s '100 Greatest Courses in the World' listing for 1983, and ranked second and fifth in that same poll for 1987 and 1989, respectively—all the while retaining its lead as the number one course in the British Isles. Muirfield's routing plan was also given the highest ranking, due to the fact that its 'circle within a circle' layout makes for an ever-varying wind direction.

This magnificent and historic course is home to The Honourable Company of Edinburgh Golfers, the world's oldest continuous golf club. The Honourable Company is a direct extension of a group known as 'The Gentlemen Golfers of Leith,' who played at Leith Links (to the west of Edinburgh), which were first used as golf links in 1593.

The Gentlemen Golfers of Leith were formally recognized by the Edinburgh Town Council on 7 March 1744, who fur-

ther presented the group with a silver golf club as a trophy for an annual golf contest. With this formal recognition, the Gentlemen Golfers set down a list of 13 golfing rules and began maintaining what has by now become the oldest continuous record kept by any golfing club.

The list of rules that they set down, originally titled 'Articles & Laws on Playing the Golf,' became generally known as the Leith Code, and was the first set of golfing rules to be written down. It was so reasonable and efficacious that the The Royal and Ancient Golf Club of St Andrews adopted it when their organization was formed in 1754.

The Gentlemen Golfers were, sometime later, further formalized as The Honourable Company of Edinburgh Golfers. In 1836,

Opposite: **Walking off the eighteenth green after a round of golf on the Muirfield links.** *Below:* **A view across the seventeenth green of the clubhouse.**

they moved from the five-hole Leith Links to links at Musselburgh, on the east of Edinburgh. Musselburgh had been a golfing ground from at least 1672.

It was at Musselburgh in 1873 that The Honourable Company consented to an agreement—with the Royal and Ancient Golf Club of St Andrews, and Prestwyck Golf Club (who hosted the first Open Championship in 1860)—for the staging of the Open Championship at Musselburgh, the Old Course at St Andrews and Prestwyck, on a yearly rotational basis.

A little over half a century after The Honourable Company had begun play at Musselburgh, they migrated once again (taking their portion of the Open with them)—to Muirfield (yet farther east, on the Firth of Forth), which The Honourable Company developed for golf, and opened for play on 3 May 1891.

David Plenderleith laid out the original course, following a plan generated by Tom Morris. In that first Muirfield layout, the course boundary included a wall where now lies the third fairway. The first Open at Muirfield was held in 1892, and was the first Open to be played over a measure of 72 holes—four rounds of 18 holes.

The present course pattern was crystallized by golf architects Harry Colt and Tom Simpson in 1926. Architecturally, it is an extremely cannily laid-out design. The nine holes 'going out' play counterclockwise around the nine holes 'going in,' which in turn play counterclockwise: due to this, the golfer at Muirfield has to adjust to an ever-changing wind.

After winning the Open Championship at Muirfield in 1966, Jack Nicklaus felt so highly about the course that he later honored it in the naming of his 'home course,' Muirfield Village in Ohio—which he designed with Desmond Muirhead in 1974.

Through the years, many extraordinary golfers have played memorable rounds at Muirfield, including the brilliant golfer Harold Hilton, who in 1892 won the first Open to be played on the course. The year

1896 saw a playoff between golfing legends Harry Vardon and John Henry Taylor; Vardon won.

Harold Hilton was the last British amateur to become a champion, and won the Open at Muirfield again in 1897, when Harry Vardon and the phenomenal James Braid were in the lists at peak form.

As of 1989, the Open Championship had been played 13 times at Muirfield. In addition to Nicklaus, Hilton and Vardon, the winners of the Open at Muirfield were as follows: James Braid, 1901 and 1906; Edward Ray, 1911; Walter Hagen, 1929;

Henry Cotton, 1948; Gary Player, 1959; Lee Trevino, 1972; Tom Watson, 1980; and Nick Faldo, 1987.

Muirfield's seaside location and picturesque surroundings offer an aesthetic banquet second to none, and its excellent clubhouse offers culinary treats that are on par with the magnificence of the golf course. It has been said that Muirfield is as close to perfection as is ever availed to earth, sky, sea—and golfing skill.

A hole-by-hole course description follows. The first hole is 447 yards from the championship tee, and is extremely well

bunkered. A horseshoe-shaped bunker lies immediately to the left of the landing spot on the fairway, and beyond this, a mound and a hollow keep the perimeter of the playing surface secure. To the left of the green approach, a pair of bunkers compose a 22-yard-long patch of sand that is one half of a 'gunsight' that makes the golfer consider a carry over the oblong bunker to the right (at the risk of landing in the large, longitudinal bunker that guards the right of the green). A bunker at left rear of the green completes a defense setup that makes for a target green.

At the second hole, you'll be playing into the wind, and the championship distance of 351 yards will be as tough a par four as was the considerably *longer* first hole. With cannily-placed small bunkers on the right and left, and a sudden slope on the fairway at the 231-yard mark, this will not be easy. The green approach demands accuracy, as a bunker and greenery to the left balance a cluster of five bunkers to the right. The 36-yard-long green is backed on the left by a slope.

The third hole is directly out of the hallowed Scottish past, when courses often as not presented golfers with 'blind' targets that lay behind mounds or other obstacles. Again a par four, hole number three lets the golfer have a good drive off the tee, to a wide fairway that is narrowed—in effect— by the wind, which on this hole, blows from left to right. The green approach has mounds left and right, which obscure the green, and front a narrow strip of fairway that has a slope to the right. You can lay up at the mounds, and try for the narrow passage between the bunkers that guard the green on its left and right. With the wind tending toward the slope, it's a risky venture indeed.

The first par three at Muirfield is the 180-yard hole number four. Once again, you're playing with the wind blowing from left to right. The split-level green lies in a depression, with a bunker on its left, and two bunkers on its right front. In addition, a mound on the right of the 'split level' adds a third level to an already complex perceptual puzzle. It's not a par three for the careless.

The fifth hole is, at 559 yards, the longest par five on the course. The wind is, again, from left to right, and as this hole lies broadside to the Firth of Forth, the full brunt of the wind will be felt here. The first hundred yards of the fairway is liberally bunkered, and the pressure for accurate play is kept on by a lateral bunker on the outer green approach. The green has bunkers left and right, and is divided longitudinally by a quick slope. A hillside lies to the rear.

There is wind at your back on the sixth hole—a dogleg left. The fairway has four bunkers inside its first turn, which also is the location of an upward slope to a plateau that gives way to a deep valley just before the green. Itself in a depression, the green is semi-hidden behind a rise on the approach, and has bunkers at right front and at left.

Hole number seven is a par three of 185 yards. Both sides of declining slope on the front of the green are protected with bunkers, and bunkers also line the left side

Facing the challenge. *At top, above:* **A threesome with caddies on the first tee at Muirfield.** *Above:* **Preparing to tee off at the eighteenth tee.**

of the green. A hillside is present on the right and rear of the green. On this hole, you play into the wind, a fact that makes the large bunkers out in front of the green especially dangerous.

A dogleg right that plays away from the wind, the eighth hole has a cluster of bunkers to the right of the landing spot, just inside its bend. Three lateral bunkers guard the green approach. The green, at 31 yards in length, is a challenging target to hit. With the wind blowing, the bunker at

left rear could easily become the resting place for overflights.

The ninth hole lies broadside to the wind, and is subject to air currents flowing from right to left. This shallow dogleg left bends around two widely-spaced bunkers and a mound. To give you an idea of its challenging properties, number nine plays as a 504-yard par five from the championship tees; or as a 460-yard par four from the medal tees. At its bend, the fairway is narrow, widening to the left and dropping into a slope on the right. An out-of-bounds further limits the scope of play on the left, while bunkers lining the right of the green approach make a declaration for accuracy: be careful with the wind here, too. At 32 yards in length, this is another target green.

Beginning with the tenth hole, golfers play in the opposite direction of that followed by holes one through nine. The wind blows left to right on hole ten, as this hole lies broadside to the Firth of Forth. Bunkers lie to the left of the landing spot, and lateral bunkers stretch across the fairway, midway to the green. The green, at 28 yards in length, is the smallest on the course, and with bunkers at right front and at left, will be a worthy challenge.

The wind comes in obliquely, from the front left, on hole number eleven. A downhill slope precedes the fairway. The fairway is guarded at its midpoint by bunkers right and left. An obliquely-set, split-level triangle, the green is guarded with bunkers on all sides, and at its rearmost point. At 29 yards across its widest points, this is an extremely difficult target to negotiate.

As the twelfth hole lies broadside to the Firth of Forth, it is subject to winds blowing from right to left. A bunker and an intrusion of rough on the left will probably stimulate you to attempt a carry to the green. It could save strokes, but it could also be an utter disaster. On the green approach, and on the right and left of the longitudinal, oblong green, bunkers await miscalculated and mis-hit shots. A hillside lies to the rear, which may also cause some unexpected disturbance in wind patterns at the green.

At 152 yards, the thirteenth is the shortest par three at Muirfield. The long, narrow green is sunk into a slight depression, with bunkers on the right and left, and a small concavity at left front. Wind currents here flow left to right.

The fourteenth, a shallow dogleg left, plays with the wind blowing right to left. Five bunkers guard the fairway at strategic plays on the left, and two on the right. The oval, 31-yard green is guarded by a pot bunker at right front, and a hillside lies to its left rear.

Wind currents flowing obliquely from the right front affect play on the fifteenth hole. A trio of bunkers at the head of the fairway represent only the first group of bunkers to challenge attempts to conquer this par four easily. Eighty yards down the fairway, staggered bunkers create a second 'line of defense,' and approximately 80 yards farther, a loose triangle of bunkers dominates the fairway at the green approach. The longitudinal, oblong green is protected by three bunkers on its right and two on its left.

The sixteenth hole is, at 188 yards, the longest par three on the course. Two bunkers are set out in front of the playing surface, and form a hazard to be carried over from the tees. The wind sweeps obliquely over this hole from the left rear, a phenomenon that increases the hazard posed by the four bunkers that protect the green approach and the right of the green. A downward slope fronts the green, and three bunkers protecting the left front and side add to the reasons for playing this hole with a sense of respect.

Broadside to the wind, the seventeenth is subject to air currents flowing left to right. A dogleg left, it has copious bunkering on the inside of its bend, and halfway down the fairway is a plateau with bunkering all across it. If you can overfly this, or bring your ball to rest in front of the bunkers, you can avoid the sand. Go a little too far, and a hillside awaits your shot. On yet another elevation, the green approach leads to a roughly triangular green with a bunker on either side of its 'chin.' The green is set in a horseshoe-shaped depression that will surely swallow mis-hits to either side and overflights to the rear.

The eighteenth hole plays obliquely away from the wind, with currents coming in from the right rear. A gunsight of bunkers at the landing spot is set up for this, with three bunkers on the left, versus one on the right. The contoured green narrows to the rear, and has a massive bunker on either side. It is not a particularly easy target to hit, and two bunkers set longitudinally in the midst of the green approach will further complicate your set-up shot.

Though you may hope for better, playing the eighteenth to par is indeed an attainment with which to proudly cap a round of golf at magnificent Muirfield.

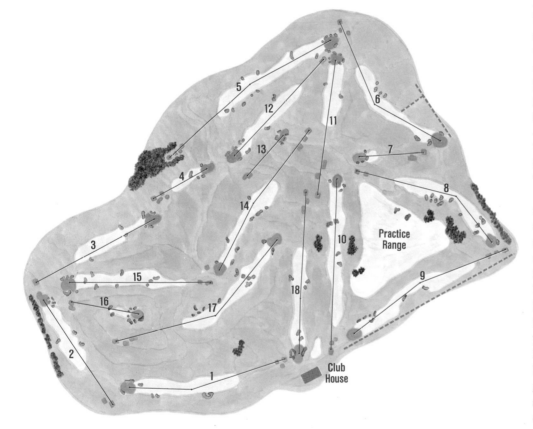

Muirfield

Hole	1	2	3	4	5	6	7	8	9	Out
Championship	447	351	379	180	559	469	185	444	504	3518
Medal	444	345	374	174	506	436	151	439	460	3329
Par	4	4	4	3	5	4	3	4	4/5	35/36

Hole	10	11	12	13	14	15	16	17	18	In	Total
Championship	475	385	381	152	449	417	188	550	448	3445	6963
Medal	471	350	376	146	442	391	181	501	414	3272	6601
Par	4	4	4	3	4	4	3	5	4	35	70/71

The National Golf and Country Club

Cape Schanck Australia

The National Golf Club was among the top 10 courses to receive an honorable mention in *Golf Magazine*'s '100 Greatest Courses in the World' listing for 1989. To quote Robert Trent Jones Jr, the architect of this great course:

'When I first saw the land on which The National was to be constructed I instantly recognized the potential it held to design a truly great international course—one that could easily be ranked with the world's best.

However, it was not until we had planned the course and cut the fairway lines that the full drama of The National became evident. We, as architects, had underestimated the full grandeur of this classic layout.'

The National is located adjacent to another of Robert Trent Jones Jr's courses—the Cape Schanck Golf Club course—on Melbourne's Mornington Peninsula, near Cape Schanck.

Although critics felt that yet another golf club in the Melbourne region—already the home of several fine courses, including the great Royal Melbourne layout—would certainly fail, The National has proven successful beyond all expectations.

Magnificent views of sights on the Peninsula, including beautiful Bass Strait, are availed to the golfer on this course—a beauty that will refresh golfers further while they engage in a very challenging round of golf.

Five separate tee markers are in place at each of The National's holes. These tee markers are black, for championship play, blue for men's play, yellow for men's social play, red for women's championship play and white for women's play.

Following is a hole-by-hole description of the course. Hole one demands accuracy, and the green is protected by a cunningly-placed bunker and a tree. Hole two, a par three, features tee positions facing left over a wooded ravine to a large but treacherous green. The third curves gracefully to the right, and has a spectacular view. Changing elevations make this very interesting—it's a downhill drive to gradated fairway, at the top of which is the green. The fairway has six bunkers, to boot.

Hole four has a large, tricky putting surface and well-placed bunkers make this a 'long' par four. The fifth's a right, a left, and right again. This serpentine catches you with bunkers, and demands accuracy at every point. The green has a pinched mouth, a bunker and pine trees. Best of luck, here. Wide, gentle dogleg right hole six drives downhill to a green protected by two massive bunkers.

The National Golf and Country Club

Hole	1	2	3	4	5	6	7	8	9	Out	
Black	344	139	473	403	521	371	308	198	390	3147	
Par	4	3	5	4	5	4	4	3	4	36	
Hole	10	11	12	13	14	15	16	17	18	In	Total
Black	358	168	511	337	342	420	390	165	475	3166	6313
Par	4	3	5	4	4	4	4	3	5	36	72

Note: all distances are given in meters

The National. *Opposite:* An oval green in a seaside landscape, with Bass Straight for a backdrop. *Above opposite:* A highly contoured green.

Hole seven is a delayed dogleg right—a fairly long drive with a bend at the end, and a tiny green protected by a stabilized sand dune. The eighth, another par three, is straightforward, with a severely pinched shot at the green. Five bunkers stand guard duty, and the green is large and sloping. A good, good hole. Hole number nine plays as a long, gentle dogleg left. Heavy bunkering on the left of the fairway, tall trees at either side of the green's mouth, and a bunker to the left make this a very nifty par four.

Hole ten is a dogleg right. You drive downhill into 'bunker heaven,' the golfer's demise—unless he's careful. A bunker waits on the right mouth of the green, and the tree on the right of the fairway, with the green bunkered behind as well, make this quite a hole. Tee shots at hole eleven must cross a deep ravine to the green, and a hidden bunker foils many shots to the left. The green slopes, to continue the fun.

The twelfth is a dogleg left that almost repents before you reach the green. Just after the elbow, the fairway pinches in, asking you to shoot for the green at risk of hitting the large bunker at fairway's end, where the range shifts sharply to a 'peninsula' which aims toward the green; bunkers trail from right, right around the green.

Dogleg right hole thirteen demands a focused drive through very crafty bunkering. The final bunker behind the green will catch many a ball. Hole number fourteen features a clump of trees which inrupt on the fairway, and a bunker at left which cuts it two-thirds of the way down into a mere neck for the rest of the way—toward a supernally well-protected green. Great views here, and great golf.

The fifteenth's two big bunkers to the right could cheat you into aiming for the two big bunkers halfway down the fairway on the left. The green is protected by two bunkers left. Hole sixteen's tees face across a ravine where bunkers catch you short and long. Then you work uphill toward the large green past the two bunkers at fairway's end. Hole number seventeen is a long shot over water to a green protected by two bunkers and water at its very edge. A very thrilling par three. The eighteenth hole is a gentle serpentine on a fairway bunkered where it does good. A bunker cuts across the approach to the green, and a large bunker at left rear of the green take the golfer's attention away from Daryl Jackson's stunningly designed course clubhouse, which has at this point come into view. A great finish to a great 18 holes of golf.

*At left: **The National's beauteous setting and strategic design combine to offer a great round of golf for players of many different levels.***

New St Andrews Golf Club

Tochigi Prefecture Japan

Tom Weiskopf is quoted in the New St Andrews brochure as saying that this course is one of the most beautiful and exciting courses he has ever played. Mr Weiskopf goes on to say, 'Come the day when it hosts a major tournament, I believe it will be recognized as one of the greatest golf courses not only in Japan, but in the entire world.'

Jack Nicklaus designed the 18 holes of the 'New Course' at New St Andrews, which fills out the original nine that form

Below: **A view of the sixth green, on the right, and the third green, directly ahead, from the sixth fairway.** *At left:* **A blossom-bedecked view of New St Andrews.**

the 'Old Course' at New St Andrews. The New Course's 18 holes provide a tremendous variety of shot values. The course is not particularly hilly, and yet elevation throughout the layout is such that magnificent views are availed to players at every fairway, tee and green.

There are valley holes, hillside holes, open links-like holes and wooded holes, straightaway holes, dogleg holes and large, double and small greens. It is a course at which you'll have to use every club in your bag. Named for the hallowed St Andrews Links (see that chapter of this text) in Scotland, New St Andrews bears the traditional insignia of the eponymous saint, with the

distinctive cross upon which he was martyred, and his famous motto, written in Latin: 'Dum spiro spero,' which is to say, 'While I breathe, I hope.' St Andrew's cross was a mark of his hope and humility—his humility was a mark of his greatness in the eyes of God.

Just so, the greatness of St Andrews in Scotland follows the Scottish *modus operandi* of taking on the forms of humble nature and elevating them to higher status—and this lineage has been passed down through one of the greatest admirers of traditional Scottish golf design, Jack Nicklaus, who has infused New St Andrews with more than a few of the traits of beauti-

Above: A view down the second fairway to the green. *Below:* A view from the tees of the seventeenth hole. The hour-glass shaped green is con- toured and surrounded with bunkers—it is a spine-tingling downhill target. *Opposite:* Another view of the seventeenth green. *Below opposite:* A view of the sixteenth green from beyond its famous waterfalls. *Above opposite:* The eighth green as seen from the tees.

ful, and challenging, humility that are to be met in the classic Scottish courses.

Its natural surroundings seem to have always held this course in their contours, and golfing here is the excitement of an intense but fair challenge. The following is a hole-by-hole description of the 'New Course' at New St Andrews. Hole number one is a brisk beginning. It's a slight dogleg right, with bunkers on its outer bend, and a lake all along the right side. There's not a lot of room between the bunkers and the lake, and for many, it'll be a water carry to the green.

A lake lies to the right of the second hole's tees, and figures in a carry to the fairway. From the landing area, it's a shot to a green having a massive bunker out front and extensive bunkering behind. A magnificent challenge. Hole number three is one of the most beautiful holes on the course. A semi-blind tee shot should bring you into good position for the shot to the green approach, which for most players will involve laying up before the carry across the tip of the lake to the green, which has bunkers and a hillside at its back. Watch out for that green approach, too—a mis-hit second shot could find the sand to the left or the lake to the right.

Hole number four is a dogleg left, with a green that is surrounded by bunkers. Additionally, the green has a split-level surface with a 'knob' in its middle. It'll be a real test to birdie here. The fifth hole is a par three that plays downhill. Its green has big bunkers guarding either side of its front, and a cherry tree guarding the right third of the green. This can be a very demanding hole. The green at the sixth hole is sandwiched between bunkers on the right and a lake on the left. A bunker also lies behind the green, and mis-hits are likely to find sand or water here.

Hole number seven has an elevated tee and a plethora of bunkers intruding on the fairway from the right. To the left is a hillside. Trees and shrubs additionally challenge all along the right. The green has heavy bunkering in front and behind, but there's a chance for a birdie here. The eighth hole is a par three with a long carry over a lake to a large green with bunkers all along the right and left side. The cant of the green is toward the lake. A truly beautiful challenge.

Hole number nine is an unusual challenge that involves a hogback ridge on the fairway that must be overcome to establish a good stance for the tee shot. The green shot will be semi-blind. You won't see the bunker at front right, for instance, until you've either put you ball in it or on the green. If you overshoot, sand and a hillside await your shot. This hole plays uphill all the way.

At the tenth hole, golfers will tee off across a valley to a landing area that is bracketed with bunkers right and left. The green has bunkers out front on both sides. It's a great start to the 'inbound nine.' At hole number eleven, players are faced with a fairway that has a gully, and has heavy bunkering on the left, and a tree on the fairway, near the green approach. Bunkers at front, left and right guard a large green that narrows to the rear.

The twelfth hole plays downhill toward a green that is surrounded by bunkers and has a scenic drop-off to the rear. In addition, this is a double green that is shared with the fifteenth hole. Hole number thirteen is a very long-playing par four, with trees and bunkers that lie in the dogleg's outer bend. The green is a split-level surface that is guarded at left front and at right rear with big bunkers. It's a tough hole to play. The fourteenth hole is a par three on which golfers tee off over a valley to a heavily bunkered green with a backdrop composed of a mound of mountain stones and boulders. It's beautiful—but potentially fatal for over-powered shots.

The fifteenth is a dogleg right with bunkers and a hillside on its inner bend, and bunkers and a depression on its outer bend. This hole has elevated tees, and plays downhill to a green having one massive bunker on its left front, and bunkering at right and at rear. The green is a double, shared with hole number twelve.

The sixteenth hole seems destined to become one of the most photographed holes in golf. A rippling series of waterfalls runs the entire length of the hole from left to right, cutting across for a spectacular hazard—and distraction—at the green approach. The green is tucked into an amphitheater-like hillside and fronts on the water, and has heavy bunkering at rear and on its exposed left face.

Tee shots at the par three seventeenth hole are severely downhill to an hourglass-shaped green that is protected all around with bunkers. The segment of the green on the left has a hog-back ridge, while the right-hand segment is bowl-contoured. This is a potentially decisive hole.

The eighteenth hole is a good, rigorous finish to a spectacular 18 holes of golf. The tee shot should pull up short of going over the top of a hill that fronts the green approach—over the hill is a valley from which it would be very tough to get to the green. The green approach shot should carry over the valley, and the intensive bunkering that fronts the green. A hillside lies behind the green.

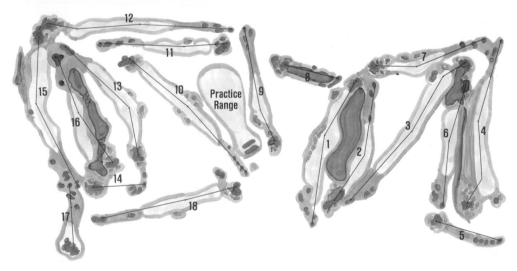

New Saint Andrews Golf Club, Japan

Hole	1	2	3	4	5	6	7	8	9	Out	
Blue	442	376	534	527	207	365	342	179	344	3316	
White	407	346	488	488	187	337	314	162	331	3060	
Red	346	282	470	466	139	314	274	93	265	2649	
Par	4	4	5	5	3	4	4	3	4	36	
Hole	10	11	12	13	14	15	16	17	18	In	Total
Blue	489	359	538	409	152	464	375	193	428	3407	6723
White	480	310	501	392	131	434	362	159	403	3172	6232
Red	427	268	460	375	102	371	295	125	324	2747	5396
Par	5	4	5	4	3	4	4	3	4	36	72

Above: A view down the first fairway from the first green. This hole will unlimber your driving muscles, but accuracy and strategy are also required here. *Below:* The third green and the green approach. The tee shot requires valor, and the green is a slippery target. *Above left:* A view of the eighteenth green and the New St Andrews clubhouse, as seen from the eighteenth fairway—an inspiring conclusion for a great round.

Pebble Beach Golf Links

Pebble Beach, California USA

The legendary Pebble Beach Golf Links was the number two course in the world, according to *Golf Magazine*'s '100 Greatest Courses in the World' listing for 1989, up from third in 1987. Pebble Beach, possessed of rare atmosphere and scenic values, is a stringent and rewarding test of golfing ability. The renowned golf writer Herbert Warren Wind is quoted as saying 'Pebble Beach… that wild and wonderful layout… may well be the best course in the world.'

A touch of historical perspective is in order. Samuel Finley Brown Morse, great-nephew of Samuel FB Morse, the inventor of Morse Code, was born in 1885. No less industrious than his famed forebear, he went to Yale University, where he became the captain of the unstoppable 1906 football team, and graduated in 1907. Morse, his wife and son settled in California in 1908, visiting the Monterey Peninsula for the first time.

As a man who would decades later be described by *Fortune* as 'one of the grand old men of American business,' the young Morse instinctively knew what he wanted. He became manager of the Crocker-Huffman Land and Water Company, in Merced. His work for the company involved overseeing irrigation projects, land development, farming and livestock development.

Sweeping ocean vistas abound at Pebble Beach Golf Links. *Opposite:* The seventh green. *Below:* The fourth green, yet another hole that is open to sea and sky. *Above:* A view of the sixth hole.

Thus he came to know the qualities of the California land well.

He became manager of the Pacific Improvement Company in 1915. The Pacific Improvement Company had extensive land holdings on the Monterey Peninsula. This reinforced his impression of the Monterey Peninsula as the venue of some of the finest land he could imagine. As an avid sportsman, he was especially drawn to the

perfect seaside linksland of the Monterey Peninsula. He moved on with his career, a definite plan taking shape in his mind.

Morse formed Del Monte Properties Company, and bought some of the Pacific Improvement Company's properties, including the Del Monte Forest and the Hotel Del Monte. The Del Monte Forest included a stretch of spectacular seaside land that was perfect for a golf course. For expert course design, Morse called in Jack Neville, a three-time amateur golf champion. Douglas Grant, the reigning state golf champion, was also called upon for help in the area of bunker design.

What they created was a course with cliff-side fairways and sloping greens, with eight holes bordering the Pacific Ocean. It was, and is, utterly spectacular. One of the few great course designs to which no major renovation has been made over the years, it is uniquely challenging. Its dramatic locale is doubly impressive in that it makes possible a great test of golf.

Two of the most revered holes are the seventeenth and eighteenth. With the ocean and the rugged, rocky coast at the back of the green, the rigorous par three seventeenth has been a 'decider' in many games, including Tom Watson's victory over Jack Nicklaus in the 1982 US Open, when he chipped in from heavy rough for

the birdie that became known as 'the [golf] shot heard 'round the world.'

The eighteenth is perhaps the greatest long finishing hole in golf. Curving gracefully along the rock-bound coast, it is beautiful and treacherous. Morse's dream was to establish this beautiful course as a public course, and so—like its brilliant design—it has remained to this day.

The course had its grand opening on 22 February 1919—first President of the US George Washington's birthday. In honor of the 'chopping down the cherry tree' fable featuring Washington as a boy, a cherry tree was planted in front of the brand-new Del Monte Lodge, an edifice that was highly touted by the *San Francisco Examiner*, which said that the Lodge 'promises in the future to be one of the favorite meeting places for society.'

Other periodicals also gave glowing reviews of the lodge. *The American* stated that 'The opening of the Del Monte Lodge, in connection with the Hotel Del Monte, represents one of the greatest all-year-round resorts available.' (The Hotel Del Monte had been completely renovated by Morse and associates.)

The very cream of society attended the opening, and it proved to be the social event of the year—spirits were high, World War I had ended just a few months before, and Americans were eager to forget the solemnities of war.

The Del Monte Lodge replaced the original Pebble Beach Lodge, a pine log structure that was opened in August, 1909 for the enjoyment of day travelers on the spectacularly scenic Seventeen Mile Drive. Guests would begin the journey at the plush Hotel Del Monte, and follow the Drive (then an unpaved road) as it wound through Monterey, Pacific Grove, the Del Monte Forest and thence along the coast to the pebbled beaches.

The Pebble Beach Lodge was a welcome pause after a day's drive in the exhilarating elements of the Monterey Peninsula. On the beach nearby, Chinese fisherman and their families set up abalone stands where travelers could refresh themselves with steaming helpings of that delectable gastropod.

The Pebble Beach Lodge burned down on 26 December 1917, and was replaced by Samuel Morse's palatial Del Monte Lodge. The Del Monte Lodge—now known as The Lodge at Pebble Beach—is a three-story structure of Spanish and Italian architectural influence. It was designed by San Francisco architect Lewis Hobart. Resplendent with tile, marble and mosaics, it has large French windows and a terraced promenade.

Above: A golfing party at the fifth tee confronts the well-treed fairway. *At left:* The distractingly beautiful tenth green. *Below:* The fairway of the sixth hole, with Carmel Bay visible on the left.

Original murals by Frances McComas and chandeliers of opaque glass further bolstered the overall sense of luxury that the Lodge exuded for the guests on opening day.

A large Turkish bath, with exercise rooms and lounges, originally occupied part of the Lodge, but has since been removed, with the spas of the adjacent Beach and Tennis Club, or the nearby Club at Spanish Bay, taking the old bath's place.

The *San Francisco Chronicle* deemed the Lodge to be 'the very ultra of exclusiveness in the way of a fashionable retreat.' The sports pages of the *Chronicle* also had their say about the new golf course. Reporter Hay Chapman quoted William Tucker, a visiting Englishman (whose native isles contain the very 'Home of Golf,' St Andrews). Tucker pronounced, 'I do not know of any course anywhere that can excel Pebble Beach from a golfing standpoint.'

By the end of the opening weekend, Douglas Grant, co-designer of the course, had the honor of the best overall score on the new course, with an 80.

Samuel Morse was 33 years old, and his public golf course was already being recognized as one of the finest in the world. Nor would succeeding generations have to see its decline in any way, for The Links at Pebble Beach remain unimpeachably great. Part of this is due to Samuel Morse's unwavering stand on preservation and ecology—he has been called 'The Father of Environmentalists.'

Under his careful consideration of land usage, native flora and fauna thrived on the Monterey Peninsula, and such civic projects as the Community Hospital of the Monterey Peninsula, Monterey Peninsula College and Monterey Peninsula Airport were granted parcels of land at below-market prices.

He was determined to preserve the coastline of the Monterey Peninsula, and did so with scenic easements in the Del Monte Forest that ensured the pristine condition of the forest land and peninsula golf courses, including Pebble Beach, Spyglass Hill and Cypress Point, for future generations.

Mr Morse's accomplishments included personal heroism, as well—in January, 1927, he rescued a cowboy, Albert Torres, who was pinned beneath his horse in Washerman's Bay, and would have drowned had Morse not come to his aid.

Samuel Morse died on 10 May 1969, and was eulogized as a man who was 'capable of preserving a garden… for millions to enjoy.' In the preceding decades he saw a lot of golf played at Pebble Beach. Fol-

lowing is a gloss of some of the great golf events played on this legendary course.

The 1929 US Amateur Championship saw Harrison R Johnston prevail over Dr OF Willing with respective match scores of four and three. Also in this tournament the great Bobby Jones lost in a first-round match to Johnny Goodman—who went on to lose to Lawson Little. Almost 20 years later, Robert H 'Skee' Riegel defeated John W Dawson to win the 1947 US Amateur Championship, with respective scores of two and one.

The young Jack Nicklaus edged out H Dudley Wysong Jr for the 1961 US Amateur Championship win—the respective scores being eight and six. Eleven years later, Nicklaus won the 1972 US Open Championship at Pebble Beach, with Bruce Crampton coming close with a 293 to Nicklaus' 290. Nicklaus' master stroke here was a magnificent draw into a strong breeze that scored a hit on the pin and landed just inches from the hole.

At the 1977 PGA Championship, Lanny Wadkins prevailed over Gene Littler at the third hole of a 'sudden-death' playoff to break their tied scores of 282. Tom Watson performed a bit of magic to win the 1982 US Open Championship. His truly great sand wedge shot from the rough on the seventeenth hole was a key to his win over Jack Nicklaus, whose 284 was not enough to beat Watson's 282.

Women's championships played on this great golf course include the 1940 US Women's Amateur Championship, which saw Betty Jameson score a six in match play to prevail over Jane S Cotton's five. Grace Lenczyk defeated Helen Siegel for the title at the 1948 US Women's Amateur Championship. Their respective scores were four and three.

Pebble Beach Golf Links

Hole	1	2	3	4	5	6	7	8	9	Out
Blue	373	502	388	327	166	516	107	431	464	3274
White	338	439	341	303	156	487	103	405	439	3011
Red	322	363	275	256	140	385	88	350	330	2509
Par	4	5	4	4	3	5	3	4	4	36

Hole	10	11	12	13	14	15	16	17	18	In	Total
Blue	426	384	202	392	565	397	402	209	548	3525	6799
White	395	374	184	373	553	366	388	175	538	3346	6357
Red	296	316	166	285	420	308	307	164	426	2688	5197
Par	4	4	3	4	5	4	4	3	5	36	72

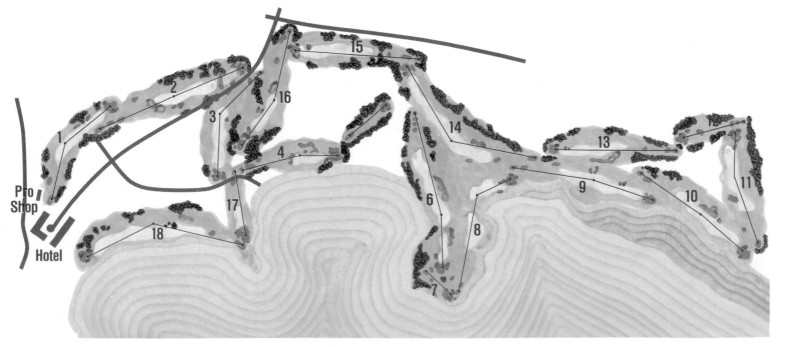

The 1992 US Open Championship will no doubt occasion yet more great golf at Pebble Beach Golf Links. Additionally, Pebble Beach is one of the three venues on which the annual Bing Crosby Pro-Am is played (the other two venues are Cypress Point and Spyglass Hill).

Stretching along Carmel Bay, the seventh through tenth holes are a great series of holes and may be likened (in their ability to test your golfing skills) to Augusta National's famous 'Amen Corner.' The following is a hole-by-hole description of this world-famous golf course.

The first hole is a 373-yard par four that is partially lined with trees. A pair of dangerous bunkers lie on the outside curve of this dogleg right, and behind each of these is a copse of trees. Long drives from the tees will have to take into account this seaside course's often unpredictable winds. The green is narrow, and a bunker at left front again strikes a note of caution, while the bunker all along the right may cause real trouble for the unwary.

Hole number two is a straightaway 502-yard par five. You'll have to carry two bunkers that preface the fairway, and the landing spot has trees off to the left and bunkers off to the right. Copses of trees offer potential disaster on either side of this fairway, but the green approach presents the most interesting problems here. Across a split in the fairway lies a longitudinal bunker, on the left of which is an overhanging tree. This tree serves to force a rightward consideration, which is dangerous in itself—as the fairway narrows to the right. One could carry over this bit of fairway, but holding the smallish, heavily bunkered green will be a bit tricky. Trees additionally complicate matters at this green.

The third hole is a dogleg left with a bunker tucked into its inner curve. The fairway is relatively uncomplicated—a 'breather' of sorts—but does feature a swale across its midsection. The green is a thick crescent that curves away to the right, behind a pair of bunkers on that side. A large bunker guards the left side of the green.

The fourth hole is the first of several holes at Pebble Beach that plays along Carmel Bay. Here, you will feel the effects of the Pacific Ocean breezes and winds quite strikingly. It is a difficult hole to calculate, especially since the tees are located in a hallway of trees, and are therefore semi-shielded from the wind. Your shot passes into the open, and must negotiate a lateral bunker that prefaces the fairway. Two layers of bunkering await windblown shots to the left of the fairway—a small bunker is cradled by an irregular, ell-shaped bunker

Above opposite: **On the fourth green.** *At top, above:* **Views of the eighth (on the ridge) and ninth holes.** *Above:* **The Lodge at Pebble Beach.**

of much larger size. The beach and the distractingly awesome Pacific Ocean waters of Carmel Bay lie to the right. The green is narrow, and two large, irregular bunkers nearly surround it with sand.

Trees provide an uneven, overhanging surround for the par three fifth hole. The green is shallower than it is wide, and is hidden behind a massive oval bunker. To the right of the green is a longitudinal bunker.

Hole number six heads out into Carmel Bay, and affords spectacular, distracting

views—and some equally spectacular winds. A gentle double dogleg. This 516-yard par five will afford plenty of driving challenge, with two long bunkers to the left, and cliffs and ocean water to the right. A split fairway complicates matters somewhat, and the narrow green with bunkers on either side is a worthy object of attainment.

The seventh hole has been cited as one of the toughest par threes anywhere, with its green situated on a small promontory overlooking Carmel Bay. The tees are set beside a longitudinal grove of trees, and a copse on the left helps to make these tee shots a matter of target practice. A crucial consid-

eration here is the wind. The green lies downhill, adding further challenge—too hard, and your ball is bound for Davey Jones's Locker. The green is surrounded by bunkers, which are fed daily by the wind and overflights.

The eighth hole is a sharp dogleg right that curves around an inlet of Carmel Bay. Cliffside and bay waters lie all along the right, and prevailing winds will sure keep you battling to get a good lie on the fairway. Beware the various incursions made by the cliffside—particularly at the nether end of the first half of the split fairway. The green approach is protected by bunkers left and right. The slender, cresent green slopes from right to left and is heavily bunkered.

Hole number nine is a straightaway driving hole that plays along Carmel Bay. The fairway is narrow, with two clusters of bunkers lying near the landing spots for average and very long hitters, and its green narrows front to rear. A small, deadly bunker guards the left front of this putting surface. Beware the cliffside incursions to the right.

The tenth hole is the final of this rugged stretch of beachside holes. You tee off over a pathway to a fairway that has a steep bank and Carmel Bay along its right. On the left is a large, complex bunker that is situated to catch windblown tee shots. The green heads into a large, wedge-shaped bunker, and has a large, oval bunker protecting its left side. The distracting beauty of the view over this green is a very special tactical problem.

Dogleg right hole number eleven plays inland from Carmel Bay. A large, oval bunker will present problems for shots that drift to the left of the fairway. The green approach is protected by one bunker on the right. The obliquely-set, narrow green itself has bunkers at left and right, and at right rear.

The wind comes from the left on the twelfth hole, Pebble Beach's third par three. Trees line the right here, and the green has bunkers directly in front and at right front, and at right rear.

The thirteenth hole's back tees lie within a narrow hallway of trees, making shot selection for the narrow, obliquely-set fairway somewhat difficult. A very large longitudinal bunker lies to the left of the fairway, and a copse of trees is close in on the right. The green is surrounded by low ridges, and has trees and a bunker on its right. Two bunkers guard the right approach.

Hole number fourteen—the longest Pebble Beach hole, at 565 yards from the back tees—is a dogleg right that curves away from Carmel Bay. Trees on the right, bunkers left and right and a fast-breaking

curve make tee shots on this hole difficult. Having gained the fairway, you're tempted to shave some strokes by cutting across the rough just shy of the trees that lie along the right. With the wind at Pebble Beach, this is a risky maneuver, and shots must needs be very positive both in force and calculation. Bunkers and low mounding on the front and right sides of the green, and trees at left and right, make this a memorable hole.

Tee shots at the fifteenth hole must clear a vegetation-filled ravine with a 135-yard carry. The fairway is straightaway and tree-lined. A bunker guards the right green approach, and the sloping green is pro-

tected at right and right rear, and at left front, by other bunkers.

The sixteenth hole plays straight toward Carmel Bay, and thus is subject to interesting wind patterns. The back tees are cradled in a copse of trees, and tee shots must carry over a path, a roadway and a large, wineskin-shaped bunker en route to a somewhat obliquely-set fairway. This fairway has a pair of bunkers at midway on the right, and a lining of trees that stretches all the way from its midway point to the left rear of the green. The green is fronted by a 'Y'-shaped bunker, and has trees close in at right and left, and a pot bunker behind.

At 209 yards from the back tees, the longest par three at Pebble Beach, the seventeenth hole heads out to the beach, and affords golfers yet more of the stunning, distracting vistas that so delight and bedevil golfers at Pebble Beach. You may want to lay up before going for the green here. A gigantic bunker lies along the left and left front of this green, and numerous bunkers guard the right, right rear and rear. Just beyond is Carmel Bay.

The eighteenth hole plays as a long, gentle dogleg left along Carmel Bay. By now your head is absolutely swimming with the astonishing expanse of sea that is so visu- ally prevalent here. Shots from the back tees must carry over the edge of a cliff at left, and a bunker at left, and trees on the fairway just beyond this narrow your play- ing options to a finely-gauged lie on the left side of the fairway, close to the hillside that leads to the water. The fairway narrows toward the green, and the green has bunkers at left, right front and right, as well as the hillside and water to the left and trees to the right.

At right and below: **The eighteenth at Pebble Beach. This is a dogleg left that plays along Car- mel Bay. Ocean breakers add exhilaration and mystique to an essentially great final hole.**

Royal County Down Golf Club

Newcastle, County Down Northern Ireland

Royal County Down Course Number One was ranked eighth in the world, according to *Golf Magazine*'s '100 Greatest Courses in the World' listing for 1989, having risen in that poll from the ninth position it held in 1987.

The Mountains of Mourne make a subtle and unignorable backdrop for this revered course, and the vistas over Dundrum Bay toward the Isle of Man and the Cumberland-Lancashire coast of Great Britain are inspiring. As can be expected, the level of play is rigorous, especially on the world-famous fourth hole, a par four that requires a shot over a sea of gorse.

It is humbling to consider that this great course was designed for the sum of four guineas by the legendary Old Tom Morris (see St Andrews Links, Old Course). It has been said, however, that the strip of dunescape on which Royal County Down was designed was practically ready to play when Old Tom Morris set his hand to designing the course. A few adjustments were made over the years—notably by James Dunn (in 1905) and Harry Vardon (in 1919), but you feel when you step onto this course that the very essence of golf is about to unfold before you.

The Mountains of Mourne slope down to the sea in the background, their contours subtly changing as the sunlight and weather over the fickle Irish Sea change—

sometimes seemingly by the minute. The links have heroic elevation changes, and are covered with gorse bushes that bedevil golfers and brighten the landscape with their ocher flowers when in bloom.

The turf is that primordial golfing surface—springy fescue, cropped close on the fairways and growing in wiry tufts on the dunes. The greens are well-kept and tend to be fast, and are somewhat difficult to read. Newcastle has five blind tee shots, as well as a number of hidden greens.

The following is a hole-by-hole description of this world-renowned golfing venue. Holes one through three play along the windswept beach of Dundrum Bay.

The first hole loosens up your driving talents. It's a straightaway, 506-yard (from the back tees), oceanside hole with a slope and a mound on the right side of the fairway, and gorse and a bunker on the left. The green approach is protected by a pot bunker at right. The green is deep, and is protected by a pot bunker on the right, and by a larger bunker on the left front.

Another straightaway hole is hole number two. Beware the tendency to overcompensate for the wind rushing in from the right, off the ocean. Those whose shots go too far right will find the gorse that lies on

Below: **The linksland of Royal County Down.** *At right:* **Preparing to tee off on the eighth hole, looking toward the Mountains of Mourne.**

that side, as well as a complex of difficult slopes that can substantially raise your score. On the left, awaiting windblown shots, is a pot bunker. Protecting the green approach is a trio of bunkers. Beyond these lies the green, with two bunkers on its left side, and a slope at right and rear.

The third hole plays close to the beach on the right. As with any seaside linksland course, the wind is as much a factor as the rolling, uneven terrain over which the course wends its way. Tee shots chance landing in one of the three (two left, one right) bunkers that guard the landing spot on this fairway. A deep incursion of rough severely narrows the fairway a short while later, and carries will chance a bunker lying left, a hidden bunker lying right and gorse off to the left. Slopes to either side of the fairway further complicate matters. The green approach is guarded by no less than four bunkers, and the green has one bunker to its left, and gorse just beyond the rough that lies behind.

The fourth hole is the longest par three at Royal County Down, at 217 yards from the back tee. From the back tee, you must tee off from amidst a veritable sea of gorse, and your shot has to pass up over a ridge (and also has to avoid a plethora of bunkers

that front the sunken green). The green is deep and narrow, is backed by mounds and has two bunkers at right rear.

Hole number five is a dogleg right, with a bunker just to the left, which probably catches more than its share of mis-hit balls on especially windy days. Bunkers to the right and left, and a trio of bunkers clustered around the center of the fairway, encourage a target approach to this part of the fairway. On the right of the green approach lie two bunkers. The green has a slope at right rear, two bunkers at left, and gorse off to the rear.

The sixth hole is a dogleg right that has a split-level fairway, with a large bunker to the lee side of the slope, and a pot bunker off to the windward side. The green features yet another elevation change. The approach is guarded with a bunker on the right, and the green has bunkers off its left front—and on its right—sides.

A par three, the seventh hole features a carry across the edge of a gorse-covered hillside to an ovoid green that has slopes at right front, right rear and on the left. A large contingent of bunkers guards this green at front, left and left rear.

Hole number eight is a straightaway hole on which tee shots must negotiate hollows and a bunker lying left, and two bunkers at right, surrounding the landing spot. The green approach is constricted by two bunkers and mounds lying left and right. The narrow green is sloped on both sides, and gorse lies at right rear.

The ninth hole features a number of elevation changes, and plays broadside to the wind. The tee shot here is quite risky, as the back tee must carry over considerable

Royal County Down Golf Club

Hole	1	2	3	4	5	6	7	8	9	Out
Championship	506	424	473	217	440	396	145	427	486	3514
Medal	500	374	473	217	418	368	129	427	431	3337
Front Medal	500	374	454	174	409	358	129	424	431	3253
Par	5	4	4	3	4	4	3	4	4/5	35/36

Hole	10	11	12	13	14	15	16	17	18	In	Total
Championship	200	440	501	445	213	445	265	400	545	3454	6968
Medal	200	429	476	422	213	445	265	376	528	3354	6691
Front Medal	192	429	476	422	202	420	236	376	528	3281	6534
Par	3	4	5	4	3	4	4	4	5	36	71/72

Above: **At the tee on the tenth hole, a gorse-lined par three with heavy bunkering in front of a tricky green. The weather at Royal County Down is as challenging as the land itself.**

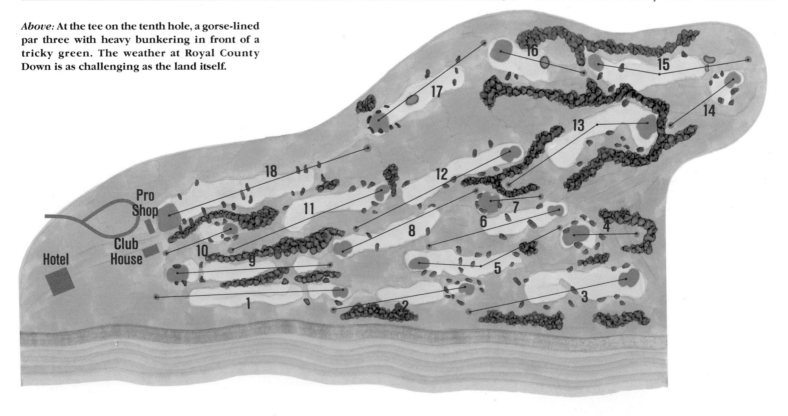

The thirteenth hole is truly lined with gorse—you could say that the hole is set amidst a sea of gorse. With slopes on either side, this is a hole for the valiant, as a mistake at any point could bring disaster. This hole is a dogleg right, with bunkers dotting its right side, and a cannily-placed bunker guarding the left front of the green. Behind this bunker is yet another slope.

The fourteenth hole is the final par three at Royal County Down. Tee shots must carry over a patch of gorse en route to a deep but narrow green that is protected at right and left front by five bunkers. Additionally—and perhaps important to remember when the wind is blowing—a pond lies to the far left, as does another bunker (both of which figure heavily in tee shots on the fifteenth hole).

Tee shots on the fifteenth hole must carry over the small pond and bunker mentioned above, and must negotiate a slope, the far side of which reveals yet another altitudinal difficulty. Careful judgement of strength and accuracy is essential here. The fairway from this point slopes down toward the gorse on either side as far as the green approach, which is guarded by two bunkers at left, and one at right. The green has slopes to its right and left, and gorse off to the rear.

Surrounded by gorse, the tees at the sixteenth hole must carry over a field of the prickly shrub, plus a ring-shaped lake. You must decide if you can indeed make the carry up the slope to the green approach—for some, laying up before the slope is wise procedure. On the left of this slope is a bunker, and just over the top from this bunker is another bunker. The green is a deep oval, beyond the rear of which lie the seventeenth tees.

Hole number seventeen is a straightaway hole with an incursion of rough on the right of the leading edge of the fairway. A bunker lies to the right of the landing spot, and long hitters should be mindful of the pond that lies in the center of the fairway 100 yards out from the green. The green approach is guarded by two bunkers at right and left, and the green is practically surrounded with bunkers.

They have saved the longest for last at Royal County Down. A 545-yard par five from the back tees, the eighteenth hole has numerous small bunkers lining both sides, and a cluster of three bunkers occupying the middle of the fairway. Additionally, gorse lies all along the left. With the exception of its very front, the green has slopes on all sides. It's a magnificent challenge of strength and accuracy with which to finish a round of golf at one of the world's greatest golf courses.

gorse. A consideration is whether to lay up on the small island of fairway that precedes a change in elevation, or to attempt the extra 45-yard carry to the main fairway. This main fairway has gorse lying off to either side, has a slope early on at the left and leads to a green approach that is protected by a slope and two bunkers, and has an additional slope and gorse to its right. The green is deep but narrow, with bunkering right and left.

A par three, the tenth hole is lined with gorse. Tee shots must carry over four bunkers that guard the front of the green—an ovoid that has a slope to its left and gorse off its left rear.

Tee shots on the eleventh hole must pass down a narrow hallway of gorse, carrying over an obstructive elevation change and

At top, above: **An escape from an eighteenth fairway bunker.** *Above:* **Gorse and a (hidden) lake threaten this tee shot on the sixteenth hole.**

find the fairway without landing in the pot bunker at left. Two ridges attempt an incursion from the left, and bunkers guard the green approach at right and left. The oval green is 29 yards deep, and has two bunkers at left front and one at right front. Gorse lies off to the rear of this green.

Hole number twelve has a split level fairway with three bunkers and a mound protecting the landing spot. The second shot will pass over the lip of a slope that has gorse off to the right. This presents a chance for daring, as from 80 to 130 yards beyond this slope are two sets of bunkers that precede a green that has slopes on either side, and gorse to the right rear.

These pages: In the rough by a green at Royal County Down. With the Mountains of Mourne as a backdrop, and volatile weather coming in off the Irish Sea, this is challenge to which traditional golfers gladly rise. Royal County Down embodies the very finest in golf.

Royal Dornoch Golf Club

Sutherland, Scotland UK

Royal Dornoch was ranked 11th in *Golf Magazine*'s '100 Greatest Courses in the World' for 1989, was 12th in 1987, and is ranked by the 1989 poll as fifth in the British Isles. The first historically documented mention of the Dornoch Links is from the accounts of Sir Robert Gordon, Tutor to the House of Sutherland and Historian of the County. He mentions the cost of the young Earl of Sutherland's 'golf clubs and golf balls' for the year 1616. His description of the golf links in 1630 was as follows (in the original orthography):

'About this town along the sea coast are the fairest and largest links or green fields in any part of Scotland. Fitt for archery, golfing, ryding and all other exercises, they doe surpass the fields of Monroe or St Andrews.'

There is no recorded mention of the Dornoch Links again until 1852, when George Dempster of Skibo, a St Andrews man, played golf with a party over the Dornoch Links. Sometime between 1616 and

Below: **A view over gorse at some of the finest linksland in the world: Royal Dornoch Links.**

1852, the Sutherland Golfing Society was established: its members played at Dornoch and at Golspie. This organization was superseded by the founding of the Dornoch Golf Club in 1877.

The Dornoch Links were, at this point, only nine holes in extent. It should be noted that the original links were formed in much the same primal way as was the Old Course at St Andrews: an Ice Age glacier carved the land and deposited sand dunes, which, over time, were stabilized by the growth of seaside grasses, and a finer grassy

texture was added via inland grass seeds deposited on the linksland via the woolly coats of grazing sheep.

In 1883, the legendary 'Old Tom' Morris came up from St Andrews to lay out a formal nine holes. In 1886, at the direction of John Sutherland, another nine were added, and Dornoch had 18 holes, as per the standard set at St Andrews 122 years earlier. (Please see the St Andrews course discussion.)

Dornoch was beginning to grow in reputation, and in 1894, its first great competition was held: 28 men from Moray met 28 men from Dornoch on the Dornoch Links. The Dornoch golfers defeated their visitors 246 holes to none, but the Moray men were so impressed by the course that, despite their defeat, they reported:

'[T]he links far surpassed anything we imagined. The turf is of excellent quality… .Everyone was charmed with the course.'

The oldest trophy to be played for at Dornoch is the Silver Medal, first won in 1878 by Alexander McHardy, and John Sutherland having won it 11 times. The most important club competition is for the Carnegie Shield that was presented to the club by Andrew Carnegie of Skibo, in 1901.

The great turn-of-the-century golfers JH Taylor, James Braid, Harold Hilton, John Low and other legends were frequent visitors to the Dornoch Links. In about 1901, advances in ball design brought about the rubber-centered ball, which travelled farther and necessitated the revamping of Dornoch Links, and the course was extended to 5096 yards, making it the fifth longest in Britain at the time.

John Sutherland, who at the age of 19, had taken over the offices of Club Secretary and Treasurer, was fixture at Dornoch until his death in 1941. The twelfth hole, for instance, is named after him, and a bunker on the right of the eighteenth's fairway is, to initiates, 'John Sutherland's Kidney.'

***Below*: Harrowing bunkers, gorse, rolling land, sea and sky at the great Royal Dornoch.**

In 1904, under Sutherland's direction, the course was extended onto nearby Embo Links. In 1906, King Edward VII granted Dornoch a Royal Charter, and Dornoch Golf Club became Royal Dornoch Golf Club. In 1909 Andrew Carnegie of Skibo funded a new clubhouse for the Royal Dornoch Golf Club.

Further course changes are said to have been carried out by Sutherland and Donald Ross in 1922. World War II saw the building of a military airport on Dornoch's Ladies' Course, and four holes of its 18 were completely destroyed.

Repairs were carried out in 1946, and a restricted nine-hole Ladies' Course, known as 'the Struie,' was built. Dornoch Links, the main course, was also modified, with a lengthening out to 6505 yards in an arrangement of eight holes out and 10 holes back. This work was done by George Duncan.

Among those whose skills were honed at Dornoch were the eminent Alexander

Ross, who won the US Open in 1907; his brother Donald—historically one of the great golf course architects; and Bob Mac-Donald, third in the US Open in 1915 and winner of the Western Open.

Located far up on Scotland's northeast coast, Royal Dornoch is far from Scotland's main centers of population, and has never hosted the more prominent national championships, but the Scottish Ladies' Championships have been held at Dornoch a number of times, as have the Northern

Royal Dornoch, on Scotland's northeast coast, is secluded, yet the natural challenge evidenced in the photo *below* is invitation to all.

Open Championship and the Scottish Professional Championship.

The Royal Dornoch Links Championship Course follows the contour of the Dornoch-Embo bays; the linksland rises in two steps, with ample width for parallel fairways. You play out the high ground, and return on the low ground. The greens here are magnificent and punishing plateaus, and the short holes are where you can make or utterly break your score.

Dornoch is quiet and memorably scenic. When Tom Watson first played the Links, he played three rounds within 24 hours. In testimony to the competitiveness and

exhilaration of playing Dornoch, he said: 'This is the most fun I have had playing golf in my whole life.....It is an experience I will always remember.'

Indeed, who can forget an outstanding round of golf played near the sea, with the sunlight filtering through that fine Scottish air, bringing into definition an ancient, yet hauntingly familiar, terrain, and a wind that both braces you and challenges your every shot?

The following is a hole-by-hole description of the world-famous, and truly great Royal Dornoch Links Course. Note that, in traditional Scottish style, each hole is

named—this adds a locally legendary quality, as it personalizes the course, and 'gets it into your blood, lad.' Also, be aware that this *is* a seaside linksland course, and the wind is always going to be a factor in play.

The first hole is appropriately called 'First.' It's a par four, and the landing spot is in the midst of a quadrangle of bunkers. A second shot should get you to the green: bunkers guard the right approach and both sides of the green front. The green slopes, but should be manageable.

The second hole is called 'Ord,' and it's a guess that this refers to the shoulder of fairway that juts out to the left ('ord' being related to the root 'harmos,' which means 'joint, shoulder'). This hole, at 179 yards from the back tee, is the longest par three on the course. It has a plateau green with two deep bunkers at right and left front. These bunkers are separated by a grassy mound, which will divert underpowered shots into one or the other bunker. Steep slopes on either side and to the rear of the green spell utter disaster for overflights or other *faux pas*.

Hole number three, Earl's Cross, is a dogleg left that slopes from left to right, with four bunkers lining the right of the landing spot. The fairway is further complicated by a transverse ridge, covered with bentgrass, about 30 yards short of the green, and beyond this, a large bunker at left and smaller bunker at right guard the approach. Deep grass lies behind the green, and hooks or slices will find the bunkers that lie on either side.

The fourth hole, Achinchanter, again slopes from left to right, where a fall of 10 feet to rough grass threatens to ruin your score. All along the left are gorse bushes an omen that overcompensation and misjudgment of wind are punished severely from either side. The green is a plateau with an undulating surface that slopes

severely on its right and rear—many balls have found the rough grass that lies at the ends of these slopes. Two bunkers lie on the left front of the green, and two more lie at the foot of the right front slope of this green.

Hole number five, Hilton, is named for the great turn-of-the-century golfer, Harold Hilton. The fairway lies 40 feet below tee level, and the hillside on the left of this hole is covered with bentgrass and gorse. The fairway slopes slightly from left to right, with numerous bunkers on the right of the landing spot, plus several roughgrass mounds of seven to 10 feet. Flag position is going to dictate tactics used on this hole. The green is a kidney-shaped plateau that presents its narrow edge to the fairway. Bunkers guard this green across its exposed face, and a sharp drop extends from the right around to the rear, where a bare lie gives way to deep grass encroachment. Two bunkers with a grassy hollow between them lie to the left of the green.

The sixth hole's name, Whinny Brae, means 'gorse-choked hillside,' so beware. This is a par three with a plateau green that is built into the side of that very hillside we have above described. A large bunker lies at the foot of the green's right slope, and three longitudinal bunkers guard the entire left side of the green. A steep, 12-foot slope extends from the right of the green around to its rear. Dense gorse lies all along the left. You tee off downhill here, and as we have indicated, if you miscalculate the green, it's a bogey at the very least.

Hole number seven plays toward the ocean, along a ridge, very much like the subject of its descriptive name, Pier. Heather and gorse lie on the left of the fairway, and gorse lies on the right. Bunkers lie to the left of the landing spot, and a bunker lying on the right of the green approach could force your shot to over-compensate into the gorse, or the bunker at left. Bunkers on the left and right protect the front of the green, and gorse lies near to the green on the left, while deep grass lies to the rear. A small seaside cliff lies to the right.

The eighth, Dunrobin, tees off over a burn, or stream, to a split-level fairway that 'breaks' on the seaside cliff that this course has as its central structural theme. A gorse-covered quarry lies to the right of the landing spot; and a sharp descent at the 246-yard point means that your second shot will be toward a lowland green approach. The green itself is sunken, with a right-lying bunker on the approach, a bunker on its right side proper, and two pot bunkers at left front. The beach—and beyond that, the ocean—is to the right.

The beach to the left of the ninth to the sixteenth holes is to be treated as a lateral water hazard. Especially on these holes, you will find that subtle variations in the direction of play from hole to hole will bring about a change in wind.

Hole number nine, Craiglaith, plays along the beach, with the Atlantic Ocean just beyond. Bentgrass and sand lie all along the left, while long grass and gorse lie to the right; a 499-yard (from the back) par five, this is an excellent and exhilarating driving hole. The green has two bunkers at right front and two off its left side; it's a frontal plateau that melds with existing landscape at rear.

The tenth hole, Fuaran, is a par three that plays to a heavily protected green. This putting surface has sharp slopes to the sides and rear, and at front has three large bunkers: its slope is to the front. The sea on the left will swallow hooked shots, and gorse to the right will swallow slices. Deep grass lies at the foot of the dropoff on the green's rear, and two bunkers additionally complicate the dropoff on its left.

The eleventh hole, A'Chlach, starts along

Royal Dornoch Golf Club

Hole	1	2	3	4	5	6	7	8	9	Out
White	336	179	414	418	361	165	465	437	499	3274
Yellow	293	164	396	395	316	145	425	377	442	2953
Par	4	3	4	4	4	3	4	4	5	35

Hole	10	11	12	13	14	15	16	17	18	In	Total
White	148	445	504	168	448	322	405	406	457	3303	6577
Yellow	138	435	463	145	438	294	395	385	442	3135	6088
Par	3	4	5	3	4	4	4	4	4	35	70

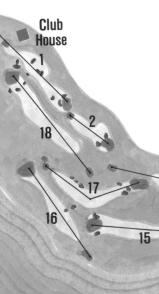

The fourteenth hole, appropriately named Foxy for its deceptively safe appearance, has a plateau green that is set on a ridge that narrows right to left. On the right of the fairway are several grassy ridges that jut into the playing area; off to the left of the fairway is a broad field of mounds with bentgrass and moss. A steep slope at the front of the green rises from five feet on the left to 10 feet on the right. This is the only hole on Dornoch Links that is bunkerless. With the ridges, mounds and wind, it is not as tame as it may at first appear.

Hole number fifteen, Stulaig, is another hole that begins near the beach and plays inland—a situation that will differ appreciably, wind-wise, from the previous hole. Along the left of the fairway lies thick bentgrass, and on the right are two rough incursions near the landing spot. At about 222 yards from the back tee lies an 18-foot-high grassy mound just to the left of center, on the fairway. The plateau green has appreciable slopes at front and rear, plus a bunker at left front, and a bunker halfway along its right side.

The sixteenth, High Hole, has a steep, uphill-sloping fairway that concretizes an old analogy comparing golf to climbing a mountain. Gorse to the right, and a large, grassy quarry on the left of the fairway toward the green end, will make this a challenge indeed. On the right of the green are several rough grass mounds. This hole plays along the beach, so the wind will be especially a factor here.

Hole number seventeen is the Valley Hole. A dogleg right, it has a diagonal, 40-foot-deep valley running across the fairway. Three bunkers on the left edge of the 'jumping off point' will endanger attempts at brinksmanship, as this hole plays opposite the immediately preceding holes: therefore, the wind will be coming right to left most often. Your second shot will be going for a plateau green that rises 15 feet above the fairway. Thick gorse lines both sides of the fairway, and several bunkers guard the approach to the green.

The eighteenth hole, Home, has rough grass on the right and gorse on the left. A gradual dogleg right, the fairway has two bunkers immediately preceding the inner bend, and three bunkers at left and two bunkers at right guard the green approach. A shallow, grassy gully, three feet deep and five feet wide, runs diagonally from front center to the right of the green.

You'll find this a course on which the play is at a high level of challenge and just plain fun. Not to be taken lightly, but to be savored, and enjoyed, as is any form of serious art. You'll never forget it.

the beach and heads back inland. A bunker at right, near the landing spot, will be dangerous when the wind is strong, as will the gorse all along the right. To the left of the green approach lies a lateral bunker, and to the left front of the green is another bunker, which lies at the foot of a slope: the green has a steep, 10-foot slope all along its left. On the right of the green is a shallow, grassy gully, and a bunker lies about halfway along this side.

The twelfth hole, Sutherland, is named for the man who gave so much to Royal Dornoch. A 504-yard par five, this is the longest hole on the course, and is a shallow dogleg to the left. A series of bunkers are to the right of the leading edge of the fairway, and heavy contouring occurs all along the right of the fairway's mid-section: the wind may make these very threatening to your

Above: **Gorse, as a decorative shrub, fronts the clubhouse, and** *(at top, above)* **covers hills to form a hazard at unforgettable Royal Dornoch.**

drive. The tee shot here is very important, as a grassy mound at left and a bunker at right create an extremely narrow approach. The green falls away to a grassy hollow, which lies behind and to the left of another grassy mound that guards the right of the putting surface.

Hole number thirteen, Bents, is the last par three on the course. Underpowered shots will surely find a bunker: one bunker lies approximately 20 yards out, and two pairs of bunkers guard the right and left fronts of the green. At right rear are two more bunkers, which will catch wind-blown or sliced shots. Between these and the bunkers at right front is a steep, 15-foot slope ending in a grassy hollow.

Royal Melbourne Golf Club

Black Rock, Victoria Australia

The Composite Course at the Royal Melbourne Golf Club has been rated sixth in the world on *Golf Magazine*'s '100 Greatest Courses in the World' listings for 1987 and 1989. This great course, composed of selected holes from the Royal Melbourne East and West courses, is part of the oldest continuously operating golf club in Australia.

In 1891, a small group of expatriate Scots agitated for the formation of a golf club near Melbourne, and soon had a prospective membership of 100 for their club. They named it the Melbourne Golf Club, and in 1895, Queen Victoria gave the club her royal stamp of approval, and the club became the Royal Melbourne Golf Club.

The first course was simply an open tract of land near the suburban Caufield Railway Station. Then, in 1901, urban growth forced the club to adopt another playing field, in suburban Sandringham. Then, the club decided to move to its present location amidst the rolling dunescape of Black Rock.

It was decided that a really good 18-hole course was required. This course, the West Course, was designed by the renowned Scottish architect Dr Alister Mackenzie. Mackenzie was invited to Melbourne in 1926 to commence the design, and, having gotten the basic idea going, left for America to design Cypress Point Golf Course and to collaborate with the legendary Bobby Jones in the design of Augusta National.

Mackenzie left Alex Russell, the 1924 Australian Open champion, in charge of the project. Meanwhile, in 1929, a general meeting of the club was held, and it was decided that a second course was needed. Since Alex Russell was already deeply involved, he was chosen as architect for this new course, to be known as the East Course.

The West Course was open for play in 1931, and the East Course opened in 1932. Both have extraordinarily good quality. The West Course has been the venue for many state, national and international championships, including the 1933 and 1939 Australian Open Championships. The course record for amateurs is 63, and for professionals is 67.

The East Course has as well hosted many championships of like variety, including the 1953 and 1963 Australian Open Championships, and the 1983 Australian PGA.

Six holes of the East Course and 12 of the West Course are used in what is internationally recognized as the Combination Course. This course was created for major championships after the traffic on the roads that divide the East and West courses into various segments became too heavy for safe crowd control.

The following is a description of the world-famous Composite Course. The first hole (West Course one) is a gentle dogleg left with intermittent greenery on the left and almost all the way along the right, save for the green approach. The green itself is practically round, of ample size (30 meters) and has a bunker just off its right front face.

Hole number two (West Course two) is a tree-lined dogleg right with a bunker set into the inside of its curve, just at the tee end of the fairway. The trees are treacherous, especially at the midpoint of the fairway, and the green has a longitudinal bunker on the front of either side. These bunkers stretch well into the green approach.

The third hole (East one) is a dogleg right, with trees lining the way from the left of the tees to the outer bend of the fairway. A huge bunker occupies the inner curve, and the green has bunkers at left front and right front, and an outer bunker on the right green approach. There are trees to the rear of the green as well.

Hole number four (East two) is a tree-lined dogleg right that tempts you to shave past the trees on the right to gain distance from the tees. The green approach has a single, massive, left-lying bunker and a string of right-lying bunkers that continue past the right side of the green to its right rear face. The green will challenge your putting capability.

The fifth hole (West five) is a par three

Royal Melbourne Golf Club has two courses—the East and the West. Heavy tournament traffic caused safety concerns, inspiring the great Composite Course, which uses holes from both. *At right:* Preparing for a round at Royal Melbourne.

that provides an avenue of trees from the tees. A slope fronts the green, and massive bunkers precede this slope at left and right. More bunkering protects the left and right, and right rear, of the green.

The sixth hole (West six) is a sharp dog-leg left with trees to the left and right of the tees. A treacherous cluster of bunkers is tucked into the inward curve, inviting a tee shot to overfly them. The fairway from this point is tree-lined, and the green approach is guarded by bunkers right and left. The green is preceded by a slope. Additionally, bunkers lie left and right of this putting surface, and trees lies beyond these.

Hole number seven (West seven) is a par three with a green that is broad but rather shallow, and may be hard to hold. Its entire right half is surrounded with bunkers.

The eighth hole (West ten) is a tree-lined

dogleg left, with a large bunker on its inner curve. The green has bunkers on its right and right rear, and a slope behind. The green is 26 yards deep, and is proportionately narrow.

Hole number nine (West eleven) is also a tree-lined dogleg left that plays in the opposite direction to the eighth. Both eight and nine are par fours, but nine is over 100 meters longer. In addition, the ninth has bunkering on the inside of its curve and on both sides of the green approach, and off the left and right front of the green. The trees on the right of the fairway can be quite perilous.

The tenth hole (West twelve) is another dogleg left, a par five that requires a tee shot over heavy bunkering on the left. The tree close in by these bunkers can cause a lot of trouble. Long hitters risk the longitudinal bunker that lies midway, on the right of the fairway. The green is 25 meters deep and quite narrow, with a bunker directly in front and a bunker on its right side. Trees are close by the right, left and rear surfaces.

Hole number eleven (West seventeen) is a long, tree-lined par four with bunkers on the right at the beginning of the fairway, and two bunkers on the left, closer to the likely landing spot. Trees cut into the fairway on the right, perhaps 90 meters from the green, pinching the green approach. A single, large, longitudinal bunker runs from the right green approach to the right rear of the green, and trees lie on the outside of this hazard.

A dogleg right, the twelfth hole (West eighteen) features a narrowing hallway of trees that forces tee shots to overfly a massive complex of bunkers on the fairway's right. A gum tree overhanging the right of the landing area further complicates this defense setup. The trees that line this fairway serve as a windbreak, so beware the large gap in this arboreal shielding on the right of the green approach. On the left of the green approach is a series of five bunkers that continue up to the left front of the green. On the right green approach is a large bunker. To the right and rear of the green lie more bunkers. It's a test that stays in the memory.

The thirteenth hole (West three) is a dogleg left, lined with trees. Tee shots must pass through a gunsight of trees to a fairway with trees close by the right, and two bunkers on the right. The green approach occupies the curve in the fairway, and the green has a slope in front, two bunkers on the left and a bunker on the right that is backed by a copse of trees.

Tee shots on tree-lined dogleg right hole fourteen (West four) must pass by trees close in on the right, and must carry over a cluster of bunkers at the beginning of the fairway, while avoiding an overflight into the trees on the fairway's left. At the midpoint, this fairway fades in from the right, leaving a gap of rough to be carried by your second shot. On the green approach, bunkers make incursions from the right, and a bunker stretches from the left green approach to the midpoint of the left green surface. On the right of the green, a single, longitudinal bunker protects the putting surface, and trees lie behind the green.

The fifteenth (East three) requires tee shots to pass through a 'gunsight' of trees to a broad, rolling fairway that is pinched in at either side by trees, near the landing area. The green has out-of-bounds behind, a bunker at left, another at left rear, another at right and a larger bunker that stretches from the right front putting surface to fifteen yards into the green approach.

Hole number sixteen (East four) is a par three with trees and out-of-bounds on the right of the tees. The green is situated at the end of a short section of fairway. Bunkers lie to the right and left of the green approach, to the left of the green and on the right front of the green.

The seventeenth (East seventeen) is a par five of 526 meters from the back tees. Tee shots must pass through a hallway of trees, and those from the back tees must negotiate overhanging trees to the right. The fairway is narrow, and curves to the right at the point that a grove of trees occurs on the left. Trees lie close by the

right of the fairway, and the green approach is narrowed by an overhanging tree at left. Bunkers march diagonally across the fairway, and the green has heavy bunkering near its right front face. Trees lie to the right rear, with the left of the green and green approach being open to the wind.

The eighteenth hole (East eighteen) is a dogleg left. Tee shots here must negotiate

overhanging trees to the right, and skim past the trees that skirt the left of the fairway. The green approach is a sea of bunkers, and the green, an ovoid 32 meters deep, has bunkering to its left and right, with a tree at left rear. A memorable finish for 18 holes of superb golfing at the Composite Course of the Royal Melbourne Golf Club.

The Royal Melbourne Golf Club East Course

Hole	1	2	3	4	5	6	7	8	9	Out	
Championship	304	402	350	192	309	160	475	427	357	2976	
Par	4	4	4	3	4	3	5	5	4	36	

Hole	10	11	12	13	14	15	16	17	18	In	Total
Championship	450	329	437	135	393	282	153	526	395	3100	6076
Par	5	4	4	3	4	4	3	5	4	36	72

The Royal Melbourne Golf Club West Course

Hole	1	2	3	4	5	6	7	8	9	Out	
Championship	392	439	324	430	161	391	135	346	370	2988	
Par	4	5	4	5	3	4	3	4	4	36	

Hole	10	11	12	13	14	15	16	17	18	In	Total
Championship	279	402	430	139	335	427	197	416	396	3021	6009
Par	4	4	5	3	4	5	3	4	4	36	72

Note: all distances are given in meters

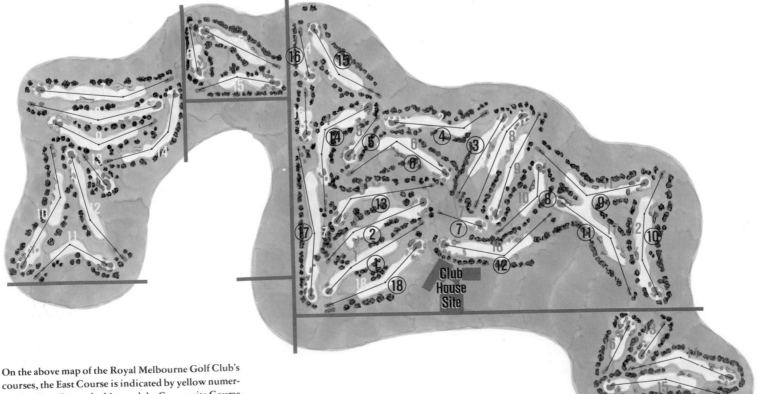

On the above map of the Royal Melbourne Golf Club's courses, the East Course is indicated by yellow numerals, the West Course by blue and the Composite Course is indicated by red numerals.

Royal Portrush Golf Club

County Antrim Northern Ireland

The Dunluce Links at Royal Portrush were rated 27th among *Golf Magazine*'s '100 Greatest Courses in the World' in 1989, ranked 33rd in the 1987 poll, and again by the current poll, is ranked 10th in the British Isles.

Portrush is located on Northern Ireland's north coast, between the town of Bushmills (of 'Old Bushmills' whiskey fame) and Lough Foyle. An outstanding local landmark is the Giant's Causeway, a nearby headland in the form of basalt pillars that have been eroded over the millennia, and resemble hundreds of square, columnar steps leading up to an off-center elevation.

The Royal Portrush Golf Club has played an important part in the development of the game of golf in Ireland since the club's inception in May, 1888. The town of Portrush, previous to its notoriety as the home of one of the world's finest golf courses, was a fishing village that was promoted in 1605, by Sir Thomas Phillips, as an outstanding site for a harbor.

By 1888, Portrush had one of the best harbors on the northern seaboard of Ireland, and had a major rail terminus as well — to serve as land transport to and

Below: **Great golfing challenge in a seaside setting are hallmarks of Royal Portrush.**

from the harbor. There was also a tramway, or streetcar line, running from the railway station to the Giant's Causeway — understandably a tourist attraction.

Excellent beaches, a first-class hotel, four churches, two banks, several pubs and Portrush's own Petty Session Court combined with a population of 1600 to make the town a fashionable Victorian seaside resort. Regular passenger boat service to and from Glasgow (bringing thousands of visitors from Scotland's Clyde region), and regular train service to and from Belfast (bringing thousands more from the environs of that city), combined with a grow-

ing local interest in the game of golf to inspire the development of a golf course.

The 40 acre patch of ground on which it would be built was known as 'the Large Triangle,' and lay near the railway station. It was owned by William Randal Earl of Antrim. The Belfast News Letter of 2 April 1888 announced the following about the new, nine-hole course:

'[O]ne of the finest golf courses in the three Kingdoms…. It abounds in hazards of the bunker type. The greens are clear and springy and completely free from brackens and from whins… .[T]here is now no necessity for our local players to cross the Channel… It is only astonishing that a ground so suitable for golf has not been utilized long ago.'

This early manifestation of the course had its official opening on 12 May 1888. There was as yet no clubhouse, and players used to keep their clubs in a covered barrel sunk in a pit during luncheon breaks.

By September 1888, the golf club at Portrush, properly called 'County Golf Club, Portrush,' had a membership of 70. By 1 January 1889, a new nine holes had been built near Salisbury Terrace: this new nine was still on the 'town side' of Bushmills Road.

In May 1889, a movement was on to construct a new 18-hole course, and it was thought that the best advisor for the job would be the by-then legendary Old Tom Morris, of fabled St Andrews, Scotland. (See the St Andrews section of this text.)

Old Tom came over in July of that same year to play Royal Belfast Club champion Alexander Day at Newcastle, County Down. Morris beat Day handily, and the two played a return match at Portrush, during which Day returned the favor and beat Morris.

While he was there, Old Tom made suggestions for the rearrangement of the extant nine, and approved terrain across Bushmills Road from the town for the construction of a new 18-hole links course.

On 5 October 1889, the first Portrush clubhouse was built, with corrugated zinc walls and a broad veranda. As of January 1890, the land for the new course on the seaward side of Bushmills Road had been bought from the Earl of Antrim.

By January of 1890, the new 18-hole course was open for play, and *The Saturday Review* proclaimed it to be 'the St Andrews of Ireland.' In April of that same year, Thomas Gilroy—the best golfer in Northern Ireland at the time—played the new course in 71 strokes (remarkably, while a

At left: **A view over the headlands of the Dunluce Links fifth, named 'White Rocks' for the natural formations that are visible from the green.**

gale-force wind was blowing), setting an amateur record for the course.

Gilroy had won the first monthly medal competition at the club in June 1888. The winners of the monthly medals faced one another in a yearly playoff for a silver cup. Gilroy won the silver cup that year, with a net score of 84 (playing off a +4 handicap).

On 13 August 1890, Alexander 'Sandy' Herd arrived from Scotland to become the first club professional. He played the 18-hole course in 67 strokes, during a six-day challenge match between him and Alexander Day. He stayed on at Portrush for two years, returning there to win the first Professional Tournament to be played in Ireland, in 1895.

By October, 1890, the club had a membership of 250, and had, with the combining of the two original nines, two 18-hole golf courses, the 'long course' being over 6500 yards, and the combined course (then known as the 'Ladies' Course') being 3738 yards. It was soon decided that, when the membership reached 300, the entrance fee was to be raised from one guinea to three guineas, to cover the cost of further land acquisition and the cost of a new clubhouse, for which the land was to be acquired.

On 27 June 1892, the new clubhouse was opened, and was acclaimed as 'the best in Ireland.' By year's end, membership had risen to 370, and the club's name changed from 'County Golf Club, Portrush,' to the 'Royal County Golf Club.' In 1895, the Royal County Golf Club became 'Royal Portrush Golf Club' when the Prince of Wales consented to become its patron. There had been some discussion about making the new name 'Royal St Patrick's Golf Club,' but 'Royal Portrush' won out by a vote of 21 to 13.

More changes were made in the 'Long Course' in 1896 and again in 1909, extending the course seaward, and bringing it up to a total of 6608 yards: the course has since been referred to as 'Old Dunluce Links.' Though a successful championship links—having hosted the Irish Amateur Open Championship in 1919, and the British Ladies' Championship in 1919—the 80 acres of untouched, undulating linksland that remained on the seaward side of Bushmills Road beckoned for a new course layout.

Sir Anthony Babington heard the call, and brought Harry Colt, the renowned course designer, to Portrush in 1923. Colt laid out a comprehensive design for two new courses. The biggest obstacle to instituting Colt's designs was proprietorship of the land. After some haggling and a gentleman's agreement, 99-year leases for two parcels of the land—of 38 and 42 acres respectively—were executed for the Club by the owners of the land, William Knox and Charles McVicker.

Upon Harry Colt's estimate of 7000-10,000 pounds sterling for the execution of the comprehensive design, the Club, uneasy at such massive expenditure, suggested that he merely shape the greens and fairways to a playable extent—and the club would arrange for the finish work. An agreement was struck. William A Murray, a Scottish international golfer and a member of Colt's golf course design staff, was the architect in charge of construction.

The championship Dunluce Course was first played in mid-spring of 1933, and its formal opening was in July of that year, with Sir Percy Greenaway, the Mayor of London, doing the honors. (He had come over to Londonderry to preside at the opening of Craigavon Bridge, as well.)

The Valley Course was next on the agenda, and was constructed piecemeal over the years; nine holes of the original Ladies' Course saw use as a nine-hole short course until well into the 1940s). Also over the years, continual additions and modifications were being made on the Dunluce Course: shelters were erected, 1000 yards of artificial burns (streams) were created, fairways were refined and new greens were laid in.

Several years before the outbreak of World War II, however, the Education Authority was eagerly seeking a site for a new schoolhouse, and offered the club a princely sum, 1700 pounds, for the necessary lands, which included that land upon which the clubhouse sat, and the first and eighteenth holes.

Of course, plans were laid for the building of a new clubhouse and course construction to compensate for the loss of the first and the eighteenth holes was planned. The war put a temporary halt to all such civilian projects, and it was not until 1946 that the problems could be dealt with again. By that time, construction costs had shot dramatically upward, and it was decided that rather than go bankrupt building a new clubhouse, the club would buy the Holyrood Hotel, with all its furnishings and equipment, for just over 18,000 pounds.

Once bought, 4000 pounds' worth of renovation sufficiently transformed the hotel to make it an excellent clubhouse, and it was dubbed 'Holyrood.'

At the suggestion of PG 'Stevie' Stevenson, the first and eighteenth holes were reconstructed across the road from the schoolhouse site. Harry Colt had approved this plan before the war. The first and eighteenth are now the eighth and ninth, respectively, as the play of the course was rearranged to coincide with the site of the new clubhouse, Holyrood.

In 1953, Rathmore Golf Club began using the Valley Course as its home course, and officialized this agreement with Royal Portrush (which continues to use the Valley Course as its 'Ladies' Course') by building its clubhouse close by that course. This arrangement continues to the present.

Below: **Putting on the green of White Rocks, the Dunluce fifth, with the rocks in view.** *Below left:* **Driving on Primrose Dell, the Dunluce Links fourth hole.**

Royal Portrush became the first Irish club to host the British Open Championship, in 1951—upon the request of The Royal and Ancient Golf Club of St Andrews. Max Faulkner defeated Fred Daly and Henry Cotton with a total score of 285 for four 18-hole rounds. During this same tournament, Jack Hargreaves set the professional record for the Dunluce Course with a round of 66 that stands to this day.

Improvements in amenities and facilities followed in the 1950s, including a piped water system to serve all the greens on the 36 holes of the Dunluce and Valley courses, in 1957, and in 1971, automatic irrigation was added to Dunluce Links.

The winter of 1982—83 produced high tides, heavy gales and concomitant coastal erosion in the Portrush area. Approximately 25 feet of earth was eroded away at

the fifth green and sixth tee, and in 1984, the shoring up of the Portrush coastal area was begun, using black basalt and white limestone facings to interrupt, and thereby reduce, wave action, and some of the beach dunescape has been recontoured and stabilized by intensive planting of marram grass.

The Harriman Cup Ulster Scratch Singles Championship was played over the Dunluce Links in 1937—39, with a hiatus for the war years, and 1946, with John M Neville of Cliftonville Club winning the last of these. The North of Ireland Amateur Open Championship is quite a tradition at Portrush, having been played on the Dunluce Links from 1947 to the present, with J Fitzsimmons of Bushfoot Club taking the first two, and other repeating champions being NV Drew, 1950 and 1952; M

Edwards, 1956-57; J Duncan 1959 and 1961; WH Rainey, 1960 and 1965; JFD Madeley, 1962—63; B Edwards, 1966 and 1973; MJC Hoey, 1968—69; BJS Kissock, 1974 and 1976; G McGimpsey 1978 and 1984; TCB Hoey, 1979 and 1983; and DC Long, 1981—82. This is as far as our records show: further information on this historic championship is available from the club.

The 1960 Amateur Championship was played at Portrush, with Joe Carr of Sutton Golf Club prevailing over Bob Cochran of the USA. More than 40 national championships have been played at Portrush, not to

Below: **Driving at Royal Portrush. The linksland contours constantly reveal new challenges.**

mention such international tournaments as the 1965 Home Internationals.

Dunluce is a 6772-yard par 72 course on which the sea winds are prominent factors in play. Each hole is named, as per long-standing linksland golf tradition, for salient features and renowned personages associated with that particular hole, or the course in general. Here the golfer, in addition to being faced with a superior challenge to his abilities, is also presented with some of the most beautiful—and at times startling—seaside vistas in the world. The following is a hole-by-hole description of the great Dunluce Links at Royal Portrush Golf Club.

The first hole, Hughies, is a 389-yard par

four with elevated tees. With the pro shop providing shelter from the wind, this hole will play with a little less than is common on this course. A bunker to the left of the landing spot will give hooked shots trouble, and a slope to the front and left of the green challenges shortfalls and hooks on the approach. Bunkers add to the defenses at left and left front.

Giant's Grave, the second hole, has two bunkers to the right of the landing spot, just where the wind may blow the tentatively hit ball. Your second shot must carry over a valley and a ridge that run laterally across the fairway, with a burn (stream) off to the right: wind could make

this a real danger. The fairway narrows after these obstacles, making for a landing spot on the approach that is rather tight, with a dangerous patch of gorse to the left, and just beyond this, three bunkers that inhabit much of the green approach. The narrow, oval green has plenteous gorse all along its left side.

The third hole, Islay, is named for the Scottish island of the same name, which is quite visible from the Dunluce Links on some days. At 150 yards, this is the shortest par three on the course. A bunker on the left and a mound on the right guard the front of the green: a slope winds around behind the green, from right rear to the mid-left side. The green surface may be rather hard to hold.

Hole number four, Primrose Dell, is cited as one of the most testing driving holes anywhere. You tee off over a burn to a landing spot that has a cannily-placed bunker on the fairway (left of center), and out-of-bounds and thick gorse bushes close by the right. Eighty-odd yards further, two more bunkers present a menacing presence near the center of the fairway. Out of bounds is still close by on the right, and gorse bushes also, again, lie close by on that perimeter. The green has a slope on its right approach, and mounds at right and left front: it's a narrow target, 30 yards deep, that slopes left to right rear.

The fifth hole, White Rocks, is named for the incredible view that is afforded of the eponymous rock formations that are situated on the far side of an inlet from the oceanfront green of this spectacular par four. A dogleg right, the landing spot is pinched by a mound on either side of the bend. Your second shot addresses a valley, and the mound that guards the green approach on the opposite side of said valley. The two-tiered green rises front to back, with a slope down to the right side, and a precipitous drop to the beach at rear.

Harry Colt's, the sixth hole, grants the golfer a grand view of the White Rocks, Dunluce Castle and, depending on the weather, the Scottish island of Islay. This par three has an elevated green with slopes at left front, left rear and right rear. On the right are a pair of mounds, and a dropoff that stretches along the edge of the green approach.

Hole number seven, Tavern, is a premium-quality par four. It's a dogleg left with a hollow and several mounds on the left of the landing spot: longer drives will be endangered by the bunker that lies a bit further beyond, just right of center on the fairway. At first, it seems it's best to go a bit long at this green: the wind comes from left front. Twin bunkers guard the green approach, and a gorse bush off to the left lies hungrily in wait. However, the green falls away at front and on the right side.

The eighth hole, Himalayas, is a dogleg right with one large mound on its inner bend and two mounds just preceding its outer bend. The green approach passes down a narrow valley to a sunken green. You'll feel you're standing at the foot those eponymous mountains when you exercise your putting on this one.

Hole number nine, Warren, is a gentle dogleg right, with three mounds on its outer bend and one on its inner bend. From here, the fairway passes down a valley, and the green approach is a transverse gully. The narrow, oval green drops off quickly to the front, and is otherwise surrounded by slopes.

On the tenth hole, Dhu Varren, the tees are backed by gorse. Near the landing spot, a lateral bunker threatens from the right. Gorse bushes lie to the right and left, and a mound lies to the left, just before a bunker that may catch wind-blown, weak approach shots. The green is protected at rear with gorse, and slopes down to the right.

Feather Bed, the eleventh hole, is wryly named, as the 'feathers' are a semicircle of bunkers surrounding all but the rear portion of the narrow, ovoid green. Out-of-bounds is close in on the left, and a watercourse lies to the right. The wind comes from the right rear on this hole.

Hole number twelve, Causeway, has bunkering on the right of likely landing spots. The green approach is guarded at right with a mound, and the green drops off on all sides, with a steep gully and a mound at right, and a bunker at left.

The thirteenth hole, Skerries, is a par four with three threatening bunkers early on the right of the fairway. A watercourse runs in front of the foremost tee. The green approach here is a diagonal rift, and a bunker guards the front of the moderately long, narrow green. This green falls off sharply to the right and rear, and has a bunker on its left side, and gorse to the left rear.

Hole number fourteen, Calamity, is a par three hole renowned for 'Bobby Locke's Hollow,' a spot on the left of the green where the great Bobby Locke always seemed to place his ball for an easy par during play in the 1951 Open. This hollow, of course, lies opposite the 'mine' on the right—a chasmic valley that cuts over in front of the tees and describes a rough arc around to the right side of the green. To the left of the green are two mounds.

Purgatory, the fifteenth hole, is where your sins of play are likely to be purged—or punished. The fairway falls off sharply to the left, and then, midway along its length, drops off to the front to a lowland that contains the green. Gorse to the right and left combine with the wind for a test of strength and finesse: the green is extremely narrow, and is pinched at the waist by a bunker on either side.

The sixteenth hole, Babington's, has an irregularly-shaped fairway. You'll probably want to lay up behind the two bunkers at right, and then try for a carry over the slopes and bunkers that lie ahead 100 yards, for a layup at the green approach—or you could go for the pin. Another slope and a bunker at right on the green approach, and a burn (stream) to the left, protect the moderately long, narrow green. Out-of-bounds lies close in on the left.

Glenarm, hole number seventeen is, at 517 yards from the back tees, the longest hole of the Dunluce Links. The leading end of this narrow fairway has a steep slope to the left, which will confine most tee shots to a layup just short of the bunker and mound to the right. The fairway jogs to the left at these, and narrows still more, with a depression at right and a ridge to the left. The green approach has one bunker on its right, and two on the left. Forty yards deep and approximately half as wide, the green has one bunker at left front, two along its right side, and a patch of gorse at rear. A thrilling penultimate hole.

With wind from left to right, it's essential to know that out-of-bounds is close in on the right of Greenaway, the eighteenth hole—named for Sir Percy Greenaway, the Mayor of London who dedicated the Dunluce Links in 1933. It's a moderate-length, 481-yard par five that plays with a prevailing wind blowing from left to right. Two bunkers at right and one at left form a deadly triangle near the landing spot; two more nearly span the fairway and will probably figure in a carry on your second shot. The green approach has two bunkers off to the left. The green is deep but narrow, with two bunkers at right front, one longitudinal bunker at left rear and a ridge along its back.

After this satisfying conclusion for one of the finest tests of golf in the United Kingdom, we would do well to consider the Royal Portrush Valley Course. This course is laid out in relatively sheltered countryside, yet while playing the Valley Course, one is close enough to the ocean to taste the salt air. There are a mere eighteen bunkers on the entire 18 Valley Course holes. One of the two qualifying rounds of the North of Ireland Open Amateur Championship is played on the Valley Course annually. A hole-by-hole description of this fine course follows. The first hole, The Narrows, is a straightaway hole that features a drive off the tees over a ridge that

Royal Portrush Golf Club Dunluce Links

Hole	1	2	3	4	5	6	7	8	9	Out	
Championship	389	497	159	455	384	193	432	376	476	3361	
Medal	381	493	150	454	386	191	420	365	476	3316	
Par	4	5	3	4	4	3	4	4	5	36	

Hole	10	11	12	13	14	15	16	17	18	In	Total
Championship	480	166	395	371	213	366	432	517	481	3421	6782
Medal	477	166	389	366	205	361	415	508	477	3364	6680
Par	5	3	4	4	3	4	4	5	5	37	73

At top, above: **Royal Portrush under a cloudy sky.** *Opposite:* **On Dunluce thirteenth, Skerries—meaning rocky islands or reefs.** *Above opposite:* **Teeing off on the fifth, White Rocks.**

precedes a small valley with sand hills and gorse on either side. The green is set into a cul-de-sac of sand hills.

Green Lane, the second hole, is a dogleg left with elevated tees. A sand hill lies to the left of the fairway, and the green is situated between bunkers right and left and a sand hill on the right. Mis-hit balls will cost heavily here.

The third hole, Fairy Ring, is a par three with elevated tees. The green has a bunker on its left side, a slope on its right rear and right side, and a 'fairy ring' of sand hills from its left rear around to its right front.

War Hollow, hole number four, is—at 534 yards from the back tees—the longest hole on the course. All along the right side are sand hills. Shots from the elevated tees pass over a ridge into a long valley. The

green is situated near a high hill that serves as the platform for the Dunluce Course's 'Calamity Corner.' Be forewarned, War Hollow is aptly named.

The fifth hole, Desert, has elevated tees that face a valley fairway with twinned sand hills on its left. An accurate second shot will attain the elevated green—providing that the two deep lateral bunkers in the middle and on the left of the fairway have been avoided. A sand hill at right rear of the green completes this scenario.

Hole number six, Curran Point, is the longest Valley Course par three, at 237 yards from the back tee. The green has a slope in front, a deep bunker at left front, and sand hills at right front and right rear.

Golfers at the seventh hole, Prospect, tee off from atop a ridge to a low hollow. From here, it's a bold shot to the green, which has a sand hill on its left front face, and a hillside acting as a backstop behind it.

Patrick's, the eighth hole, has a 'gunsight' composed of sand hills that force tee shots down the middle. Those going awry will cost you at least a recovery shot. The green approach is a long, narrow valley, and the green has a slope at left and a sand hill behind.

Royal Portrush Golf Club Valley Links

Hole	1	2	3	4	5	6	7	8	9	Out
Championship	349	385	141	534	336	237	453	409	320	3164
Medal	339	374	135	520	324	231	441	399	311	3074
Par	4	4	3	5	4	3	4	4	4	35

Hole	10	11	12	13	14	15	16	17	18	In	Total
Championship	496	140	465	486	421	165	360	384	192	3109	6273
Medal	472	130	452	458	412	155	349	382	170	2980	6054
Par	4/5	3	4	4/5	4	3	4	4	3	33/35	68/70

carried over to the green. The green has a pot bunker on its left front, and falls away to a grassy hollow on the right.

The thirteenth hole, Valley, requires two long shots to reach the green. The first of these must carry over a right-lying pot bunker. A sand hill lies to the right of the fairway at about the midpoint of same. The green is prefaced by a slope and a left-lying sand hill, and has two sand hills at left rear, and a slope at right rear.

St Andrew, the fourteenth hole, requires a drive through a narrow valley to a wide, flat landing spot. Two sand hills require a shift to the right for the second shot, but beware the right-lying bunker. The green has a pot bunker on its right face, and a rough-covered slope at rear.

Hole number fifteen, a par three named Recess, features a long tee shot to a narrow green that is guarded with bunkers on the right, and a sand hill on the left.

The sixteenth, Bunker's Hill, doglegs gently to the left. A bunker and a low ridge guard the left of the fairway, and a series of rough-covered sand hills guard the right of the fairway. Therefore, the tee shot requires more than a modicum of accuracy. The green is protected by bunkers at left front and at right front.

The Valley Course's eponymous hole, Valley, the seventeenth, plays down a narrow valley between sand hills to a plateau green that is guarded by a slope at front and a bunker at right front. At the rear of this green is a very dangerous lateral hollow.

The eighteenth hole, Stevie's, requires a shot from elevated tees to a plateau green with a deep hollow in front of it. Bunkers lie to the left and right of this green, and rough lies to the left. Accuracy is paramount here. A splendid finish for the Valley Course at Royal Portrush Golf Club.

Hole number nine, Cradle, is a slight dogleg left that, as its name suggests, is cradled between a series of sand hills lying left and right before, at and beyond the green approach. The green is hidden from less-than-perfect placements for the second shot. Additionally, the approach is very narrow, so it's quite clear that the drive from the tee is crucial.

The tenth hole, Switchback, is a straightaway hole whose fairway has three valleys to be negotiated en route to a green that has slopes at right and at rear. Two sand hills, some gorse and a tree are located on the left of the fairway.

Mann's, the eleventh hole, is a par three with elevated tees. The green has two bunkers out in front, and sand hills at left and behind.

Hole number twelve, Middle Green, features a gunsight of sand hills at the beginning of the fairway. A bit further down, a triplet of sand hills lies to the right, and the fairway falls into a valley, which must be

St Andrews Links (Old Course)

St Andrews Scotland

It is almost an understatement to say that the Old Course at St Andrews ranked seventh in *Golf Magazine*'s '100 Greatest Courses in the World' listing for 1989, as it was for 1987, and is, by the 1989 poll, ranked second only to Muirfield in the British Isles. After all, the Old Course at St Andrews is the undisputable 'home of golf,' and is known to have been in play at least as early as 1552. The Old Course is, therefore, of undeniable antiquity, and remains the prime example of a truly natural linksland golf course. You see, it was never 'designed' in the way that word is used today. Its design was accomplished not by purpose of man, but by millennia of geologic processes working ceaselessly.

The prime integer of the playing surface and underpinnings of the St Andrews linksland are Ice Age sand dunes—long since stabilized by salt-tolerant marram grass, and seeded with finer, short grasses by grazing sheep herds. The rolling dunescape, in combination with the short grass which let a lying ball be struck easily, and find a firm place to 'lie' when it came to rest, offered itself naturally as a venue for the game of golf.

The game itself seems—even early on—to have had a peculiarly obsessive appeal. In 1457, King James II of Scotland observed that his archers were spending all their time knocking a feather-filled ball around the linksland, when they should have been preparing for the upcoming British invasion. Infuriated, the monarch outlawed the game, saying 'That fute-ball and Golfe be utterly… nocht usit.'

The ban did not last in Scotland, however, as the year 1502 saw King James IV sending a special order to his bow maker in Perth: the order was for a set of golf clubs and balls. Indeed, while rival claims as to the origins of the game exist, Scotland is the place where the game was developed from its primal state to the sophisticated sport that it is today.

The golf organizations were formalized in Scotland. As we mention in the Muirfield section of this book, a group of golfers who had been playing on the primordial links at Leith were formally recognized by the Edinburgh Town Council as the world's

first golf club, 'The Gentlemen Golfers of Leith.' This club was to later be known as The Honourable Company of Edinburgh Golfers. Ten years later, the golfers who called the Links at St Andrews home were formally recognized as the Society of St Andrews, and when, some time later, King William IV became patron of the Society of St Andrews, he conferred upon them the title of 'The Royal and Ancient Golf Club of

St Andrews,' and in 1834, he declared them the chief arbitrating body for golf.

To this day, the Royal and Ancient Golf Club of St Andrews shares its role—as arbitrator for golf worldwide—only with the US Golf Association.

Thus it was that the Royal and Ancient Golf Club established the championship game that was to evolve almost immediately into the first Open Championship.

Back in 1764, after a round of 121 strokes played by William St Clair, it was decided to reduce the number of holes at St Andrews from 22 to 18. Due to St Andrews' later prominence as a legislative body, this number of holes was to become the world standard.

The idea of a championship to be played over the length of 18 holes was conceived and brought to fruition at St Andrews in 1858. Allen Robertson, already considered the finest golfer, won the match, but died in 1859. This forced the notion of a new match to establish a new champion.

Since another match had to be held, Major JO Fairlie of Prestwyck Golf Club took up the matter, and introduced the basic format of the Open Championship as it is known even today. There were some ruffled feathers, however. Major Fairlie invited only professionals for the 1860 Open, and there was a huge outcry from the many fine amateurs throughout the land: if the contest was to determine Scotland's finest golfer, they felt that the field should truly be open. So it was that, the next year, Major Fairlie was compelled to announce that the contest was to be 'open to all the world!'

However, the first 'professionals only' 'Open' was played over the 12 holes of the Prestwyck Club, with 36 holes of golf (three rounds at Prestwyck) determining the victor. The means by which the champion was decided was another milestone.

Previous to this Open, competitive golf was a matter of match play, with betting and so forth on the results of each hole. In the Prestwyck Open, however, the means of scoring was by the overall number of strokes. Thus, this first Open also introduced stroke play as the scoring mode of all following Opens.

The winner of that first Open was Willie Park of the Honourable Society of Edinburgh Golfers, who won by two strokes over Old Tom Morris of St Andrews. The Championship was held for the next 12 years at Prestwyck, until, in 1873, an agreement was struck between the Royal and Ancient Golf Club of St Andrews, The Honourable Company of Edinburgh Golfers and Prestwyck Golf Club to play the Open on a year-to-year, round robin basis at those three organizations' respective golf facilities.

The progenitor of an early Open dynasty, Old Tom Morris went on to win the Open in 1861, 1862, 1864 and 1867. The trophy was a silver-trimmed red leather Championship Belt that was traded back and forth

The renowned Home of Golf, St Andrews Links. *At left:* Teeing off on The Old Course first hole, Burn, so named for troublesome Swilcan Burn.

among champions until someone won it three consecutive times. Willie Park won in 1860, 1863 and 1866, and Andrew Strath won in 1865.

Old Tom Morris' son, 'Young Tom' Morris, then won the Open in 1868, 1869 and 1870, taking the red leather Championship Belt for his very own with his consecutive wins. Unfortunately, Young Tom, who had made the first hole-in-one in Open history in 1868, died of a broken heart in 1875, following the death of his wife.

As for the Open, after Young Tom had claimed the belt, a substitute trophy had to be arranged. It was deemed that the new trophy would be a silver claret jug, and the trophy itself would never be the property of any winner. The trophy remains the same even today, and the winner receives a replica of it.

The Open was played at St Andrews for the first time in 1873, and two rounds of the course's 18 holes was the prescribed distance. Tom Kidd won that year. The 1876 Open at St Andrews saw competitor David Strath storming away from the course over a ruling on one of his shots, leaving his would-be playoff competitor Bob Martin.

And so the years rolled on, with the Royal and Ancient Golf Club of St Andrews making slight alterations in the rules of the Open to make it an even more competitive championship. For instance, the Open was extended to 72 holes in 1892. In 1920, the Royal and Ancient Golf Club took over the Amateur Championship, which had been held first in 1885 at Royal Liverpool.

As of 1977, the Royal and Ancient Golf Club had expanded the rotation for the Open to Muirfield, Royal Troon, Turnberry

and St Andrews; and had included the English courses Royal Birkdale, Royal Lytham and St Anne's, and Royal St George's. Everyone who has ever been anyone in golf in this century has either played, or wanted to play, on the Old Course at St Andrew's.

Modern course design depends in great part upon the architect's perfect use of earth moving equipment. By contrast, St Andrews Old Course was formed by 'the winds of God' that shaped the dunes into intricate and complex forms that were and remain indifferent to the whims of mankind. Therefore, play on the course takes on the similitude of man's struggle with powers mightier than he, and is an education in itself as to how one might best struggle through the vicissitudes of life.

It is a commonly held opinion that the more you know St Andrews, the more you

come to respect the course. For one, this course, as the only remaining course of what were at least several that had their roots in medieval times, is the very archetype of all courses in the world today.

The Old Course at St Andrews has survived by struggle and good fortune. First of all, the course lies on the commons of the town of St Andrews, which commons were ceded as part of that village back in 1140: this gave some protection to the grounds themselves. Then, the game of golf survived King James II's anti-golfing edict, but a 100-year legal battle was fought against rabbit ranchers who wanted the linksland for their bunnies to nibble to the quick.

Municipal bankruptcy then threatened

Below left: **An aerial photo showing the nearness of St Andrews to the sea.** *Below:* **A view right of the fairway on the fourteenth.**

the town (and by extension, the golf course). At another point in time, the sea threatened to overwhelm the fairway of the 'Burn' hole, number one, and old fishing boat hulks were loaded with ballast and sunk in place to act as a dike.

Finally, legislation passed in 1974 put the land under the direct responsibility of the St Andrews Links Trust for all the foreseeable future. This, then, is a course that has come down to us from another age, and is the only one of its distant contemporaries to which we have access. It is a primordial linksland course, the likes of which is not to be found elsewhere. While there are linksland courses aplenty today, they have been shaped in a few years, by the hand of man. This course, on the other hand, cannot be adequately described, for it was shaped by other means.

Nor should one be discouraged if, when playing the Old Course at St Andrews, one is confronted with a half-obscured flag pin, or a blind drive toward that which one cannot hope to know until he's actually crested the hill and seen the other side. Remember that the course and the game itself came about in an age when men knew beyond a doubt that they were 'at the mercy' of God, and therefore, it demands a good deal of faith and willingness to take one's lumps, if only to come out of the experience better than before—and it is an unforgettable experience.

Consider, also, that the players who called St Andrews their golfing ground would have played the course thousands of times in a lifetime, and therefore, they would have been quite familiar with the course, and its various veilings and obscu-

rities would serve to enhance what was to them the challenge of a lifetime.

With six massive double greens, various plateaus, mounds and elevations, and the classic 'eternal return' hole pattern that culminates in holes one and eighteen playing side-by-side, tee to green, the Old Course at St Andrews is the original design that countless golf courses throughout the world have emulated.

Yet, as you will see, there is every evidence that not many of these courses have even approached the quality and challenge of the original. The following is a brief description of the Old Course at St Andrews: the holes are generally named for those salient features that serve to fix them permanently in the minds of those golfers who have played them.

The first, also known as the Burn Hole (a 'burn' is a Scottish brook), is named for Swilcan Burn, and is 370 yards from the men's tees. It's a straightaway drive to the left of the fairway, away from the out-of-bounds to the right. Swilkin Burn winds directly across the front of the green, and has been the demise of many a long drive. The green slopes from left rear to the front, with rough all along its back.

Hole number two, the Dyke Hole, is blind from the back tees. Gorse bushes lie along the right, and from 190 to 210 yards, a series of pot bunkers guard the right side of the fairway. You can, however, see Cheape's bunker over to the left, just in front of a small mound that is parallel to the Black Sheds that figure prominently in the seventeenth, the Road Hole. You will probably

want to circumvent the gorse and the bunkers by driving just to the right of Cheape's, and then going for the green. A pronounced longitudinal ridge, and several other changes in elevation, make the green surface and the approach complex. Not a hole for the timid, winds are always changing, and you could easily find the gorse no matter what shot you attempt. On the right of the approach is a quadrangle of pot bunkers. The green is likewise protected at front and rear with bunkers, and the rough is close in behind.

At the third hole, the Cartgate Hole (Outward), tee shots must pass between gorse bushes on a line with the right of the fairway. A series of shallow bunkers along the right of the fairway will pose a problem if your accuracy is not up to par, and a plateau

of sorts preceding the fairway will be a slippery place to try to lay up. Just on the left of this plateau, where it winds around to the left front of the green, is the crescent grin of the Cartgate Bunker. Depressions criss-cross this hole where an old cart path was continually changed as the carts' wheels broke through the sod and the carts bogged down in the deepening grooves. The green slopes gently away to the right rear from the rise behind the Cartgate Bunker. However, near the right rear perimeter of the green is a sudden dropoff.

The Ginger Beer Hole, St Andrews' fourth, was once known as 'The Hole of Cunnin Links,' 'cunnin' being the old Scots for rabbit, as this hole was once let out for a rabbit warren. As we have previously said, a century-long lawsuit put a stop to that

practice. The pin is partially visible from the back tee here, and a mound lies just to the left of the apparent line of flight. Any shot to the left of that mound will encounter several small bunkers and the 'Cottage,' a massive bunker that immediately presages a goodly carry over a patch of bunker-dotted rough. More adept golfers may want to go straight for the green, a narrow passage down a valley of bushes, slopes, mounds and bunkers. Any shot to the green, however, will have difficulty holding the putting surface, which slopes from left to right. In addition, bunkers rest in the green's 'wasp waist' and to the right. A mound lies at right front.

The fifth hole, or Hole O'Cross (Outward), is loaded with severe bunkering, including the very dangerous Spectacle

just in front of the green, and while it is not visually impressive, it is a serious threat. The green is ample, with a slope from the right, and rough and gorse bushes lie directly behind.

The High Hole (Outward), St Andrews' seventh, is a dogleg right. You tee off over gorse and rough, and hopefully find a favorable landing spot in the series of elevation changes that lie on the 'elbow.' Grass here is not guaranteed as to manicure, but assurances are that it is 'usually kept at a friendly length.' The large and highly dangerous Shell Bunker (accompanied by two small bunkers off to the right) lies like a gaping maw on the green approach, and the green has several gentle 'draws' or depressions. Hillside rough rises behind the green. The beach is along the rear of the green.

St Andrews bunkers *(above)* **include such legendary traps as the Beardies, Hell and the Principal's Nose.** *At left:* **Teeing off on the fourteenth.**

Bunkers. From the tee, the left-hand Spectacle Bunker is visible, and you may be able to see the flag just to the right of it. The Spectacles are of the utmost difficulty, so avoid them at all cost (playing left or laying up short of them are the suggested means of doing so). A gentle valley lies between the Spectacles and the green. Rough guards either side of the green approach. Likewise, gentle depressions in the green make putting a challenge, but the crucial factor here is that the green is 80 yards deep. Therefore, your strategy will rely emphatically on pin position.

At the sixth, or Heathery Hole (Outward), golfers once again face a patch of rough and gorse off the tee. A loose grouping of seven bunkers on the right side of the fairway beyond the rough further add to this hole's demand on strength and accuracy. A shallow, transverse depression lies

The eighth hole, appropriately named the 'Short Hole,' is the shortest on the course, at 166 yards from the back tees. One of only two par threes on the course, it presents you with a long carry over rough (and a few gorse bushes) to the green. Guarding the front of the green are two bunkers, one of which is pronouncedly to the right, and the other of which is almost dead on with your probable line of attack. This latter is the infamous Short Hole Bunker, and is of the utmost danger. However, this is a deep, flat green, and may well be a pleasure to play. This hole has remained unchanged from time immemorial.

The ninth, or End Hole, is the end of your outbound nine. This fairway was once covered with heather, but was reworked with grass in the nineteenth century. Heather rough lies to the left, and supreme accuracy is required of any golfer wishing to accomplish this in the allotted four strokes. You tee off over rough and gorse, with

St Andrews Links—Old Course

Hole	1	2	3	4	5	6	7	8	9	Out
Mens	370	411	352	419	514	374	359	166	307	3272
Ladies	339	375	321	401	454	325	335	145	261	2956
Par	4	4/5	4	4/5	5	4	4	3	4	36/38

Hole	10	11	12	13	14	15	16	17	18	In	Total
Mens	318	172	316	398	523	401	351	461	354	3294	6566
Ladies	296	150	304	377	487	369	325	426	342	3076	6032
Par	4	3	4	4/5	5	4	4	4/5	4	36/38	72/76

bunkers lying near the likely landing spot for a high lob over the bushes. Then you must avoid Boase Bunker, and End Hole Bunker—both likely to shave distance from any escape shot—en route to a large, flat green. Remember that the heather on the left gives new meaning to the word 'rough.'

We turn right around at this point, and proceed to play inward on the tenth hole. In 1972, the great American golfer Bobby Jones was made a freeman of St Andrews, and at the request of the St Andrews Council, this hole was named 'Bobby Jones.' You tee off over obscuring gorse and rough. Just beyond this lies three bunkers that will likely capture short landing shots. The fairway widens to the left after this, and the green is guarded by a steep bank at its front; however, the green is 40 yards deep and concomitantly wide. After the trials comes the reward.

The eleventh, or High Hole (Inward), is the second and final par three on the course. This famous short hole features a carry that passes not far off the tip of Shell Bunker that we met at hole seven (High Hole Outward), and hopefully carries over Strath Bunker, a hazard of deadly intensity should it swallow your ball. The wind is pronouncedly a factor here, and club selection is very important: too far, and you're in the 'savage rough' that rises on the steep bank behind the green like a petrified tidal wave. The green rises from front to back and has a number of surface complexities. (Long ago, the Eden River flowed along the back of the green.) Off to the left front is infamous Strath Bunker. You will not have an easy putt here.

Hole number twelve is Heathery Hole (Inward). Stretching down the surface of the fairway—from the swale just off the tees to the green approach—are six

bunkers of a middling difficulty. Only one of these bunkers is openly visible to the approaching shotmaker. A heroic, 215-yard shot would carry them all, but, barring such a valorous attack, the rough of the left is said to be merciful. Go left or right if you please, depending on pin position. The sea is off to your right here, and its primal call may well distract you. A dangerous bunker guards the front of the green from the midst of the green approach, and a lateral ridge rising from the left and running across to the right of the green makes putting quite complex, depending on your shot placement and pin position.

Hole O'Cross (Inward), the thirteenth, is the home of that ominously-named group of bunkers, 'The Coffins.' You tee off over the edge of a right-lying rough that is festooned with huge clumps of gorse. The way to the extremely deep green lies down a valley formed by said rough on the right, and Nick's Bunker and The Coffins on the left. At about the 250-yard mark, heavy incursions of bunker-bedecked rough pinch the approach from either side, and a steep slope prefaces the green. The green, though very deep, is contoured on the right, where also lie two severe bunkers and a grassy hollow.

The fourteenth is aptly named the Long Hole, for, at 523 yards from the back tee, it is the longest on the course. Again, you tee off over gorse-dotted rough, hoping to avoid the dangerous Beardies Bunkers that lie just beyond—and are hidden from view by—said rough. The second shot requires extreme valor, for a long drive to the green will have to carry over severe Benty Bunker and the all-too-aptly-named Hell Bunker to a green that slopes very sharply away from a steep frontal elevation. An alternative is to play to the left of Hell Bunker—actually onto the fifth fairway,

At right: On the eighteenth, Tom Morris. Note the bridge over Swilcan Burn. *At left:* Putting on a typically large green at St Andrews.

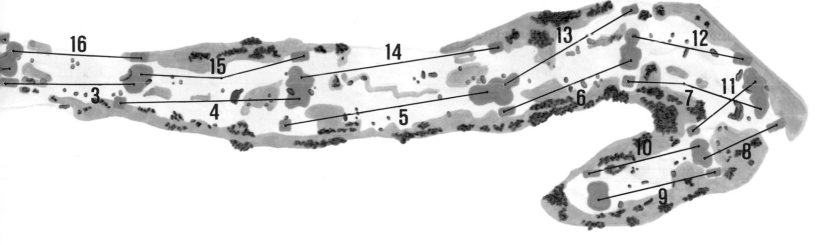

and to approach the green over the Grave Bunkers. No matter what approach you take, the green is very, very hard to hold.

The fifteenth, the Cartgate Hole (Inward), plays down a narrow fairway bounded on the right by gorse-dotted rough, and on the left by Cottage Bunker and Sutherland Bunker. Humps exist on either side a bit farther on, and serve to obscure the three dangerous bunkers that lie at the 300—320 yard mark. The green has a dangerous bunker at left front, but should be rewarding to a practiced putter.

the railroad was dismantled some time ago. The landing spot widens a bit to the right, and a second shot must negotiate the narrowing passage between rough on the left and right, and the Progressing Scholar's Bunkers to the left: accuracy in making this second shot is emphasized by the presence, toward the green, of the vicious Road Hole Bunker on the left of the green, and the road on the right. The front of the green is elevated, and a fine touch is needed in this shot to an unnerving green. The wall which is first encountered at the tees has

The Cartgate Bunker lies to the rear of this green. A bit of local history has it that Sutherland Bunker was filled in by the St Andrews Committee, but there was such an outcry that on the morning of the Biblical third day, the golfers found the 'grave opened.' Sutherland has not been tinkered with since.

The sixteenth is known as the Corner of the Dyke Hole. It is the home of the famed Principal's Nose Bunkers and Deacon Sime Bunker. You tee off with the out-of-bounds very close to the right. The Principal's Nose and Deacon Sime lie left from 200—225 yards. The prevailing wisdom is that a drive to the left of Deacon Sime will set you up for a less perilous approach that will, however, involve Grant's Bunker and Whig Bunker, both of which are quite dangerous. The green requires strength on the approach, as a high bank lies to its front.

The seventeenth is the famous and feared Road Hole. You tee off over the Black Sheds—actual reconstructions of black railroad sheds that were destroyed when

Above: **Looking toward the clubhouse, with the first hole on the left and the eighteenth hole on the right.** *At right:* **Teeing off on the Burn hole.**

been in place since at least the first half of the nineteenth century.

The eighteenth is the Tom Morris Hole, named in honor of an exceedingly great golfing name (see our previous text about Old Tom and Young Tom Morris). From the tee, the Royal and Ancient Golf Club clock steeple looms directly behind the (at this point of your round unseeable) green. Thus, it is a time-honored 'pointer' that many a golfer has aimed at when making that first shot over Swilcan Burn. The road lying at the fairway's midpoint is not considered a hazard. The green approach is made complex by a rise and a dropoff to the right. The Valley of Sin protects the front of the green, which slopes from right rear to left front: better to go long here than fall into the depths of the Valley of Sin. It's an extraordinary finish to an unforgettable round of golf at the great and venerable Old Course at St Andrews.

SentryWorld Golf Course

Stevens Point, Wisconsin USA

Robert Trent Jones Jr incorporated over 300,000 geraniums and marigolds in this stunning masterpiece. He is quoted as describing it in SentryWorld's press kit as 'very possibly my Mona Lisa.'

Sentry Insurance is the corporation that developed SentryWorld. Its former chairman John Joanis, a 14-handicapper who played globally, conceived the idea of building a truly magnificent golf course for public use.

In 1984, SentryWorld was chosen as the best new public course in the United States by *Golf Digest*, which also rated the course as the best in Wisconsin and as one of the best 25 public courses in America. In addition, *USA Today* asked the American Society of Golf Course Architects to compile a

Above: The 'flower hole' sixteenth at Sentry-World Golf Course. *Below:* One of the flower gardens that adorn this fine course.

survey of the best designed courses in the United States in 1984, and SentryWorld was chosen as among the top three (designed after 1962) of the top 130 courses in the United States. The criteria used in this polling were natural beauty; design aesthetics; drama and subtlety; fairness; and playability.

In 1985, Arnold Palmer, Jan Stephenson, Betsy King, Miller Barber, Bob Toski and Dave Marr were the featured players at the $50,000 Sentry Challenge Cup, hosted by SentryWorld. In 1986, this fabulous course was host to the USGA Ladies' Public Links Championship.

Mr Jones carefully cut this jewel of a course out of the native Wisconsin countryside. Always taking care to meld his

courses into the existing environment, Mr Jones decided to do something a little different for the course's famed par three sixteenth hole: a concentration of 90,000 flowers literally creates an explosion of color on an already colorful course.

The greens, tees and fairways were seeded with Penneagle Creeping Bentgrass—a hybrid which was developed by Doctor Joseph M Buich, professor of Turfgrass Science at Pennsylvania State University.

Roughs in sunshine areas were seeded with a mix of Adelphi Kentucky bluegrass, Barron Kentucky bluegrass, Negget Kentucky bluegrass and Pennlawn creeping red fescue. Roughs in shaded areas are seeded with Barron Kentucky bluegrass, Pennlawn creeping red fescue and Dawson creeping red fescue.

The following is a hole-by-hole description of this great public course. At hole one, players tee off to the fairway which lies, and continues curving, to their left—errant shots will find the bunkers to the right and to the left, which provide for a well-protected green. Hole number two is a slight curve to the right. Again, a bunker catches the unwary—on the left perimeter of the

fairway, just past the bend—and the approach to the green is pinched by two bunkers, with an additional bunker just to the right.

Tee shots on the third travel for a good distance over a stream which extends out from one of the course's ponds. Strong hitters chance landing in a bunker that lies directly in the well-placed ball's path, on the opposing side of the fairway. Then it's a fairly straight—but pinched on the approach—shot to a well-protected green; overshoot the green, and you're in the water—in the form of a narrow neck which

Above and below are further views of the sixteenth hole, ablaze with flowers. They may be pretty, but those flowers are as much a hazard as a lake or a stream. This is not an easy hole to play.

connects the course's two ponds. Golfers at hole four can 'go for it' by carrying over an inlet of the pond, or they can play it safe by hitting for the right side of the well-protected green, so accuracy—no matter what route you take—is the key here.

The fifth bends around a pond, describing a near semicircle to the left. A long shot onto the fairway is likely to land just where the fairway makes its first major bend, the outside bend of which is guarded by three bunkers—each attuned to the various tee placements. A bottleneck here forces shots to the left—just barely avoiding the rough to the left—and encourages a ball flight directly at the large bunkers situated just where the fairway makes its second major bend. From here, it's a shot to a well-bunkered green.

Hole number six shares its back tee with hole twelve. Hole six itself is straightforward, excepting that the tee shot must avoid the bottleneck and bunker that is situated just where most tee shots will land comfortably, and another bunker diagonally across the fairway from it will catch inaccurate long shots. Then, it's a straight approach shot toward a green which is well protected by two bunkers situated in the right hollow of said bottleneck.

The back tee of hole seven carries over a stream to the green, which is actually larger than the fairway. The fairway is massively bunkered on both sides and the green is bunkered in back—perhaps a good hole on which to forego the fairway altogether. Hole eight's a demanding tee shot, an immediate skew to the left with a bunker right, then a serpentine tending right with bunkers left—at least one shot has to pass over a bunker. At the end of the fairway is a rough, and then a slender, hourglass-shaped green bunkered front and left.

The ninth has a fairway which is broken by a stream. After the stream, the fairway tends toward the left, with a subtle hook to the right as it approaches the green—of course, on the leading edge of the 'hook,' where it is likely to catch the unconsidered shot, is a large bunker. Play is then right, across an extension of the same stream encountered previously, to a smallish, triangular green—the base of which faces the fairway, and the sloping sides of which are cut into by bunkers. It's a very dangerous green. Continuing on with this extraordinary course, hole ten describes a long arc to the left, dotted with bunkers leading to a triangular green whose 'chin' faces the fairway, and which is protected on three sides by bunkers.

Hole eleven is fairly straightforward, after a long tee shot onto the green, up until the fairway widens and doglegs left—at precisely which point Mr Jones has placed a bog to the left, extending from this bend up to and accompanying the left bunker,

SentryWorld Golf Course

Hole	1	2	3	4	5	6	7	8	9	Out
Championship	417	409	399	177	513	407	196	357	501	3376
Intermediate	382	375	371	140	492	372	152	331	469	3084
Club	369	362	361	121	450	346	130	320	441	2900
Forward	331	329	334	92	413	306	102	295	417	2619
Par	4	4	4	3	5	4	3	4	5	36

Hole	10	11	12	13	14	15	16	17	18	In	Total
Championship	391	533	216	389	509	448	166	406	417	3475	6851
Intermediate	380	492	183	363	475	398	135	370	406	3202	6286
Club	342	454	146	342	452	353	115	339	383	2926	5826
Forward	315	425	105	309	416	281	108	317	302	2578	5197
Par	4	5	3	4	5	4	3	4	4	36	72

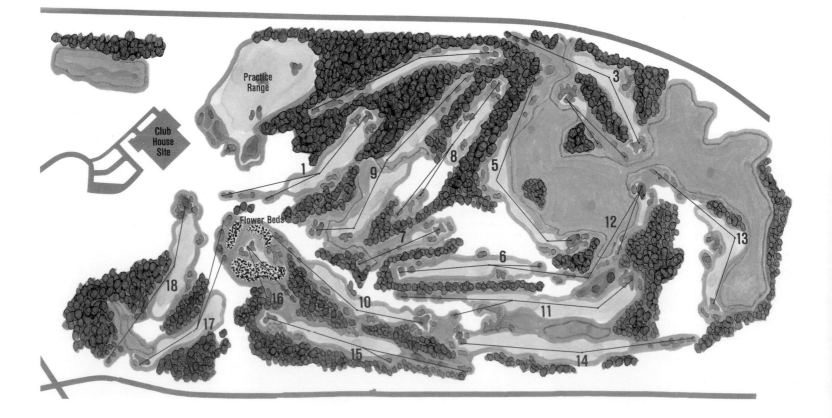

which defends the green. The green itself is also bunkered right, and tapers in between the two bunkers. Any errant shots on this last stretch—dogleg left and green—are in serious trouble.

The front three tees of hole twelve have the option to carry over water, with the back tee carrying a long distance over same. The layout of this hole wraps the play around an inlet of one of the course's ponds. Combine a teeing off distance to the fairway with the fact that the fairway itself is no longer than this distance, and you have an interesting golf puzzle to solve—with a pinched approach to the green (which itself is protected by bunkers on both sides, and of course by the pond which lies to the left).

The thirteenth is a severe dogleg right, which, as it doglegs, slips in closer to the pond which lies to its left. There is a long carry from tees to fairway, with the line of flight head on toward the bunkers in the dogleg's inner bend. Overcorrection will take you into the pond. Then, it's a drive toward the green, which lies, bunkered behind, at the end of a concave arc which curves away from the pond—shots had best be accurate here, or it's 'in the drink' for going left, and in the trap for going too long. An intriguing and very beautiful hole.

Hole fourteen combines a challenging tee shot to a fairway with a large pond on the right. Well-distanced shots are important here; and from this point, shots tending toward the right—which is the fairway tendency—will find the large bunker at right. At any rate, the green is secluded by

Above: A golfer chips out of a bunker on one of SentryWorld's many water holes. *Below:* Lining up a putt on the sixteenth hole: mums add distraction to a good, challenging hole.

its smallness and the armada of bunkers which surround it. Hole fifteen's straightforward fairway suddenly develops a case of the wobbles toward the green end. Neatly tucked into these wobbles are several hungry bunkers which will tempt you into going for a carry over onto the boot-shaped green, the heel of which is likely to let your ball kick off into the rough. You'll love it.

The sixteenth is the famous and fabulous 'flower hole'—perhaps the one hole in all of golfing that is likely to be known on sight by many non-golfers. The play on this hole is magnificent, the scenery, breathtaking. Tee off across a beautiful bed of flowers—which in effect is a water hazard—toward a short, narrow fairway which leads to a triangular green set with its chin buried in the fairway. Many golfers will go for the green immediately, though—and the green is trapped left and right, for short shots and long shots. In addition, another strand of flowers hungers to mulch over-long tee shots. This is a very tricky hole, a delight to play and is visually an utter astonishment.

Hole number seventeen continues the pace with a long carry to a quick dogleg left, then down the fairway's 'shin' to small green trapped behind and protected at right by a small pond, which forces a bottleneck green approach, tending toward the left—a dangerous setup, as the green curves toward the right beyond the water.

The eighteenth hole is a marvelous finish to eighteen holes of golf. All but the innermost of the four tees have a long carry over a slender pond surrounded by rough to the fairway, which curves to the left and is bunkered at a likely place right. Bunkers dot the right side of this fairway, which leads toward a very pinched approach to the green, which is bunkered right and left. Unsubtle shots will find the two right bunkers as well as pot bunkers in back of the hole—these provide the ultimate challenge for a sand wedge shot. A great finishing hole, and more than enough reason to head for the clubhouse—which lies directly in your line of sight at this point—to celebrate an outstanding round of golf.

Add to this as complete and varied a practice range as one could imagine, and you have one of the finest courses in the United States—a course which has features found nowhere else in the world. Robert Trent Jones Jr has created a real gift to the public, under the auspices of the late John Joanis and Sentry Insurance. For golfers of all capabilities, SentryWorld truly is a 'Mona Lisa'... in Wisconsin.

At left: **SentryWorld has challenge, accessibility and excitement. It is one of the very finest public courses. Now, one last look at the sixteenth....**

The Links at Spanish Bay

Pebble Beach, California USA

We are much indebted to the California Coastal Commission for certain information which they provided us on the development of this excellent course.

Opened in 1987, the Links at Spanish Bay golf course was built on some of golfing's most hallowed ground—the pebbled beaches of the Monterey Peninsula, not far from the Pebble Beach Golf Links, which is considered by many to be the premier golf course in the world. Adjacent to the Pebble Beach Golf Links, there is beautiful Spyglass Hill, designed by Robert Trent Jones Sr (this is ranked by *Golf Digest* as one of the top 40 courses in America) and in Monterey is the classic Del Monte Golf Course,

the oldest course in operation west of the Mississippi.

The Links at Spanish Bay was collaboratively designed by Robert Trent Jones Jr, world-famous professional golfer Tom Watson (winner of five British Opens), and former USGA president and renowned amateur golfer Frank 'Sandy' Tatum. Together, they formed a team which beat the very stiff competition—which included Jack Nicklaus and Arnold Palmer—who were vying to be the designers of this course.

Given the restrictions imposed upon the Monterey Peninsula by the California Coastal Commission, Spanish Bay is proba-

bly the final course that will be built here. With his nearby Poppy Hills course ranked among these crown jewels of the Monterey Peninsula, Spanish Bay makes Robert Trent Jones Jr the *only* designer to have *two* courses here on the Mount Olympus of golf.

Design rights for this course were hotly contested because, as Hugh Delehanty stated in the *San Jose Mercury News* of 7 April 1985, '[I]t may be the last course in the United States built on a piece of true linksland, the rolling type of seaside landscape on which the game was born in Scotland. Being asked to build a links-style course in Pebble Beach, says [Robert Trent

Jones Jr] is like "being commissioned by the Pope to paint a section of the Sistine Chapel.'"

The goal was this: to build the first and only true links-style course outside of the British Isles. This was to be an outstanding achievement, and to all current appearances, it certainly is. As Robert Trent Jones Jr says, quoted in an article by Ted Blofsky, in the *NCGA News* of July 1987: '... Spanish Bay will yield to good play and thinking; this course is totally Scotland.' Adds Tom Watson: 'We hope you can hear the bagpipes in the background when you play the links.'

The open arms of the golfing world were, for awhile, counterbalanced by the opponents to the project, who claimed that the large resort hotel and condominium which were part of the project would create additional traffic burdens for the area, and would create, during their construction, a serious nuisance to local residents.

Below left: **A daunting array of fairway bunkers on the third hole.** *Below:* **Monterey Peninsula weather is evident in this view of the thirteenth green.** *At right:* **The tenth green.**

This grand undertaking is located near Asilomar State Beach, on a tract of land that was barren waste before work on the project began. Approximately 530,000 cubic yards of fresh sand was transported from two miles away by a special conveyor system, to replace that which was actually quarried from the site earlier in this century.

This, in combination with improved public access to the nearby Del Monte Forest, can definitely be seen as a conservation-minded move. In a sense, it could be said that the golf course project financed and implemented the restoration of the area, which had been ravaged for its sand. Severe erosion would shortly have affected the coastline at this point had not the developers restored this area to something approximating much of its original condition.

Mr Jones, along with Mr Watson, Mr Tatum and the Pebble Beach Company (developers for the project) saw it as a positively transformative development — a restoration of the coastline to its former

Seaside linksland. *Above:* **The first green at Spanish Bay.** *Opposite:* **The first green as seen from the eighteenth tees.** *At right:* **The fourth, with the Inn at Spanish Bay in view.**

beauty, and the building of a recreational site that both golfers and non-golfers could enjoy.

The California Coastal Commission backed the plan initially, but complete approval was suspended for some time due to the protests. A gamut of lawsuits—on the part of the cities of Monterey, Pacific Grove and Carmel—had to be run. The opposition was vociferous, but the Spanish Bay project won out.

It was a very intense battle, and one that the golfing world will be glad—for some time to come—was won. The Links at Spanish Bay evoke the spirit of traditional golf.

The civic-minded builders of the course graciously provided public access to Asilomar State Beach and a nearby state preserve. The Pebble Beach area in general is being made accessible to the general public via biking and walking trails that were being built as part of the project.

In addition, this magnificent golf course is available to the public.

Also, some 340 acres of Monterey cypress trees have been retained on the grounds of the Spanish Bay development. Natural habitats are being protected, and any rare flora that would be interfered with by the building of the course were transplanted to a location which was suitable to California Coastal Commission specifications. The dunes of the Asilomar beach area are distinguishable from those elsewhere in the vicinity of the Monterey Peninsula by their brilliant white sand.

Likewise, various species of fauna associated with the dunes had to be protected. All in all, a massive project, but one which has been successfully executed. Indeed, one is likely to encounter a wide spectrum of bird life—ranging from red-tailed hawks to red-winged blackbirds—while playing or even just strolling these links.

In a sense, this was not only the building of a major golf course, but was also a major restoration project for the area. In keeping with Robert Trent Jones Jr's penchant for including native habitats in his courses, it could be said that nothing could have

The Links at Spanish Bay

Hole	1	2	3	4	5	6	7	8	9	Out	
Championship	500	307	405	190	459	395	418	163	394	3231	
Middle	461	265	334	176	405	345	382	148	357	2873	
Forward	434	224	285	127	349	301	342	98	326	2486	
Par	5	4	4	3	4	4	4	3	4	35	

Hole	10	11	12	13	14	15	16	17	18	In	Total
Championship	520	365	432	126	571	390	200	414	571	3589	6820
Middle	464	318	406	99	535	342	157	369	515	3205	6078
Forward	401	285	341	76	475	296	130	321	476	2801	5287
Par	5	4	4	3	5	4	3	4	5	37	72

Club House

Hotel

13 12

11

10

14

6

5

4

7

9

18 1

2

3

8

15

16 17

Spanish Bay

Pacific Ocean

suited his very special talents better. It was, even so, a tough battle to get things rolling—and now, with many Coastal Commission conditions to have been met, one of the finest new golf courses in the world adds to the very substantial golfing glories of the Monterey Peninsula.

Says Sandy Tatum, 'It's a great satisfaction to know we've made something useful and beautiful here.'

The Links at Spanish Bay includes no gimmicks—just terrific golfing. The course measures 6820 yards and is rated at par 72. The fairways are rolling and narrow, and the roughs at The Links include a stabilized sand dune 24 feet high on the ninth fairway. Pacific winds, and the well-known fog of the Monterey Peninsula, contribute still more challenges at The Links. The large, undulating greens of The Links are an additional challenge. The majestic, 100-foot-tall Monterey pines of the Del Monte Forest line many of these holes, and form a beautiful and otherworldly frame for the playing surfaces of this great new golf course.

The eleventh green has, even this early on, added a new phrase to golfing's fond jargon of famous course features, such as the 'Road Hole' at St Andrews. At Spanish

At top, opposite: **The seventh green, open to the sea salt air.** *Below:* **These golfers show perplexity at having lost a ball on the ninth hole's notorious block-long sand hill, just one of many evocations of Spanish Bay's Scottish roots.**

Bay, the talk already turns to the 'Top Hat' green at the eleventh hole.

On the weekend of 16—17 January 1988, The Inn at Spanish Bay hosted the official grand opening for the resort and golf course complex. Among the guests were film star (and, at the time, mayor of the nearby city of Carmel) Clint Eastwood, and film star Sidney Poitier. The architect showed up in a green top hat—an obvious allusion to the eleventh green.

The following is a hole-by-hole description of this fine new golf course. Hole number one plays toward the ocean, with bunkers right and left off the fairway. Just before the green, a couple of fairway bunkers at left harmonize with the two bunkers on the left of the green to keep your shot tending right. The second hole plays inland, and the green is right under the Inn at Spanish Bay, which is perched on a hill overlooking the course.

There is a truly spectacular ocean view from the elevated championship tee at the third hole, which is a 405-yard par four, describing an extreme dogleg left, that breaks at a series of interior bunkers and heads toward a contoured green, with the ocean in sight all the way. The short but tough fourth hole incurses sand dunes with its putting surfaces.

Hole five is a long dogleg that faces tee shots with three pot bunkers in a row set into the fairway. It doglegs right and heads

toward a green which has a bunker at left front. The sixth hole has a contoured fairway having almost a dozen bunkers sprinkled on and around it! All your golfing skills are called for on the approach to the oblong green.

Hole seven's fairway has bunkers right, at the bend of the shallow angle it makes in breaking for the green. A hazard again must be overcome en route to the second stretch of fairway, which angles to the left and has a prominent bunker set into the green approach. If you look to the left of the green, you'll see the marsh which forms a hazard at the eighth.

Tee shots at hole number eight carry over a marsh. You can hear frogs, and you'll see plovers and redwing blackbirds who are nesting here. The contoured green will test your putting, and the wildlife will enchant—and distract—you. The ninth plays away from the marsh, and has a 24-foot sand hill all along its right, and fairway bunkers along the way—it demands the straight and narrow approach, and a good hand on the green!

Hole ten is a long, meandering double dogleg, with a bunker outside its first bend. Toward the end of the fairway, three bunkers lie in line to the green approach, and a bunker to the right of the fairway, and another behind the broad, shallow green complete the challenge. The famous Top Hat green at the 365-yard par four eleventh

Above, clockwise from photo left: Holes seventeen, fifteen, eighteen and one. ***At left:*** The seventeenth hole—with Spanish Bay Beach and the Pacific Ocean on the right.

hole features a flattened hummock in its center, and the hole itself describes a dogleg right with strategically located traps.

Hole twelve has a straight-ahead fairway, with a bunker left and a bunker right. The green is set sideways, with heavy bunkering at its right front and right. Tee shots at the very short thirteenth hole carry over a very deep ravine. Set end-on, its oblong green is bunkered right and left.

The fourteenth features tees which are essentially a series of buttes stepping down to the fairway. This entire hole is a long downhill toward the ocean, and is quite spectacular. Bunkers start at the left of the long, long fairway, and march across the fairway to the lower right end, and include a deep bunker directly in the middle of the fairway near the green approach. Directly on the right front of the narrow green is a pot bunker which will further add to the excitement here. Off to the left, in the triangle formed by the fourteenth green, the eighteenth green and the fifteenth's tees, is

a conservation area in which blackbirds are nesting.

You'll see redwing blackbirds near the tees of hole fifteen, as their nesting sanctuary is off to the left of the tees here. This hole is a dogleg right with a two-part fairway, which has bunkers on the right of its first half. The second half faces five bunkers set to the left half of the green, which is irregularly-shaped and curls around one of the bunkers. The sixteenth is a par three, 200-yard hole whose tees face an obliquely set, oblong green having numerous strategically-placed bunkers.

Hole seventeen plays along Spanish Bay beach, and has the Pacific Ocean all along its right. The fairway consists of two parts, the first of which has a cluster of bunkers two layers deep on its right edge. The second part of the fairway has a single bunker at its right, and the kidney-shaped green has a bunker left.

The eighteenth hole plays also to broken fairway, the second part of which branches into two prongs, and brings into mind Robert Frost's poem 'The Road Not Taken.' Talk about coming to a crossroads! The left 'prong' is preceded by a pot bunker, and the wine flask-shaped green is set narrow end first, to the left, with bunkers guarding it to the right. To the left of the green is the redwing blackbird sanctuary, and considerable charm—and distraction—will be availed to golfers during the final strokes of their round. This is an exciting hole, and an apt embodiment of Robert Trent Jones Jr's 'great risks, great rewards' philosophy.

This is a fine conclusion to 18 holes of challenging golf. The Links at Spanish Bay course has been planted, after much consideration, with fescue grass—the putting surfaces being a mix of bent grass and fescue. It was felt that this seeding would produce a surface that would be ideally resilient in, and tolerant of, the often very dry conditions of the Monterey region.

This grass treatment will enhance the qualities of ball movement which are necessary for the windy peninsula upon which the course lies—conditions which are very similar to those at classical Scottish oceanside linksland courses. Fescue is, after all, the very green that is to be found prominently on most Scottish courses.

The majority of the 18 holes of this course provide awesome Pacific Ocean views, and the closeness of that huge liquid body, its waves smashing grandly on the shore, will provide stimulus and distraction. This is a strategist's course, and calls for meditative, yet powerful and accurate, golf. It should be very rewarding for those who are willing to take risks for the truly good shot.

Spyglass Hill Golf Course

Pebble Beach, California USA

Spyglass Hill Golf Course is one of the several legendary courses that are located in the golf-rich countryside of California's Monterey Peninsula. Rated as the toughest course in California from the championship tees, Spyglass is also widely recognized as one of the finest courses in the world. Also, *Golf Digest* has ranked Spyglass Hill among the top 40 courses in America.

In accordance with golf tradition, each hole is named for a significant person, place or thing. In this case, the names come from Robert Louis Stevenson's *Treasure Island*—uncannily appropriate for a golf course. Stevenson lived in California for a good part of his life, and it was he who metaphorically metamorphosed the Monterey Cypress trees (some of whose gnarled trunks are bleached white by the

Links. The following is a hole-by-hole description of the great Spyglass Hill Golf Course.

The first hole, Treasure Island, plays downhill, affords ocean vistas, and gets you limbered up for a demanding test of golf. An unusual first hole in that it's the longest on the course, this 600-yard (from the back tees) dogleg left plays around a grove of trees that follow the line of Spyglass Hill Road. These trees, close in on the left, and additional trees that severely pinch the green approach, make this hole a very challenging start. There is the opportunity to let out your driver a bit, and also the necessity of paying close attention to strategy and accuracy. This is not the end of travails on this first hole, however, as the green is fronted by a huge bunker that is at least 60 yards deep—incidentally, you'll be facing the ocean wind here. Additionally, on the right and left frontal areas of this irregular green, two more bunkers serve to further tighten the defenses.

Hole number two, Billy Bones, demands a carry over a drainage ditch to a fairway that has a dangerously-placed swale. You play uphill on this hole. The rough cuts a wide swath across the green approach, and the green is long and narrow.

The third hole plays into the wind, and is all-too-appropriately named The Black Spot. This par three, quite scenically situated atop a high plateau, has a green that is irregular and is set obliquely to the tees. Conviction and carefulness are the keys here, for a weakly-hit shot will be windblown into the large bunker at front right. Also, the rough is perilously close on all sides of this green.

Blind Pew, the fourth hole, is a dogleg left that hooks around the edge of a pine grove, effectively hiding the green from the elevated tees. Again, you're playing into the wind, and the trees along the left form a hazard, indeed. The 50-yard-long (but comparatively narrow) green has one small bunker on its left side and another bunker at right front, with rough all along the right. The oceanward slope of the land here is quite pronounced.

The fifth hole, Bird Rock, may afford a birdie—but you should beware that, at

The famed golf course designer Robert Trent Jones Sr designed this course, which was opened for play in 1965. Its 18 holes wind their way up, down and around Spyglass Hill, affording an excellent level of playing challenge, and spectacular views.

Spyglass Hill Golf Course received much acclaim. It is, with Pebble Beach and Cypress Point, one of the three sites on which the world-famous Bing Crosby Pro-Am is played, and is a regular venue for the AT&T Pebble Beach National Pro-Am. Spyglass is also the home of the Northern California Golf Association.

Tall pines and undulating sand dunes make for a memorable aesthetic experience, and combined with the exhilarating vistas availed to golfers on this course, make for a golf outing that is truly unforgettable.

Spyglass Hill hole names were taken from *Treasure Island* by Stevenson. *Opposite:* Israel Hands, the sixth. *Above:* The tenth, Captain Flint.

elements) into 'ghosts fleeing before the wind.'

The Spyglass Grill provides refreshment before or after your round of golf. Its menu includes choices for breakfast, lunch or snacks, from early morning until late afternoon.

In addition to the Spyglass Grill and a full-service golf shop, visitors to Spyglass Hill are also availed the luxuriant amenities of The Inn at Pebble Beach, which offers epicurean dining, excellent equestrian facilities, a first-class beach and tennis club, boutiques, Old World service and award-winning conference facilities. For historical detail on The Lodge, please see the chapter of this text on Pebble Beach Golf

times, it's perilously hard for the 'birds' to get a purchase on the 'rock.' This 180-yard par three is tied with the twelfth hole for the honors of being the longest in yardage of the par threes on this course. Again, you play into the wind, and it's necessary to overfly some greenery en route to the green, which has a troublesome trio of bunkers on its left front, and a not-to-be-ignored large bunker on its right. This irregular green widens to the rear, where the steep slope down to the beach awaits over-long shots. Easily-distracted golfers should be on their guard here, as panoramic ocean vistas form a backdrop for this green.

Israel Hands, the sixth hole, plays uphill and is a slight dogleg right on which the wind is at your back. Trees line the right side of this hole, and a grove of trees on the left further creates a 'hallway' effect. Bunkers left and right near the landing spot, and the persistent presence of trees on the right, may cause trouble if you fail to gauge your shot to conditions. The green presents a very narrow face that is brack-eted by bunkers, and widens front to back.

Hole number seven, Indian Village, presents another set of challenges. Playing relatively sheltered by trees along the left, it has a 'gunsight' of trees at the beginning of the fairway, plus a pair of bunkers to the left of the landing spot, and a cart path winding along the right. Set off to the right, behind a grove of trees on the green approach, is the green. A lake occupies the space where one might expect to find the green. Therefore, position at the green approach is all-important. A lie to the left will mean a carry left to right across the lake to the green. A lie on the right will grant you a tree-skimming shot to the green down the right side of the lake. From the former, the green presents its broad side to you, but is quite shallow; from the latter lie, the green is long but narrow. As they say, you've got to 'know the forest,' and its ways.

The eighth hole, Signal Hill (perhaps named for the location of its green), is situated parallel to and above the previous hole, availing ocean views to players here. Signal Hill is lined with trees on the left, and has two pines encroaching on the fairway on that same side. The wind can play tricks here, so beware those trees, which are, after all, to the lee. The green is uphill of the fairway, and has a cannily-placed bunker on its right front face. Trees on either side of the green complete the scenario.

Spyglass Hill Golf Course

Hole	1	2	3	4	5	6	7	8	9	Out	
Back	600	350	150	365	180	415	515	395	425	3395	
Middle	551	325	125	347	138	377	474	367	408	3112	
Forward	481	230	75	300	107	330	455	305	385	2668	
Par	5	4	3	4	3	4	5	4	4	36	
Hole	10	11	12	13	14	15	16	17	18	In	Total
Back	400	520	180	440	555	130	465	320	405	3415	6810
Middle	371	485	148	418	514	104	434	308	383	3165	6277
Forward	360	419	95	386	475	102	403	293	355	2888	5556
Par	4	5	3	4	5	3	4	4	4	36	72

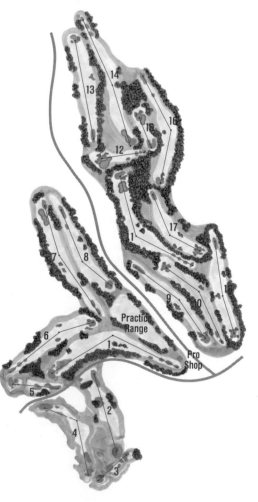

Captain Smollett, hole number nine, is situated on the lower of two hilltop plateaus, and plays fairly level up to the green approach, which features an elevation increase to a plateau green. This hole is a slight dogleg right, with gaps of ocean view between the intermittent trees on the right, and a lining of trees on the left. This can create a complex wind situation, with 'avenues' of wind coming in through the gaps in the right-hand 'windbreak.' Also on the right is longitudinal bunker, situated to catch over-corrective tee shots. The green, which widens front to rear, is guarded on either side of its narrow 'chin' by two large bunkers, with a pot bunker off to the right.

The tenth hole, Captain Flint, plays downhill from the tees. The fairway is difficult, and includes a dangerous bunker on

Opposite: **Where golf and nature meet: two stags engage in combat near Blind Pew, Spyglass Hill's fourth hole.** *Above:* **Bird Rock, the fifth hole.**

the right, and a pair of trees on the left. This creates a 'gunsight' situation that requires very good accuracy. The green is deep but narrow, and has bunkers front and back on both sides.

Tree-lined hole number eleven, Admiral Benbow, is a sharp dogleg right, with trees very close in on either side. Particularly, there is an incursion of trees on the inside curve that could cause real trouble. The green approach is occupied by a lake, and the green is ample, but with a bunker on its wide right face.

Facing the ocean—and situated on the edge of the highest plateau of the course— the twelfth hole, Skeleton Island, features

trees on either side of the tees, making for a broad hallway. This 180-yard par three is one of the two longest par threes on the course (see also the fifth hole). A lake guards the entire left side of the obliquely-set, peanut-shaped green. The windward, leeward and starboard (to use suitably nautical terms) sides of this green are guarded by bunkers. This is an 'island' that will not be easily conquered.

Tom Morgan, the thirteenth hole, is a straightaway par four with trees all along its right side, and a bunker just to the right of the landing spot. On the left lies an intermittent line of trees. The green is narrow but deep, and is guarded right and left with bunkers.

Long John Silver, hole number fourteen, is an appropriately serpentine hole with a

hallway of trees at the tees. Further making this a 'target' situation are the trees on the fairway at left and the trees close in on the right. The fairway widens a bit for your second shot, and the green approach is occupied by a lake. The green is 'ell'-shaped but shallow, and wraps around the left rear of the pond. Trees closely guard the rear and left side of the green. This is one hole that could very easily 'Shanghai' the golfer who's not fully awake and in control.

A par three, the fifteenth hole, Jim Hawkins, challenges tee shots with a grove of trees that partially obscures access to the green on the right. The left side of this hole is open to the wind. The green wraps around the left rear of a lake, and is backed by two bunkers. It is a pleasantly challenging hole that could be considered to be quite even-handed and fair.

The sixteenth hole, Black Dog, is another matter. Of course, it's a *dogleg* (right) with trees on both sides, and its inner curve contains an encroachment of trees on the fairway. This will force your shot left, where a second shot must clear two bunkers on the left front of the green. This green is a gentle cresent backed by trees and a cart path. It should be noted that the green approach is open to the wind on the right side. This hole practically comes alive with a challenge that can be said to possess the quality of *tenacity*.

Benn Gunn, hole number seventeen, is a dogleg left. Tee shots must pass down a hallway of trees to a broad fairway that has trees close in on the right. One bunker on the inner curve, and two on the outer curve, further guard this playing surface. The green is a smallish, irregular target set among four large bunkers that are evenly spaced in a box formation, and one pot bunker directly in front of the green. Trees close in on the right and rear additionally add to the challenge here.

The eighteenth hole, Spyglass, is a straightaway hole that has trees on all sides, save for the right green approach. A clump of trees on the left and a bunker on the right, near the green approach, create a target situation. The second shot faces an uphill green that is set amidst a 'box' of four bunkers (similar to that on the seventeenth hole). This green is additionally set back amidst a cul-de-sac of trees. This hole's commanding height above the surrounding countryside allows views of the ocean through gaps in the trees. It's an exhilarating finish for a great 18 holes of golfing challenge.

At left: **A view down the eighteenth, toward the tees. This hole, Spyglass, commands the surrounding countryside from its lofty perch.**

Sugarloaf Golf Club

Carrabassett Valley, Maine USA

Robert Trent Jones Jr's Sugarloaf Golf Course was chosen as one of *Golf Digest*'s best new courses of the year in 1987. The February 1987 issue of that magazine states that 'Sugarloaf provides a visual feast for the golfer. Several tees are elevated 50 feet above the fairway. The eleventh through fifteenth holes play along and over the South Bend of the Carrabassett River, a gurgling stream dotted with white rock. Our panelists gave it the highest numbers for aesthetics of any new course in all categories.'

The course is the product of a joint agreement between the town of Carrabassett Valley, developer Peter Webber and the Sugarloaf Mountain Corporation; specifically, this scenic layout is owned by the town of Carrabassett and is leased to Mountain Greenery, a joint venture between Sugarloaf Mountain Corporation and Peter Webber.

Initial discussions for the course were begun in the winter of 1983, and Robert Trent Jones Jr began work on the course the following spring. Over 100 workers were on the site at peak construction. To create the 100-acre course, 155,000 yards of fill, topsoil and beach sand were trucked in, and more than 4000 cords of wood were cleared.

The Sugarloaf brochure quotes Mr Webber on the philosophy behind the creation of Sugarloaf: 'The concept all along was that we had to have a great golf course. People won't travel here just to play any golf course, and that's why we had Bobby design ours. We had the best designer, the best site, and the result is absolutely spectacular.'

Each hole is closed off from the others by dint of the course having been created from mature forestland—the trees are dense, and each hole has a very marked feeling of individuality. Yet the course does exist very strongly as a whole, so that the overall effect is very much like a Beethoven symphony; strength upon strength—a very spirited and exquisitely beautiful course. Robert Trent Jones Jr himself is quoted in the Sugarloaf brochure as saying 'Of all the golf courses I've designed, this is one of my favorites.'

Above: **A view from the tees of Sugarloaf's first hole.** *Opposite:* **A view of the fifteenth hole, with the Carrabassett River running along its side.**

The course has Penneagle Bentgrass on the tees and greens, with combination bentgrass on the fairways, and the course, despite being closed during the winter, is kept in absolutely first class condition. Its popularity is growing very rapidly. Excellent facilities await golfers in Sugarloaf's 'Stay & Play' program: the beautiful Sugarloaf Mountain Hotel is seven stories of comfortable accommodations at the base of Sugarloaf Mountain. The Sugarloaf Inn is another hostelry which is affiliated with the program, and is home to the fine cuisine of the restaurant known as The Seasons.

Three more fine restaurants lie within easy walking distance of the Sugarloaf Mountain Hotel—the Gladstone, specializing in gourmet veal dishes; the Truffle Hound, well known for its French cuisine; and Gepetto's, which provides meals with an American accent. Both the hotel and the inn have swimming pools and tennis courts, and regional activities include fishing in the pristine local streams and incredible rafting on the Kennebec and Dead rivers.

In addition to Sugarloaf's acclaim in the February 1987 *Golf Digest*, that magazine and the magazines *Golf Traveler* and *The Golf Club* have published feature stories about this marvelous, mountainside course. Sugarloaf has also appeared on the

covers of *Golf Traveler* and *The Golf Club*. *Golf Magazine* has also featured this course.

The championship tees are 6900 yards total, and front tees are 5400 yards. At this point, the course appears to be a real 'comer,' and considering its auspicious beginnings, could well become a golf legend.

Sugarloaf/USA's *News From the Mountain* of May 1987 quotes Robert Trent Jones Jr as saying—in an article authored by Chip Carey—'We tried to do something quite different for this part of the country in that it's a mountainous setting. It's a deep wilderness course, which is Eastern, and we used some of the third dimensions that are apparent in Western golf. The combination is unique in the whole country, where you have a wilderness course and occasionally a moose will come and add a little interest to the shot and each hole is virtually separated from each other... .'

The course is very interesting both from a scenic and from a golfing point of view. This is an excellent golf course, a sure test of your skills that challenges and rewards with great generosity—which is not to be confused with unremittent ease, but is to be equated with the very best that golf has to offer for all levels of golfing skill. This course is truly 'a cut above....'

The following is a hole-by-hole description of this beautiful, white birch- and river-adorned golf course. The holes start out playing downhill, and follow a big spiral around and up the hillside, for a variegated sense of play and a visually stunning variety. Hole number one is a dogleg right with multiple bunkers just beyond the bend of a tree-lined fairway, and heads toward an obliquely-set green having bunkers left and right. Trees all around add beauty, and of course, something to stay away from!

The second hole is a double dogleg—first right and then left. Tee setups include a back tee with a stream which must be accounted for inrupting from the right and trees pinching in from the left—or a much more open tee setup which avoids the stream altogether. The first bit of fairway here arcs around to the right, and has the stream on its edge at right and trees left. From this fairway you cross the stream to another bit of fairway which has a massive bunker lying in wait for overpowered shots, and has the stream at left for underpowered shots. Finesse here! To the left is a green which is well-bunkered on its right and left, with trees behind.

At right: **As this view down the fairway illustrates, you'll have to carry over a large bunker to reach the green on the tenth hole.**

Hole three is a short, straight hole with almost equisized fairway and green, but having a bunker dangerously set in the slight notch cojoining the fairway and green. Trees are at left, rear and right rear. Hole number four is a tree-lined, stretched-out dogleg left, with a small bunker incursing from the left almost immediately. The bend in the fairway may cause some over-shooting to the right, into the trees, and the bunker left almost at the end of the fairway will keep shots dangerously right—three bunkers surround the green, and two lie rightward.

The fifth hole is a dogleg right whose back tee has a narrow passage around some trees leaning in from the right. Trees close on both sides here, and the green lies at the end of a narrow, recurving bit of fairway with large bunkers at right and left front. Trees and another bunker on the left and rough behind make this a challenge.

The sixth plays downhill to a landing area and doglegs right 90 degrees—then it goes sharply uphill over a series of bunkers. You've got to risk the bunkers, but it's worth it—for that green is a wonder, with the typically rolling eastern-US Bigelow Mountains for its magnificent, scenic backdrop.

Hole number seven plays straight away on a dogleg right with a bunker just beyond its bend, and plays up to a highly irregularly shaped green having trees close by and bunkers at right front and left rear. The eighth is a beautiful par three, and players here tee off a green with a pond at its entire front, a bunker right, and trees at left and behind.

Hole number nine tee shots must carry across a stream—directly toward an 'X'-shaped bunker which is situated just where most shots would land on the fairway; a companion bunker lies to the right, just off the fairway: lay up or go for broke. The fairway tends left here, and to make it even more interesting, a tree incurses from the left just a bit farther on: accuracy is needed. Then it's a shot to a rolling green having a bunker on its left approach and trees at left, right and behind.

As quoted in the Sugarloaf brochure, Robert Trent Jones Jr describes hole ten, in particular, and the second nine, generally: 'Number ten starts from on high and plays up the throat of the Carrabassett River. Then the next series of holes plays down, over and around the river like a chain of diamonds—these are the sparkling holes.'

Indeed, hole ten tee shots have to pass through the trees straight toward a fairway with serpentine sides: in the convolutions are hidden three large bunkers, two left and one right. This heads into a green

approach which is blocked directly with one frontal bunker, two bunkers left and one right, trees to the left and the Southern Carrabassett River slanting from right to rear. Absolutely great!

Hole eleven features tee choices similar to hole number two: three tees must carry the river to the green, and two tees shoot down a narrow hallway of trees with no river crossing. The green itself has a bunker at rear, a tumble downhill to the depths of the forest at right rear, a massive bunker all along its right and the river close on the left. With white birches in evidence,

and the mountains in the distance behind, hole eleven is a glorious par three.

The twelfth plays down a narrow hallway of trees to a divided fairway, the first half of which tends to the right, leaving most shots headed for the grove of river-front trees to the left—double jeopardy, trees and water. Shots too far right from here will find the bunker near the fairway break, which break is protected by three bunkers all across. The second half tends left, straight at the river, and the green is canted slightly left so that its left side is on the water. Bunkers left and right pinch the

Opposite: **With a massive bunker on its right, and the Carrabassett River on its left, the eleventh green is a challenge—and a scenic delight.**

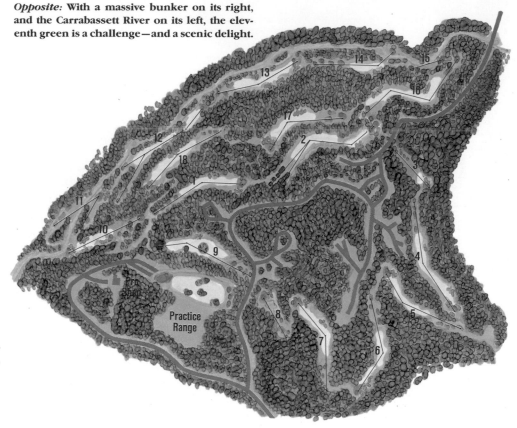

Sugarloaf Golf Club

Hole	1	2	3	4	5	6	7	8	9	Out
Championship	416	550	217	533	405	403	380	187	417	3508
Regular	400	518	190	508	385	361	354	172	392	3284
Club	366	487	169	456	361	338	327	150	364	3018
Forward	333	463	155	396	328	307	308	120	339	2749
Par	4	5	3	5	4	4	4	3	4	36

Hole	10	11	12	13	14	15	16	17	18	In	Total
Championship	355	222	554	405	367	180	530	384	417	3414	6922
Regular	275	200	520	373	327	167	509	365	384	3119	6403
Club	255	176	505	360	291	133	455	353	367	2895	5913
Forward	222	151	443	320	250	110	437	305	337	2575	5324
Par	4	3	5	4	4	3	5	4	4	36	72

approach, and a grove of trees will swallow shots too far to the rear.

Hole number thirteen's fairway curves to the left along the river. Tee shots too far left could find the bunker which incurses from the fairway's left, or the riverfront trees there, or the river itself; and shots too far right will find one of two bunkers on the fairway's right. The green approach is over a stream and is pinched by two bunkers at right. Hole fourteen drives straight at a fairway which has a bunker at right, just where unthought-out tee shots may find their way. From here, it's a sudden dogleg left between trees and across the river to a small green which is cannily bunkered rear for over-reaching shots, and has trees left and river all along its front and right.

Tee shots on the fifteenth have to carry across one of the river's meanders and a sand bar to a green having huge bunkers at its right, and a smaller bunker—and of course the river—at its left. The forest lies dead ahead. In the autumn, the foliage will easily outclass any other generally available distraction, as is the case with any hole on this course—the eastern American autumn is, in a word, spectacular! Hole fifteen is an unforgettable par four.

Hole number sixteen forms a right angle dogleg right which then repents itself into a more graceful dogleg left. On the inner bend of the first dogleg, bunkers lie in wait, and at the end of the comparatively long stretch to the second big bend, bunkers await overreaching shots on the outer bend. The green heads into an arboreal corner, with a bunker even deeper in to catch shots too strongly hit; the call is for accurate landing and restraint here. Hole seventeen is a dogleg left with a bunker early on, on the fairway's right. Then it's a drive to a green with two 'X'-shaped bunkers right out front, and a copse of trees on right, rear and left.

The eighteenth hole drives obliquely onto a fairway having a very deadly bunker set to the right, in perfect alignment with most tee shots. From here, it's a drive down a long fairway to an ovoid green which is canted to the left and has two bunkers left to protect that vulnerable side, and one bunker at right rear, to catch overflights from the left. Trees lie directly behind and to either side. A good, clean finish to an exciting and exquisitely beautiful 18 holes of golf.

This course demands every club from the golfer's bag, and yet—with its multiple tees and tee placements—is geared to challenge any golfer's talent at his or her level of capability.

At left: **An aerial view of the tenth, showing Sugarloaf's verdant mountain surroundings.**

Turnberry Hotel and Golf Course
(The Ailsa Course)

Ayrshire Scotland

The Ailsa Course at Turnberry was 19th among *Golf Magazine*'s '100 Greatest Courses in the World in 1989,' and 18th in that same listing in 1987. Additionally, the Ailsa Course was ranked by the 1989 poll as the sixth best course in the British Isles.

The course is located in Ayrshire, homeland of Scotland's renowned Robert Burns. Indeed, a vivid sense of the poet's rugged and beautiful sensitivity hangs over the course. Of all the great Scottish courses, the Ailsa Course is the most strikingly beautiful: it is situated on a dramatic, rocky coast above the golden sands that frame Turnberry Bay, with compelling vistas of such Firth of Clyde landforms as Ailsa Craig, the Mull of Kintyre and the Isle of Arran—and off in the distance, the coast of Northern Ireland etched clearly upon the sea and sky.

Of course, the weather here is as legendary as the view, and often overshadows everything with a proper Celtic mist. The wind is, also, a powerful influence on the locale—and aesthetics, weather and wind combine to present the golfer at Turnberry with an ever-changing variety of playing situations. While this is not a locale to be taken for granted, it must be said that Ailsa and its companion course, Arran, are in play throughout the year.

Turnberry has hosted every major British championship, including the Open, the Amateur, the Walker Cup and the Home

At left: **A view of the eighth fairway from the green. Behind this trio of golfers is the grand Turnberry Hotel.** *Below:* **Teeing off at the sixth tee.** *Above opposite:* **Inspiring golf at Turnberry—the sea, the links and the sky.**

Internationals—as well major PGA events. The history of Turnberry as a golfing ground is a fascinating tale of seemingly sure destruction and resurrection.

It all began when the Marquis of Ailsa, captain of the Prestwick Golf Club, decided that the considerable trek from Turnberry to Prestwick warranted a golfing venue that was altogether closer to home—and might bring in a profit as well. The Marquis was well aware of the scenic glories of Turnberry, and felt that a golf course would be a splendid impetus for tourists to visit Turnberry.

The chosen architect was respected greenskeeper Willie Furnie, who designed two courses—Number One, which measured 6115 yards, and Number Two, 5115 yards. Then the Marquis struck an agreement with the Glasgow and South Western Railway, whereby a railroad was built to communicate directly with lines to London, and a railway station was built at Turnberry, as well as a magnificent hotel overlooking the golf courses. The station, hotel and one of the courses were complete in the spring of 1906, and by the spring of 1909, the second of the two courses was finished.

Willie Furnie's son, Tom, became Turnberry's first golf professional. Turnberry was just beginning to establish a name for itself—Gladys Ravenscroft won the Ladies' British Open Amateur Championship on the Number One Course in 1912.

However, the First World War interrupted Turnberry's development in a very direct way: the golfing grounds and hotel were requisitioned as training runways and officers' mess for the Royal Flying Corps and other Commonwealth flying units. The War Memorial, which stands on the hill beside the Ailsa twelfth green, commemorates the brave flyers who gave their lives in that conflict. Altogether, the facilities were under military control for five years.

After the War Office relinquished control of Turnberry, the damage was swiftly repaired when the Carters firm of Raynes Park was called in to construct a new Number Two Course. This course was such a success that the numerical ranking no longer hinted at the relative merits of each course. Therefore, when the London Midland and Scottish Group assumed control of the Glasgow and South Western Railway, and took over ownership of Turnberry from the Marquis, the names Ailsa and Arran replaced the old numerical designations for the two courses.

A succession of Ladies' championships preserved Turnberry's championship status through the years up to the Second World War. The Ladies' British Amateur Championship was played on Ailsa in 1921 and 1937. The phenomenal Cecil Leitch battled it out with Joyce Wethered and the great American Alexa Stirling for the 1921 title, and Jessie Anderson won the 1937 title. Scottish Ladies' Amateur Championships played at Turnberry in those interwar years were 1924, 1930, 1933, 1936 and 1939, and they were won by CPR Montgomery, AM Holm, MJ Couper, Doris Park and Jessie Anderson, respectively.

Back in 1926, the London Midland and Scottish Hotels Group assumed control of Turnberry from the Glasgow and South West Railway. Arthur Tawle was the man in charge for the new directors. He was succeeded sometime later by Frank Hole—a man who was to play a pivotal role in the history of Turnberry.

Perhaps because men's championships had not been forthcoming, well-known golf architect Major Cecil Hutchison was called in to remove some of Ailsa's blind shots, and to add yardage—a task that was completed in 1938, to the commendations of well-known critics of the day.

Unfortunately, Turnberry's location was considered of great strategic importance, and the War Office commandeered

the facilities once again. This time, however, the RAF Coastal Command wreaked absolute havoc upon the courses. The RAF flattened the whole facility with bulldozers, and paved it over with macadam and deep, foundational concrete for the substantial runways required by the heavy RAF Liberators and Beaufighters of the Second World War era.

The end of the war saw Clement Attlee's Labor government pushing a mild socialist program that included the nationalization of rail lines. Thus, the London Midland and Scottish Hotels Group, holders of many rail lines, was assumed into British Transport Hotels, Ltd, the Chairman of which was Frank Hole.

Frank Hole was now in charge of the Turnberry facilities, and he began a battle with the British government in 1948, seeking the compensation for damages to the golf course that would enable its reconstruction to begin. This was in the face of widespread pessimism that declared that

Below: **An approach shot to the eighth green.** *Below left:* **In a bunker at the seventeenth.** *At left:* **A tee shot with Turnberry Lighthouse in view.**

golf at Turnberry was never again to be experienced. Hole called in the celebrated architect Mackenzie Ross, who made a detailed relief model of his conception for resurrecting Turnberry's Ailsa Course.

Eventually, the desired compensation for wartime damages came through. It was to be a massive undertaking, as concrete blockhouses, hangars, permanent runways and other aeronautical appurtenances covered over what had once been the Turnberry golf courses. At the end of June, 1949, Martin Sutton and Company were awarded the contract to commence clearing the airfield and to begin realizing Ross's design.

A large amount of the excavated concrete and tarmac was used to fill in low points and to create mounds and hills, and thousands of tons of excess fill were hauled to the neighboring village of Maidens, and were used to build a new sea wall.

Topsoil had to be replaced—30,000 yards in all. Light, sandy loam from an adjoining field was combined with granulated peat to provide the ideal combination for a seaside course. Every inch of tee, green and fairway on each and every hole

had to be turfed, requiring the moving of immense amounts of topsoil for a single green.

The golfing world has found that it was all worth it: Ailsa opened in 1951 to a fanfare of jubilation. The Arran Course, meanwhile, had suffered even worse damage than had Ailsa. James Alexander, Superintendent of British Transport Hotels' golf courses, produced the design for the resurrected Arran Course. He also instituted the spectacular promontory back tee on the Ailsa ninth hole.

Arran occupies flatter, more sheltered land than Ailsa, and is in many respects the perfect complement for Ailsa. Arran, opened in 1954, is a target course, wending its way through the gorse, and emphasizes control from the tee.

The resurrected Turnberry's rise to the highest ranks of golf courses was swift. Upon the opening of Ailsa, offers for staging championships poured in, and the golfers and fans who came to the championships were faced with the question of why they had not been to Turnberry before, as it is as visually stunning as it is challenging.

As per the latter consideration, the Ailsa Course provides an extraordinary, yet fair, challenge for golfers at all levels, thanks to its variant tee settings.

The latest chapter in the Turnberry ownership story was generated by the Margaret Thatcher government, whose privatization policy resulted in the selling of the railway hotels, and Venice-Simplon Orient Express Hotels became the new owners of this great golf complex.

The following are the championships, plus winners of same, that have been played on the Ailsa course in the years since its reopening—up to the date of this writing: the 1952 West of Scotland Championship, John Panton; the 1954 Ayrshire Amateur Championship, JR McKay; the 1954 and 1960 Scottish Ladies' Amateur championships, Mrs RT Peel and Miss JS Robertson,

Below: **A valiant golfer readies his escape shot from a deep bunker at the eighth green; Turnberry Lighthouse is in the distance.**

respectively; the 1954 and 1959 Scottish Professional Championships, John Panton—both; the 1957, 1960 and 1963 PGA Matchplay Championships, Christy O'Connor, EC Brown and DC Thomas, respectively; the 1960 Home Amateur Internationals, no winner listed; the 1961 and 1983 British Amateur Championships, MF Bonallack and Philip Parkin, respectively; the 1963 Walker Cup, the US team; the 1972 and 1973 John Player classics, RJ Charles and Charles Coody, respectively; the 1975 Skol Lager Tournament, P Dawson; The 1975 Double Diamond World of Golf Classic, the 'Americas' team; the 1977 and 1986 Open Championships, Tom Watson and Greg Norman, respectively; the 1979 European Open Championship, Sandy Lyle; the 1980 British Club Professionals Championship, D Jagger; the 1984 PGA Cup Matches, the Great Britain and Northern Ireland teams; and the 1987 Seniors British Open, Neil Coles.

As is evidenced by the above, the Royal and Ancient Golf Club of St Andrews admitted Turnberry to the prestigious Open rotation, and the first Open held at Turnberry (in 1971) was one to be remembered as a classic display of golfing genius: Tom Watson and Jack Nicklaus played it down to the last shot, with Watson posting 65 and 65, and Nicklaus posting 65 and 66, for the last two days of the tournament. Watson broke the overall record for any Open by eight strokes and Nicklaus by seven.

Mark Hayes set the lowest individual round Open record at 63, but could not keep the pace. Lest anyone think this was all due to 'softness' in the course, only one other player—third place finisher Hubert Green—broke par for four rounds, and he finished 11 strokes behind Watson.

Watson was literally one stroke ahead of Nicklaus at the final hole, so that, even then, the outcome was in question. The two great players each scored a three on the

final hole—with Nicklaus placing a near-miraculous pitch to the green from under a branch of a gorse bush (see the description of the Ailsa eighteenth hole, below)—and Watson won.

The 1986 Open was memorable, as well, with Greg Norman winning his first really big tournament on a course that—as those who have played the Ailsa Course well know—is utterly different depending on the weather. The following is a hole-by-hole description of the world-famous Ailsa Course at Turnberry. Note that, in the Scottish tradition, each hole has a descriptive name as well as the usual number.

The first hole, Ailsa Craig, is named for that feature of the Firth of Clyde that is visible from nearly everywhere on the course. This hole doglegs gently to the right, and has a cluster of bunkers on the inside of the dogleg. Rough lies to the left, so you must split the difference here, or make a carry for good position from which

to carry over the right front bunker guarding the green. This is considered a relatively benign starting hole—but beware, the first six holes of Ailsa are renowned as a difficult beginning.

Hole number two is called Mak Siccar, which is Gaelic for 'make sure'—an admonition that had best be heeded. This hole plays along a ridge that lies on the right side. On the left, the ground slopes sharply down toward the third fairway. Bunkers at left center in the fairway are just far enough from the green to be deceptive. In addition, bunkers lie at right front and left front of the green—and it can be hard to get out of these.

The third hole, Blaw Wearie, is definable as 'out of breath,' which describes the state of many golfers as they play against and ever-present head wind. Severe rough lining this dogleg right is a definite concern, and the bunkers guarding the green are often beneficiaries of the aforementioned

wind. From here to the eleventh hole are some of the most extraordinarily scenic holes in the world of golf.

Hole number four, Woe-Be-Tide, is obviously named for the shorefront of the Firth of Clyde, which lies immediately to the left, and lies down a pronounced slope from this par three. This hole has an elevated green, and any shot missing the green will be hard to recoup from. Among the more obvious hazards to be encountered when going for the pin is a big bunker that lies down a steep slope from the right front of the green. It's the shortest on the course, at 167 yards from the rearmost tee.

The fifth hole, Fin Me Oot, is in translation named 'Find Me Out,' as it is a subtle hole, indeed. This hole is a dogleg left, with bunkers on the inside of the dogleg, and four more bunkers strategically located to protect the green. The bunkers at left of the fairway will definitely come into play from the back tee.

The sixth hole, Tappie Toorie, which means 'hit to the top,' is named for the playing action of this par three hole, on which tee shots must cross a shallow valley to a high green that is tilted and deeply bunkered at left and right. The wind here can be a cross wind or a head wind, depending on conditions.

The seventh hole, Roon the Ben, signifies that you'll have to 'go around the mountain' on this hole. From the rearmost tee, this is the longest hole on the course—a 528-yard par five. However, from the inner tees, it is a 465-yard par four, and from the closest tee, its is a 424-yard par five. This hole embodies an unusual versatility for a really top-ranking course. Tee shots on this dogleg left must carry from a tee that is elevated in the dunes down to a fairway that is preceded by a stream running along the

Turnberry Alisa Course

Hole	1	2	3	4	5	6	7	8	9	Out	
Championship	350	428	462	167	441	222	528	427	455	3480	
Medal	362	378	393	167	411	222	465	427	413	3238	
Ladies	345	367	381	112	393	219	424	385	372	2998	
Par	4	4	4/5	3	4/5	3/4	4/5	4/5	4	34/35/39	

Hole	10	11	12	13	14	15	16	17	18	In	Total
Championship	452	177	441	411	440	209	409	500	431	3470	6950
Medal	430	157	391	379	400	168	381	487	377	3170	6408
Ladies	339	130	358	338	395	160	343	401	374	2838	5836
Par	4	3	4	4	4/5	3	4	5	4	35/36	69/70/75

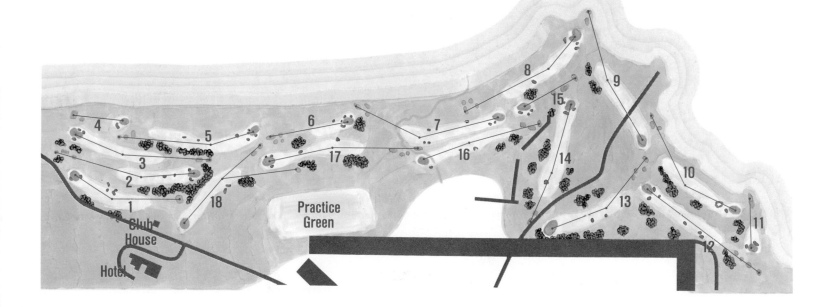

floor of a small and rugged valley. The fairway is slightly cupped and is lined with very dangerous, rolling rough on the left. Bunkers on the left and right present some difficulty in the winds coming off Turnberry Bay. The impression here is of everything funneling in toward the green. As you drive the fairway, it's best to go right. Two bunkers lie to the right of the green. There were four eagle threes here in 1977.

Hole number eight, Goat Fell, is named for the highest peak on the Isle of Arran, across the Firth of Clyde to the northwest. The entire fairway slopes to the right, its left side ascending the sand ridge to the left that drops off to the beach. A single fairway bunker on the right lies at driving length from the championship tees, and demands a little extra bit of effort. Less capable players will probably want to go left of this bunker. Massive bunkers lie to the left and right of the green approach. Best to stay to the right on this approach. A single bunker

Above opposite: **The eleventh fairway, from the tees.** *Below opposite:* **The eleventh green, facing the tees.** *Below:* **Turnberry Lighthouse.**

guards the right front of the split-level green.

The ninth hole, Bruce's Castle, refers to the ruins of Robert the Bruce's castle. These ruins lie on the promontory between the eighth green and the ninth tee. The ninth championship tee is the most photographed tee in Britain, and probably one of the most photographed in the world. Mackenzie Ross designed this hole from the elevated medal tee, but James Alexander, Superintendent of British Transport Hotels' golf courses back in the 1950s, produced the design for this spectacular championship tee (see text, above). The vertiginous, promontory tee lies below the line of sight, and some 200 yards across a rocky cove from the fairway: a rock cairn serves as the sight marker—go for the cairn to hit the fairway. This hole plays as a dogleg left, and the fairway is heavily contoured. The green is 45 yards broad, but comparatively shallow.

Dinna Fouter—'don't fool around'—is the tenth hole. Off to the left of the elevated tee is the gleaming, white Turnberry Light-

house. The tenth is a dogleg left, and hooked drives may well find the beach to the left. This hole defends itself psychologically, with the ominous spectacle of a massive lateral bunker that guards the green approach, and another bunker that lies to the right a little further on. Though these complicate the green approach immensely, they can be overcome, providing your presence of mind triumphs over your trepidations. The green is friendly, except on the left, where a slope will lead your ball to the rough.

The eleventh hole, Maidens, is so named for the village immediately to the north of Turnberry. This par three is the last of the glorious seaside holes that began at the fourth. With attentiveness to the wind, you could have a birdie here. The back tee is elevated and plays down to an ample green that has a large lateral bunker protecting its left front half, and a smaller bunker on the right side. An out-of-bounds fence lies off to the left.

The twelfth hole, Monument, is named for the monument on the hill above the

green that commemorates the airmen of the First World War who were stationed at Turnberry (see text, above). A new back tee added 50 yards to this hole in 1986. The fairway rolls heavily. The new tee brings into play the three bunkers that guard the left side of the fairway. The green is built up, with a slope to the front, and slopes left to right.

Hole number thirteen, Tickly Tap, is so named because you are here faced with a 'tricky little hit' on the green approach. The fairway is deceptively flat to the eye, and though the two fairway bunkers look sufficiently far left that you'll have no trouble going right, the wind and the ground condition may well tell another story. Beware those bunkers. Likewise the apparently defenseless green, where a slight dip in front precedes a sharp rise to the putting surface. Additionally, the ball may well be hard to stop here.

The fourteenth hole, Risk-an-Hope, lives up to its daunting name. For the first two shots on this par four (par five or more for most players), a single bunker on the left is a threat, and gorse lines the right. This situation narrows the fairway considerably, and the green is protected at right front by a massive, lateral bunker that is the bane of many attempts to carry to the putting surface. Large bunkers guard the right and left side of the green. The putting surface slopes back to front, and the wind—which is often a headwind—is a big factor here.

The name of the fifteenth hole, Ca'Canny, is an admonition to 'be careful.' It's a very punishing hole for mistakes. On this par three hole, shots from an elevated tee carry over rolling rough to a green having three deep bunkers guarding its left side, and a steep slope downward on its right. Hit for the middle of the green.

As its name in translation would suggest, the sixteenth hole, Wee Burn, features a slender rivulet among its defenses. A single bunker lies on the left of the fairway near the landing spot, and Wilson's Burn wends its way across the green approach. Like Swilcan Burn at the Old Course at St Andrews (see that section of this text), Wilson's Burn is a small but irreducible obstacle that strikes fear into the hearts of golfers. The banks of the stream decline into a narrow, deep ravine. Any shot just short of the stream will dribble down the bank and into the water: any shot that hasn't established itself on the putting surface proper will likewise find the water. The green slopes back to front, so it's best to go beyond the pin.

The seventeenth hole, Lan Whang, or 'good whack,' demands a strong tee shot for a good setup. The fairway runs through a shallow valley, and bunkers lie on its right side, the second of which is concomitant with a lateral ridge that demands a good second shot on your part. An uneven, narrow stretch of fairway leads to the green. The wind is all important here—you could attempt a carry over the ridge, or lay up for a long pitch to the green. The green is protected by one large bunker on its left, and two bunkers on its right.

The eighteenth, Ailsa Hame—as the name proclaims, the home hole of the Ailsa Course—uses the eighteenth tee of the Arran Course for championship play, which makes the Ailsa eighteenth a sharp dogleg left. The medal tee, however, is straightaway, but faces a ridge of heather. Though the carry over this is only 100 yards or so, it can produce feelings of insecurity in those standing at the tee. Two bunkers lie left on the fairway, and the playing surface is full of bumps and hollows, but is quite forgiving. These same bunkers figure in a carry from the championship tee. A gorse-overgrown bank lines the right of the fairway, and is to be avoided at all costs. Some swales and unevenness accompany the green, but all in all, this is a forgiving green. It's a fine finish for one of the world's outstanding golf courses.

Wild Coast Country Club Golf Course

Transkei South Africa

Robert Trent Jones Jr's beautiful course qualifies as the best in South Africa. Nestled just inside the Transkei border—about two hours' drive down the South Coast Road from Durban—is the Wild Coast Sun Hotel, Casino & Country Club. Though the hotel is fully equipped and offers elegant service, the most striking element in this compound is the fabulous golf course, which exists in the minds of many of the golfers who have played it as the word 'Magic.'

Sculpted out of naturally hilly, undulant terrain, it creates for golfers an ever-changing variety of exquisite Indian Ocean coastal beauty. The course is situated in a conservation area and has been designed to blend into its surroundings—which is, of course, a characteristic of Mr Jones' marvelous course designs.

In 1987, Wild Coast was host to its fifth Golf Classic, the Yellow Pages Skins tournament—the biggest Skins tournament ever held in South Africa—with special guest pros Nick Faldo, Bernhard Langer, Curtis Strange and Lanny Wadkins.

Something of the beauty of this magnificent course can be imparted in words.

Standing on the first tee, a gentle, almost still, lagoon forms the backdrop which leads onto a virginal hillside abloom with tropical trees which are silhouetted against the sea and sky. This is not an uncommon view on the front nine, and golfers may chance to see whales spouting just off the coast, and ships passing serenely by.

The back nine moves inland: the contours here frame visions of hidden valleys, tree-filled gorges and gently rippling lakes which are incorporated into the play of each hole. In the grand Robert Trent Jones

Below: **The first green, with Thompson's Lagoon beyond.** *Above:* **The dogleg of hole twelve, looking toward the green. A lake, barely seen in the foreground, figures in play from the back tees.**

Jr style, this course both involves itself with, and incorporates into its challenges, the natural wonders and beauty with which its venue is endowed.

Following is a hole-by-hole account of this unusual and highly playable course. The wind from the ocean becomes a factor on some days; on other days, the limpid stillness causes attention to flag in favor of simply savoring one's surroundings—a challenge, and what a pleasurable challenge it is.

Hole one plays down toward Thompson's Lagoon in a dogleg left. The fairway is squeezed between two opposing bunkers, and an overhanging tree at left. The green is bunkered left and at rear, and has the lagoon at rear and all along its right side. The second hole plays away from the lagoon to a sharply right-curving fairway which leans out from a bunker on its inner curve. The narrow green has two bunkers right, and one bunker left.

Hole number three plays onto the narrow end of a fairway which is pinched between opposing bunkers. The fairway widens after this—a watercourse follows the right side at this point—only to pinch down again near the green. This time the bunkers lie right, and the fairway is at this point a narrow neck which leads to the triangular green, which is itself bunkered on all three sides.

Hole four plays toward the sea, to a small, roughly triangular green having bunkers at left and at right front. A slope guards all along the right. The fifth plays along the crest of a high dune, and is comprised of a fairway—having three mounds on its right hand leading edge—which curves gently left to a rounded, triangular green having bunkers at right and at left front. A slope lies to the right and the rear.

Hole number six plays downhill onto an abbreviated fairway, or more directly, onto its actually larger green, which widens toward the rear after its two bunkers at right front and left front. A slope guards the rear, and could lead errant balls to the depths of the nearby Umtamvuna River.

The seventh has a long, serpentine fairway having three bunkers hidden in the folds along its left side, and having one bunker strategically placed on the right. A pinched approach leads to a green having three bunkers at rear and right rear, and a large bunker left.

Hole eight's back tees carry a lake, which lies left, to a contoured green having a massive bunker at right. Short but deadly. The ninth has a dogleg left having a mass of bunkering on its inner 'knee,' and a green which is basically surrounded with bunkers.

The tenth features a right-tending fairway which has two side-by-side bunkers just in line with any straight tee shot, and is lined along its right side with a series of bunkers which are likely to cause consideration on any shots to the right of the green. The green has a bunker at front right and another, 'outrider' bunker amongst the trees at right.

Golfers at hole eleven tee off to a very nearly equisized fairway/green combination, wherein the fairway has a massive bunker on its left, and the green is backed by a slope all around to the bunkers on its left front and right front. The ball had better stop where you see it must.

Hole number twelve is a water carry off the tee, involving part of the large, spike-shaped lake which also involves hole eighteen. You then must thread the 'needle's eye' which is posed by the right-lying bunkers, encountered early on the fairway, and the left-lying bunkers which guard the green approach. The contoured green could mislead you to the bunker at left rear, or the general rough at rear. The fairway is lined with trees and a watercourse at left.

The thirteenth is as sweet, scary and ingenuous as any hole you're ever likely to play. Pouring into a tree lined gorge is a beautiful, robust natural waterfall. This natural marvel is a real challenge for many golfers, as hole thirteen demands that you tee off over said gorge to a green which is large enough—but it seems small, compared with the hefty bunker at its back.

This bunker is calculated to gather in all overpowered shots; of course, all underpowered shots will find rest far from the worries of the game at the bottom of the gorge.

Hole fourteen's fairway bends to the right, and has a bunker designed to keep tee shots to the right on the fairway. Watch out for the water hazards which cut across the fairway at the one-third of the way point. Beyond these is a small garden to the left, and the green—having a large bunker at left front.

Hole number fifteen has a welcoming committee on the fairway, composed of a large bunker crossing, and two opposing large bunkers and a smaller pot bunker a tad farther up on the right. This precurses a roughly heart-shaped green having a bunker at right front and at left front.

The sixteenth plays into a valley. Its fairway describes a slow arc around to the left, with two ponds on its inner curve and a bunker right to keep things even, and a lake guarding the entire right half of the green. How wet was my valley.

The player at hole seventeen has to tee off across a tree-lined ravine to a broadside fairway having a green which is accessible from the tees, but which is protected from them by bunkers at left and right on its green-facing side. Short shots find the ravine or the bunkers, long shots find the slope to the rear. Hit it on the lip or sink the ship.

At the eighteenth hole, play commences with a carry across the foot of the spike-shaped lake that we visited on hole twelve. The fairway rides the high ground, and has two pinching, opposing bunkers early on—make that tee shot down the middle. From here, no less than four bunkers stagger across the fairway in quick succession on the slope to the green, which itself is set fortress-like—bracketed by a massive bunker at left, a bunker at right front and another at right rear.

Wild Coast Country Club Golf Course

Hole	1	2	3	4	5	6	7	8	9	Out
Championship	368	335	500	112	387	182	512	171	366	2933
Club	363	305	472	102	362	161	477	143	340	2725
Casino	324	280	449	83	337	142	442	108	315	2480
Par	4	4	5	3	4	3	5	3	4	35

Hole	10	11	12	13	14	15	16	17	18	In	Total
Championship	353	189	457	175	400	374	515	160	346	2969	5902
Club	338	163	437	150	372	350	492	141	323	2766	5491
Casino	295	140	388	131	320	309	449	138	286	2456	4936
Par	4	3	5	3	4	4	5	3	4	35	70

Above opposite: **The magnificent sixteenth hole—water everywhere.** *Below opposite:* **An aerial view of the eighteenth, with greenside bunkers and the Indian Ocean in the background.**

Wild Dunes

Isle of Palms, South Carolina USA

Wild Dunes is a 1600-acre private, oceanfront resort and residential community, located 15 miles north of historic Charleston, South Carolina. Situated on the northeastern end of the natural linksland environs of the Isle of Palms, Wild Dunes has two outstanding golf courses—the great Wild Dunes Links Course, and the acclaimed Wild Dunes Harbor Course.

Designed by Tom Fazio in 1979 and opened for play on 1 September 1980, the Wild Dunes Links Course has skyrocketed to fame: it was rated 57th among *Golf Magazine*'s '100 Greatest Courses in the World' for 1989. *Golf Digest* acclaimed the Links Course as one of the top 25 resort courses in the US, and *Golfweek* selected the Links Course as the best in South Carolina. The Links course measures 6715 yards from the championship tees. The RJ Reynolds Classic and the PGA Sectionals are played here.

The Wild Dunes Harbor Course, also designed by Tom Fazio, was opened in March, 1986, and plays parallel to the Intracoastal Waterway. The *Toronto Globe and*

Beautiful Wild Dunes. *Above:* **A view of the eighteenth on the Harbor Course.** *Below:* **The seventeenth fairway of the Links Course.** *Opposite:* **The eighteenth hole of the Links Course.**

Mail has dubbed the Wild Dunes Harbor Course 'The St Andrews of the South,' because of its preserved prehistoric sand dunes, and the very active role that atmospheric elements take in affecting play on the course—'it never plays the same way twice.'

The Wild Dunes Resort was honored as one of the 12 best resorts in the US by being awarded *Golf Magazine*'s Gold Medal Resort Award in October, 1988. The Isle of Palms venue of the resort was never cultivated, and therefore, when the resort commenced construction in 1976, the preservation of this unblemished natural seaside land was a major concern.

When Tom Fazio laid out his course designs, preservation was likewise a part of his considerations. Therefore the name, 'Wild Dunes,' is particularly appropriate, with ancient, stabilized sand dunes and extremely variegated wild vegetation informing the aesthetics of the resort development.

In the true Scottish linksland tradition, golf courses have a 'rough at the edges' appearance. The entire area has rolling sand dunes and heavy forestation, including palmettos, pines, magnolias, cedars, myrtles and live oaks, some of which are 300 years old. Sporting about in and around this vegetation are 20 mammalian species, including white tail deer, oppossums, raccoons, grey squirrels and rare, beautiful fox squirrels.

Reptiles and amphibians—including alligators—and over 100 bird species—including pelicans, ducks, herons, ibis, egrets hawks and terns—inhabit the property. Wild Dunes is zoned for 2500 residences, but in order to maintain the wonderful diversity of flora and fauna now present, the number of units completed falls intentionally short of the zoning maximum.

An expansion development is planned for a segment of land along the Wando River, 10 miles east of Charleston. This is to be called Dunes West, and will be the product of a joint venture partnership between Wild Dunes Associates—the owners of Wild Dunes—and the Georgia-Pacific Corporation. Arthur Hills has been hired to

design an 18-hole golf course for that project.

Wild Dunes is not only the home of some of the world's greatest golfing adventure, but also features the Wild Dunes Racquet Club, with 19 Har-Tru courts, including a stadium court for televised events, and one hard surface practice court. The Racquet Club is ranked among the nation's top 50 by both *Tennis* and *Tennis Week*, and has consistently earned *World Tennis*'s Five-Star Resort rating.

The current site of the US Men's Clay Court Championships, and sometime host of the Lincoln-Mercury Tennis Classic, the $75,000 Women's International Tennis Tournament and other prestigious events, the Racquet Club enjoys an exalted status in the world of tennis.

Swimming accommodations include not only the Atlantic Ocean, but also a variety of swimming pools, from Junior Olympic-size to kiddie pools (as well as private pools at homesites). Wild Dunes Yacht Harbor is an inlet of the Intracoastal Waterway that offers 10 feet of water at low tide, and is one of the finest yachting facilities anywhere. A 24-hour general store and fuel dock, plus a restaurant and full service facilities— including sailboat and powerboat sales— are available to boaters at Wild Dunes. Fishermen also have a full range of facilities and tackle to choose from, and the environs of the Isle of Palms avail extremely fine fishing to the patient angler.

Golf, tennis, family, honeymoon and other special personal events are catered to via Wild Palms' special rental package plans, featuring a wide range of housing types and more than 10,000 square feet of meeting facilities—to ensure that business and pleasure can indeed be combined here.

The Island House Restaurant specializes in fine seafood cuisine—as well as serving informal local specialties, while The Club offers prime cuts of beef and other savory dishes. The restaurant at the Yacht Harbor offers special menus suited to a casual setting.

Hurricane Hugo savaged the South Carolina coast in autumn, 1989. The hurricane swamped Wild Dunes, causing power outages and the need for building repairs and a massive cleanup. The damage to the courses, however, was thankfully not permanent, and months of hard work had the courses in good playing condition once again.

The golf courses at Wild Dunes are, as we have indicated, exceptionally fine, and offer challenging play to golfers at every level of play, thanks to a multiple-tee system. While most courses in the coastal lowlands of South Carolina are more or less flat,

the Links at Wild Dunes has a mile-long, 50-foot high sand dune that serves as the 'backbone' for its back nine, and exhibits great topographical variety.

There are holes that are carved into marshland, and holes that climb the flanks of the giant sand dune, as well as other situational variants. On one hole, the fourteenth, is said to be the fateful tree that figures in Edgar Allen Poe's eerie tale, 'The

Gold Bug.' The seventeenth and eighteenth holes play along the Atlantic Ocean.

Meanwhile, the 6709-yard Harbor Course features a great variety of its own, with two holes that play across an inlet of the Intracoastal Waterway, the lower end of which is Wild Dunes Yacht Harbor.

Terry Florence is the golf pro at Wild Dunes, and may well be one of the most envied professionals in the game, with two excellent golf courses under his influence. It is worth our while to consider both of these courses, as they each offer unusually good tests of golf. First of all, let's take a look at the already world-famous Links Course: the following is a hole-by-hole description.

Links hole number one is a moderate par five of 501 yards from the back tees. You start off playing up over a hill, and the green is protected by a bunker and a pond on its left, and trees and bunkers on the right. The green rises toward the middle, and the trees behind it will spell trouble for mis-hit balls. The pond stretches up along the left of the green, adding to the possibility of lost balls. Putt your best here.

The back tee at Links hole two is in the midst of a marsh, and from it, this hole plays as a dogleg right, with complex mounding on its outer bend. The marsh, a danger in

windy conditions, extends along the right side of the fairway to the green approach, and trees line the left of the fairway. The green has a general slope from back to front, and at 22 yards by 22 yards, will be a 'target,' indeed.

The back tee is again situated in a marsh at the third Links hole. Also as with hole number two, the Links third plays as a dogleg right from the rearmost tee, but golfers here will have to carry over a bunker on the right of a narrow fairway: hit your tee shot too hard, and you'll find the trees that line the left of the fairway. Golfers at the inner tees have a narrow, tree-lined passageway through which to place their shots to the fairway.

Midway down the Links third's fairway, a glint of water through the trees may distract you. The green approach is narrow, and the green slopes to the left front, with a pond, marshland, a large bunker and trees on the left. The bunker wraps around to the rear, adding to the hazard provided by trees in that location and trees to the right.

The fourth Links hole is, at 165 yards, the shortest par three on the course. With marshland behind, to the right and in front of the tees, you should be aware of the wind before you tee off. The shot to the fairway must negotiate a narrow 'gunsight' of trees—which, forming a double row on the left, also serve as a bit of a windbreak, so that it is possible to find the rough on the right of the fairway through overcompensation on the tee shot. The green slopes back to front and, lying obliquely, forms a wide but shallow target. Bunkers on its right may catch the unwary golfer's shots.

Tees at Links hole number five are set in a cul-de-sac of greenery, and trees line the entire left side of the fairway, with several close by the playing surface, and with a small opening in the wind break that could cause trouble for tee shots. On the right, there are trees, then a swath of water and then a longitudinal mound, all on the perimeter of the fairway. Past the mound, the water reappears some yards off the green approach, on the left of which is a longitudinal bunker. The green slopes back to front, and is protected by bunkers at right and left front.

Links hole number six is a dogleg left. Its back tees face heavy vegetation, and thus provide a challenging shot to the fairway, indeed. There is water to the left and right of a tree-lined fairway, and the sun gleaming off it may cause distraction at the landing spot. In addition, a right-lying hump and a valley stretching across the fairway complicate attempts for a good layup to the green approach. A lake off to the right rear, and trees at rear and on the left frame the green, which slopes from the right rear to the left front. A large bunker on the left front, bridging over from the green approach, may be the repository of shots that catch a gust of wind from the open right side.

The seventh Links hole is a tree-lined dogleg right, with a wind passage across the path of most tee shots. On the outer bend of the dogleg is a longitudinal mound. The green approach narrows to a few yards, and the crescent-shaped green presents a relatively wide, but very shallow, target. A pond off to the left will provide distraction, and a cul-de-sac of trees on the right and rear may swallow overflights and balls blown by the wind.

Links hole number eight is, at 203 yards from the back tee, the longest par three on the course. The back tees must carry over a 40-yard (more or less) lake, and down a hallway of trees to a fairway that widens toward the green approach, and has a long grass bunker on its right. Golfers going

directly for the green may encounter one of the two grass bunkers on the left front of the green, or the sand bunker at left rear, or the grass bunker at right front. The green slopes back to front, and is framed by a stand of trees that stretches from left rear all the way down the right side of the fairway.

The wind comes in from the almost entirely open left side of the ninth Links hole. At 451 yards from the back tees, this is the longest par four on the course. Trees line the right side, and the rearmost tees must carry over a lake to the fairway. A

bunker 246 yards down the fairway lies to the right. The green approach has water all along its left, and this water extends up along the left of the green itself. The small green has a complex slope, back to front, and right to left—the first slope acting almost as a 'chute' into a bunker on the right front of the green, and the second slope providing a similarly treacherous path to the water on the left. Trees line the right and rear, and a bunker is situated at left rear.

With Links hole number ten, you encounter some very interesting fairway

Wild Dunes Links Course

Hole	1	2	3	4	5	6	7	8	9	Out	
Blue	501	370	400	165	505	421	359	203	451	3375	
White	474	332	357	147	472	375	343	180	375	3055	
Gold	410	308	315	125	417	307	255	165	328	2630	
Red	388	268	301	93	408	259	252	113	326	2408	
Par	5	4	4	3	5	4	4	3	4	36	

Hole	10	11	12	13	14	15	16	17	18	In	Total
Blue	331	376	192	427	489	426	175	379	540	3335	6710
White	293	355	169	387	477	362	133	364	518	3058	6113
Gold	248	332	118	338	402	340	125	325	392	2620	5250
Red	227	287	118	330	396	269	100	275	392	2394	4802
Par	4	4	3	4	5	4	3	4	5	36	72

topography. No less than five valleys and two mound ridges stretch across the playing surface. A tee shot to the top plateau will make for the easiest approach on this dogleg right. An oak tree close by the fairway on the right, and two grass bunkers on the right of the green approach, add to the hazards to be avoided here. The green slopes back to front.

The eleventh Links hole is a straightforward, moderate-length par four. Trees line the fairway, and a grass bunker lies to the right, just before the green approach. The green is elevated, and lies in a cul-de-sac of trees. A grass bunker guards the inner curve of the green crescent, and a sand bunker guards its back. Set edge-on to the fairway, and slanting front to back, it will be a worthy challenge to your skills.

Wind will be a factor in the playing of Links hole number twelve. This hole plays downhill to a green that slopes left to right, and has a grass bunker on its right front approach.

Links hole number thirteen is a dogleg left, with a large sand mound on the 'shin' of the dogleg. In addition, dunes are found along the entire left side, where you may seek to shave a stroke from your score—beware the dunes. The green is long and narrow, and slopes back to front.

Trees and a waterway must be carried over from the tees of tree-lined Links hole fourteen. A big oak tree stands in the midst of the fairway near the landing spot—prevailing wisdom dictates driving to the left of this tree. A large bunker lies to the right of the green approach, and trees lie to the left. At 24 by 34 feet, the green presents itself almost broadside, and slopes from the left.

The fifteenth hole of the Links Course heads straight toward an inland pond. This hole is lined with trees, except where a tip of a marsh runs across in front of the tees. The marsh continues behind the trees, down the left side of the fairway. A pair of bunkers cut into the fairway from the right at the 248-yard mark, and the green is deep but narrow, with a nine-yard wide 'wasp waist.' On its left and left rear are trees, and just off its rearmost segment is the pond.

Par three Links hole sixteen has its back tee in the midst of a pond. The fairway is sandwiched between a marsh on the left, and a tree-bedecked dune and the pond on its right. You will probably go for the green, and it's said that a birdie is almost in hand here. Miscalculate, however, and four bunkers—ranging around the back of the green from its left to its right—are arranged to catch your ball. Extreme errors will find the marsh, the treed sand or the pond.

Depending on the wind at your back, your tee shot at Links hole number seventeen could go farther than you think it might. Trees line the right side of this hole, and sandy beach—with Dewees Inlet of the Atlantic Ocean just beyond—lines its left side. The green here is shaped like a link of sausage, curving away to the right. It's 16 yards narrow, and slopes from back to front. Between the trees, sand and ocean proximity, it's an exciting penultimate hole.

The eighteenth hole of the Links Course is a 540-yard par five. A superb driving hole, it also develops and culminates the oceanside theme promulgated by hole seventeen. Sandy beach all along the left, and trees interspersed along the right, give this dogleg right just the right amount of reso-

Above: **With the ocean beyond the trees and a lagoon just ahead, the Links Course fifteenth green presents an exotic sunset image.**

nance to call to mind the classic oceanside linksland of Scotland. On the inside of the dogleg bend lies a grass bunker—stay to the left of this, and avoid the right-hand side at all costs, but beware of the beach incursion about halfway down the fairway. Another grass bunker lies on the right of the green approach, and a sand bunker exists just to the left of dead center. The green slopes back to front.

It's an exhilarating finish to a spectacular and unusually well-balanced 18 holes of golf.

The Wild Dunes Harbor Course is an apt complement to the great Links Course, and contains its own share of outstanding challenges. The following is a hole-by-hole description. Harbor hole number one gives

ample opportunity for a good drive off the tees—straight up the middle of the serpentine fairway. Beware the cluster of bunkers and mounds that impinge on the right of the green approach. The green, at 39 by 28 yards, is a good-sized target to hit. Do not, however, underestimate the presence of a grass bunker on its right front face.

The second Harbor hole is a dogleg right. All tee shots have to carry over a marsh, and weaker shots will have to contend with two mounds early on the fairway, while those following the dogleg may find the grass bunker that lies on the 'elbow.' A mound on the left of the green approach will cause many golfers to go right—watch out for the ever-present marsh on the right side. The green slopes from right to left; there is a grass bunker on the left, a sand bunker all along the right, and trees behind.

Par five Harbor hole number three is, at 566 yards from the back tee, the longest on the course. With marsh all along its right—and making two deep incursions on the hole—all but the innermost tee face a carry over same. At the first landing spot, prepare for yet another marsh carry to a complex second fairway, having a 'gunsight' of palm trees that must be negotiated, grass bunkers all along its left, and on the left of the green approach. Trees and the marsh lie to the right of the green approach, and the green slopes back to front; a sand bunker protects its left front.

Tee shots at Harbor hole number four must carry over wetland (and also must overfly a grass bunker on the very tip of the fairway). A mound and trees lie to the left at the 239-yard point, and two grass bunkers lie on the left of the green approach, while a third protects the leftmost tip of an irregular green. Shaped like a wine flask, the green points its chin to the right of the fairway, and has a small crescent bunker on its own right front. An immense waste bunker lies all along the right of this hole, and behind the green, which slopes from back to front, is water.

One of two par threes on this course that measure 177 yards from the back tees, Harbor hole number five features a long carry over marshland from the back tees. An immense bunker protects the entire front of the green. Deeper on the right than on the left, the green slopes toward the right, and is protected on that side by a sand bunker sandwiched front and rear between two grass bunkers.

At 564 yards (nearly the length of hole three), Harbor hole number six is surrounded by marsh and has two grass bunkers at the midway point on the left. A bunker close by on the right—and another

impinging from the left—on the green approach, present hazards to be taken into account when going for the green. It is said that this is a good birdie opportunity. Sloping back to front, and with a grass bunker to catch overflights to the rear, this is a green that should be a gratifying attainment.

The seventh hole on the Harbor Course has two sand bunkers incursing on the fairway from the left, and two grass bunkers further on, also on the left, near the green approach. Sand bunkers and grass bunkers fill the green approach. The green slopes front to rear, and a pair of grass bunkers guard the rear. It is possible to reach this green from the tees, but a layup is the best approach.

The eighth Harbor Course hole is the shortest on the course. A 143-yard par three, it is sandwiched by marsh on the right, and marsh and water on the left. A large sand bunker on the left of the narrow green approach, and two sand bunkers sandwiched front and rear by two grass bunkers, guard the right of the green. A mound directly behind, and a sand bunker at left rear, plus marsh on the left, complete the defenses here. A 44-yard deep green, it is only 15 yards wide, and slopes to the left front.

Harbor hole number nine plays over marshland from the back tee, and is a dogleg left, with marsh all along its left side. Its

Above: **The seventh Harbor Course fairway, with the Intracoastal Waterway close by.** *Below:* **The fifteenth and sixteenth Harbor holes.**

two-tiered green slopes toward the front, and has grass bunkers at left front and left rear and at rear, and a combination of sand bunkers and grass bunkers at right rear, right and right front.

The tenth Harbor hole is a narrow, straightaway driving hole, with water and trees for much of its length along the left. A grass bunker lies to the right of the tip of the fairway, and another lies to the left about two-thirds of the way down, where the water leaves off. The green narrows to

the rear, slopes to the front, and has four mounds at left front, left, rear and right. Additionally, grass bunkers lie on the right rear and right front of the green. There is fun to be had on this driving hole.

Harbor hole eleven is a dogleg right, with a bunker off to the right early on, and a grass bunker on the right 24 yards farther on. A large mound occupies the middle of the fairway approximately four-fifths of the way down, and to the left of this is a longitudinal bunker. A sand bunker occupies the green approach, and mounds protect the left front and left rear of the green, while a sand bunker protects the right side. The green slopes to the right front.

The twelfth hole on the Harbor course is the second 177-yard (from the back tees) par three on the Harbor Course. It's endowed with a beautiful, panoramic view of the Yacht Harbor and the complex inlet system of the Intracoastal Waterway. You'll tee off across the inlet to a green that lies on Waterway Island. A segment of marshland fronts the green, which slopes down from a ridge to the front. Pay attention to the wind here, for a sand bunker exists just off the right front of the green, and is accompanied by two mounds close by. Mounds additionally occupy the right rear of the green, and trees form a loose perimeter to the left rear. It can be a difficult green to hold.

Harbor hole number thirteen plays back across the inlet, and it has marshland all along its left. The back tees have an extensive marsh-and-water carry to make. This hole has been dubbed the 'Marsh Monster,' which reinforces one's qualms about the difficulties to be encountered here. A massive sand bunker lies along the right side of the green, and a mound and a grass bunker protect the rear.

The fourteenth Harbor Course hole also plays with its entire left side in the marsh. It's a straightforward driving hole, with a pair of trees at the halfway point to the right of the fairway, and, just beyond them, in a chain leading up to the green approach, a sand bunker and three grass bunkers. On the left, opposite these, is a large pine tree. The green slopes to the front and to the left, with marsh, of course, on the left, and trees on both sides and behind.

Hole number fifteen on the Harbor Course is a dogleg left, with Palmetto Lake all along its left side. Sand bunkers and grass bunkers on the 'shin' precurse a large sand bunker sandwiched between two grass bunkers in a progression that crosses the green approach on a diagonal from left to right. A tree on the right side of the green, and a sand bunker behind it, complement a defense scheme that includes the lake flowing all along the left. It's a broad green of intermediate depth, and the really valiant (but perhaps foolishly so) may attempt a stroke-saving carry over the left of the fairway, across the lake and to the green. The ever-changing winds at Wild Dunes being what they are, you'd better check your windage. The best bet is a layup short of the green approach, for a chip to the green.

Harbor hole number sixteen also plays along Palmetto Lake, and is a straightaway driving hole. Beware of the wind, however—as much danger as there is of having your ball blown into the lake, there is equal peril that it will find the 'blind' formed by three trees and a sand bunker that are grouped just off the left side of the fairway. The green approach is protected by a large, sand bunker on the right, and the green has three grass bunkers on its right,

and sand bunkers at rear and on the left. The green surface slopes to the left, toward the lake.

The seventeenth is a classic buildup to the eighteenth; a 154-yard par three, it presents golfers with a large green that slopes toward the left front, and the water that lies all along the left of the hole. A grass bunker on the right of an abbreviated fairway will catch underpowered shots, and an array of one sand bunker immediately behind the green, with four grass bunkers arranged in a 'corona' still farther back, will capture the majority of over-powered balls.

The water on the left side of the Harbor eighteenth can be a real threat on a windy day, as can the right-lying 20-foot mounds at the 342-yard mark. A drive to the left of center is the best attack to use on this par four hole. On the right front of the green lies a grass bunker, and to the left rear lies a large sand bunker. This tiered putting surface slopes back to front, thus rendering the water that lies to the left front of the green yet another hazard to be avoided in conquering this excellent finish to a very fine 18 holes of golf.

With the superb Wild Dunes Links Course *and* the Wild Dunes Lagoon Course to offer, Wild Dunes is a golfing paradise in the American South.

Wild Dunes Harbor Course

Hole	1	2	3	4	5	6	7	8	9	Out
Championship	330	342	566	306	177	564	319	143	443	3190
Mens	315	253	545	286	154	455	266	130	336	2740
Ladies	266	210	471	213	127	356	224	93	243	2203
Par	4	4	5	4	3	5	4	3	4	36

Hole	10	11	12	13	14	15	16	17	18	In	Total
Championship	489	361	177	464	434	561	437	154	442	3519	6709
Mens	474	348	168	416	425	546	421	144	426	3368	6108
Ladies	375	276	118	317	321	413	342	105	344	2611	4814
Par	5	4	3	4	4	5	4	3	4	36	72

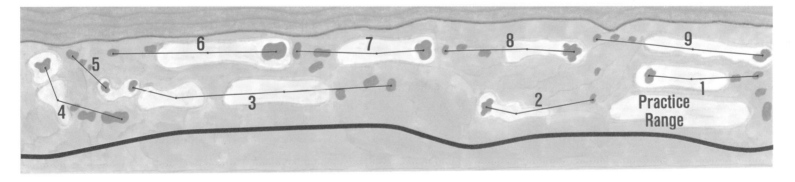

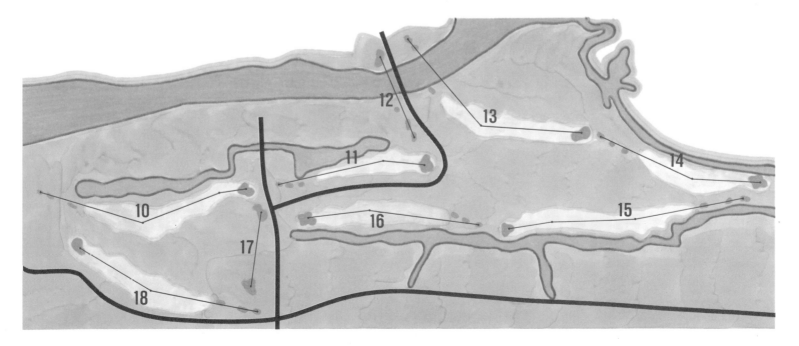

INDEX